Venice, Verona, Lake Garda & the Dolomites with Kids

2018

Ariela Bankier

All rights reserved, ©Ariela Bankier. No part of this book may be reproduced in any form or by any electronic or mechanical means, including information storage and retrieval systems, without written permission from the author.

Photos are used by permission and are the property of the original owners. All photos credits appear at the end of the book. If your photo appears without a credit, or isn't credited properly, please let us know and we will fix it immediately.

Front cover photos: ESB Professional/Shutterstock.com and xbrchx/Shutterstock.com

Back cover photo: Sergey Dzyuba/Shutterstock.com

Managing Editor and Author: Ariela Bankier

Editor: Irene Hislop

With contributions by: Flavia Canestrini

Maps: © OpenStreetMap contributors, under CC BY-SA license.
Created by Julie Witmer.

Fact checking: Irene Loiudice

Disclaimer: Although the author of this guide has made every effort to provide readers with the most accurate and up-to-date information (as of the date of publication), she accepts no responsibility for any damages, loss, injury, or inconvenience sustained by readers of this guide. The author makes no warranties or representations of any kind regarding the accuracy of the information (text, photos or maps) listed in this guide, including the completeness, suitability or availability of the products and services listed, and does not endorse, operate, or control any of the products or services listed in this guide. The author is in no event liable for any sort of direct or indirect or consequential damages that arise from the information found in this guide. If you have come across any errors in this guide, please let us know so we can correct our future editions. If you have any comments or concerns, please write to this address: info@travel-italy-guru.com. Thank you!

General note: Travel information tends to change quickly. In addition, the recent economic crisis has influenced many businesses and attractions, including restaurants and hotels. Shops may close without notice, and some sites may change, or reduce, their opening hours unexpectedly. For this reason, we recommend confirming the details in this guide before your departure, just to be on the safe side.

Also by Ariela Bankier:

Florence & Tuscany with Kids

Venice & Verona for the Shameless Hedonist

Tuscany for the Shameless Hedonist

Table of Contents

Introduction 7
How to Use this Guide 9
Planning Your Trip 14
Getting into Italian Mode 22
Moving Around in Italy 31
Staying in Venice 39
Eating and Drinking in Venice, Verona, Lake Garda
and the Dolomites 44
Traveling with Kids 55
How to Build a Family Trip Using this Book 61

Chapter 1
Venice. **65**
Venice—An Introduction 66
Planning A Family Visit to Venice 71
Sample Itineraries for Families (A, B, C) 76
Three Self-Guided Walking Tours in Venice 84
    Tour N. 1 84
    Tour N. 2 103
    Tour N. 3 118
Kids' Corners 123
Eating in Venice 134
Sleeping in Venice 140
Special Events in Venice 141
Special Activities in Venice 145

Contents

Chapter 2
Day Trips from Venice 149
Itinerary N.1 - Lake Santa Croce and the Caglieron Caves 150
Itinerary N.2 - Ferrari, Lamborghini and Ducati Museums 155
Itinerary N.3 - Jeslo 159

Chapter 3
Verona 166
Walking Tour of Verona 167
Eating in Verona 183
Sleeping in Verona 185
Special Events in Verona 185
Special Activities in Verona 186

Chapter 4
Lake Garda 187
How to Build a Family Friendly Itinerary in Lake Garda 188
Lake Garda Itinerary: From Sirmione to Salo 198
Eating in Lake Garda 217
Sleeping in Lake Garda 221
Special Events in Lake Garda 225
Special Activities in Lake Garda 227

Chapter 5
Day Trips from Lake Garda. 235
Itinerary N.1 - Lake Molveno 236
Itinerary N.2 - Castel Beseno 238
Itinerary N.3 - Lake Ledro 239
Itinerary N.4 - Trento and Lake Tenno 242
Itinerary N.5 - Sigurta Park and the Nicolis Museum 247

Contents

Chapter 6

The Dolomites **252**
Planning Your Visit to the Dolomites 253
    Itinerary N.1 - Merano 259
    Itinerary N. 2 - Passo San Pellegrino and Moena 262
    Itinerary N. 3 - Lake Carezza and Pass Pordoi............................264
    Itinerary N. 4 - Ortisei and the Seceda..268
    Itinerary N. 5 - Santa Cristina and Panaraida 271
    Itinerary N. 6 - the Marmolada and Serrai Canyon 273
    Itinerary N. 7 - Dobbiaco and Lake Braies 276
    Itinerary N. 8 - Gilfenklamm Gorge and Racines Mines...............280
    Itinerary N. 9 - Alpe di Siusi..284
    Itinerary N. 10 - Cortina d'Ampezzo and the 5 Torri.....................287
Kids' Corners 290
Eating in the Dolomites..293
Sleeping in the Dolomites 295
Special Events in the Dolomites..297
Special Activities in the Dolomites..297

Chapter 7

Top of the Top. **305**
Index 309
Photo Credits...313

Introduction

Venice, Verona, Lake Garda and the Dolomites are four of the most popular tourist destinations in Italy, and it isn't difficult to see why. Venice, with its enchantingly beautiful canals and world-famous art is a pivotal stop in any Italian tour. Verona, the city of love, has been immortalized in Shakespeare's work and is the epitome of Italian charm. Lake Garda's picturesque villages and many kid-friendly attractions make it an almost obligatory stop for families. And the Dolomite Alps are a UNESCO world Heritage site featuring magnificent views and some of the best hikes in the country. With so much to see, do and enjoy, how can anyone resist this stunning part of Italy?

Why Do We Need a Travel Guide?

Today, the abundance of online information about Venice and northern Italy seems to make a traditional guidebook almost superfluous. But in reality, nothing could be farther from the truth. These days, travelers are bombarded with "Top 10" lists and all sorts of endorsed reviews; every restaurant is described as "the best meal I had in Italy," and every minor sight and attraction is said to be "incredible." For this reason, it is essential to find a reliable source of information—a serious guide that will help you sift through the plethora of opinions and recommendations and zoom in on what is truly worth your time and money. That way, your family trip will actually be as spectacular as you hope and deserve.

Luckily, we're here to help! *Venice, Verona, Lake Garda & the Dolomites* is the most comprehensive guide for families visiting this part of northern Italy. It is the result of over a decade of traveling, and contains everything you need to know to build the perfect vacation for your family, from dozens of practical tips to information on adventure and amusement parks, medieval castles, kid-friendly museums, fun festivals, beaches, ice cream shops, and excellent family restaurants and B&Bs.

Introduction

We're honest about which places shouldn't be missed, which places aren't worth your time and effort, and the best ways to navigate your way when you (and your kids) are short on stamina. Additionally, you will find several unique features in this guide, such as Kids' Corners, detective missions, insider's tips, and money-saving ideas. And all is presented in a friendly, easy-to-use format. In short, your next great vacation starts here.

Welcome to Italy, and have a wonderful trip!

Ariela Bankier

How to Use this Guide

This book is divided into four main chapters—Venice, Verona, Lake Garda and the Dolomites. Each chapter features a varying number of easy-to-follow (but detailed) self-guided itineraries that cover the best sights and attractions in that area. At the end of each chapter you will find sections dedicated to the best family-friendly restaurants and hotels, as well as special events and activities that are especially interesting for kids. The last chapter includes a review list of the best activities, hikes, parks, and museums for the entire family.

Q: Why is the guide divided into itineraries?

Several travel guides offer lists of sights and attractions in a given region, but ignore most of the activities that could interest families, such as amusement parks, water parks and medieval festivals. Other guides set out a one-size-fits-all list of attractions, but they don't explain how to create a fun, sensible itinerary that everyone—even young children and teenagers—will enjoy. Our itineraries give readers a sense of which sights and attractions go well together, and they are built so that families can follow them to the letter or use them as a general reference point, whichever they prefer. And since the itineraries are organized by geographical order and proximity, you can easily mix and match them, and build a day with your favourite activities from two or even three different itineraries.

Q: What unique features does this guide offer?

We have included a number of unique features in this guide to help get your kids involved and have a great time. **The first feature is our "Missions",** a series of fun, detective-style missions that kids can complete when you visit a sight or museum. **A second feature is the "Kids' Corner"** that you will find at the end of most itineraries. These include fun facts, stories, and anecdotes, everything from cool facts about Gondolas in Venice to stories about mysterious animals that live in the Dolomite Alps. These facts and stories are meant to get kids curious about their surroundings while having fun and exploring. **A third feature is the "Special Events in the Area" section,** which covers the main family-friendly events, from medieval feasts to jousting matches and carnivals. If you are traveling to northern Italy in June through September, there are at least 10 big events to choose from,

How to Use this Guide

and we highly recommend working one of them into your schedule. There is nothing quite like hearing drums beat in the background while a procession of men and women dressed in medieval clothes marches by, waving flags. Bigger events, like sporting contests, races, and jousting, will probably be one of the most memorable parts of the trip. A fourth feature is the "Special Activities in the Area" section, dedicated to all the fun stuff kids and teenagers love to do: horseback rides, thermal springs, adventure parks, amusement parks, and more. You will find several suggestions for every itinerary, and we highly recommend selecting a few activities and trying to work them into your schedule. A guided hike with Alpacas or a visit to a farm might be the most-talked-about part of your trip for your 8- or 12-year-old. An adventure park, after a long day of sightseeing, can make all the difference between cranky kids who feel they "aren't doing anything fun" and happy kids who get to run around, tire themselves out, and then fall asleep early, letting you enjoy a quiet evening to yourself. **A fifth feature is the emphasis we put on practicality.** We've included dozens of useful tips throughout the guide, to help make our readers' experience as smooth as possible. We make suggestions on where to park, when to visit certain sites and not others, how to save money and skip unnecessary lines, and how to avoid the common pitfalls of traveling in Italy.

Q: Some attractions in Venice, Lake Garda, Verona and the Dolomites aren't mentioned in this guide. Why is that?

It's true, not every sight and town are reviewed (though the best and most important ones absolutely are). In fact, if you would call this guide opinionated, you wouldn't be wrong. If we think a medieval village is no more than average, we won't hesitate to say so, and if we believe a certain attraction isn't suitable for most for families, we will express that clearly.

The reason for this approach is that we feel describing every single miniscule museum, park and hamlet (and there are literally hundreds of such sights) as wonderful, charming, and quaint is unfair to our readers. If you have a month to tour the back roads of northern Italy, then discovering tiny, unknown areas can be a real treat. But if you have about a week in the area, like most travelers, you'll have to be picky about where you spend your time and money. There is no reason to drive 30 minutes to a pleasant but entirely unimportant town when just a few kilometres away sits a much more interesting sight that you and your kids will probably enjoy more.

We know that you've worked hard to be able to take your family on this vacation, and we want you to have the best possible experience. Hopefully,

How to Use this Guide

our recommendations will be able to help you do just that. We are, however, always happy and grateful to hear any comments and suggestions from our readers. If you believe we haven't covered a sight, town, or attraction that should be featured in this guide, please let us know.

Q: I'm still not sure traveling to Venice and northern Italy with my seven- and nine-year-old children is a good idea.

Traveling with kids can be challenging, but it is also a wonderful adventure. Very few experiences in life are as character-building, eye-opening, horizon-expanding, fun, and instructive as travel. Seeing the heart of European culture with their own eyes and touching 1000-year-old monuments will teach kids more about history and mankind than one hundred books or movies. The daily contact with different cultures, languages, and customs will help them develop as people and understand the world in a way that only travel can do. Even the more annoying aspects of travel have their advantages: Learning to handle complicated situations that require patience and thinking outside the box, adapting yourself to the unexpected, tasting new (sometimes weird and sometimes delicious) foods, living outside your comfort zone, and daring to try new things are all experiences that teach children to become more resilient, confident, and mature. It also helps them become more open to the world and curious about their surroundings. Travel can and usually does bring families closer, and the memories from the trip will stay with your kids long after you go back home.

In our experience, kids don't always get enough credit for what they are able to understand and enjoy on a trip. While it is true that most (okay, all) kids would pick a visit to the amusement park over a visit to the museum, there is no reason you can't do both. The fact that your nine-year-old won't spend four hours in the Guggenheim Museum in Venice, expressing his thoughts about the art in a series of perfect sonnets, doesn't mean that he can't enjoy (or at least be intrigued) by a 40-minute tour of the art collection there, if properly prepared in advance. Kids are naturally curious, and if you find a way to get them involved, they will gain a great deal even from the most unlikely tours and activities.

Q: Are the maps in this guide enough, or do I need a GPS/other maps?

You will find some maps in this guide, but they are only meant to give readers a general sense of direction, and aren't enough for easy navigation. We encourage you to use a GPS or a good road map, as well as to pick up

How to Use this Guide

detailed city maps at the tourist information offices in cities like Venice and Verona. A detailed city map can be useful for one simple reason: Italian towns and villages are filled with tiny alleys and hidden piazzas that can't be shown with enough detail in our guide. In any case, you should also know that once you get used to the way Italian towns are built, you won't get lost; all of the attractions are usually concentrated in the historical centre—"centro" or "centro storico" in Italian—which is marked on road signs with a bull's-eye.

Terms You Will Find Throughout the Guide

As you tour northern Italy, you will notice you keep coming across a few technical terms or words that are useful to know in advance:

Duomo—the central church/cathedral in town. Every self-respecting town, even the smallest ones, has a duomo, which is usually considered the focal point of the town. In most cases, if you are trying to get to the historical center (the centro storico), ask where the duomo is.

Fresco—churches (and sometimes private homes, too) in Italy are decorated with frescoes (affresco, in Italian). This term refers to paintings painted directly on the plaster walls.

Baptistery—next to most duomos, you will find the baptistery (battistero, in Italian), where, you've guessed it, infants were baptised.

Piazza—town square. There are several piazzas in every Italian town. In Venice, a town square is called campo, not piazza. The only piazza in Venice is Piazza San Marco.

Piazzale—a larger piazza.

Palazzo—though it sounds like "palace", palazzo actually means "building". In some cases, it means very fancy buildings and even small palaces. The plural of palazzo is palazzi.

Ponte—bridge.

San—saint.

Borgo—any small fortified medieval village.

How to Use this Guide

Uscita (pronounced "ushita")—exit.

Entrata—entryway/entrance.

Via—road/street.

Fermata—stop (usually used for bus stops).

Stazione—station (either for buses or trains)

Parcheggio (pronounced parke-jo)—parking lot

Planning Your Trip

Choosing When to Travel

Venice is busy year-round, but between May and September the city is positively packed with people. In Verona, the Dolomites, and Lake Garda, the busiest months are July through August. There are pros and cons to summer travel in Venice. The pros are obvious—most of the cultural events and festivities (not just in Venice but in the entire region) take place in the summer. The days are longer, which means you can get more done. And the fine weather permits you to explore every angle without worrying about storms or the "*acqua alta*" (the periodic rising of the water level in Venice, which leads to extensive flooding in the city). Additionally, hours of operation for attractions are longer, as they are adapted for the influx of tourists. The cons, on the other hand, are also quite clear. During the summer months, everything is extremely crowded, especially the public transport system and the popular sights. There are hordes of people in every canal and piazza, and there are long lines for every major attraction. Hotel prices are also higher; a well-located apartment or room in a popular hotel can cost 35% to 40% more during the summer months.

The loveliest times of the year to visit Venice, in our opinion, are May through June, and September. Though you may come across the occasional storm and grey skies, for the most part the weather is pleasant, the shops and attractions are open, and the city is relatively calmer and less crowded. From November to March, rain tends to spoil most of the fun.

The best times to visit the Dolomites and Lake Garda are late-June—mid-September. That is when the weather is warm enough to go for a swim in the lake, enjoy the hikes in the mountains, and join the many family activities in this area. Verona can be visited year-round.

Documents You'll Need before Leaving

If you are an **EU citizen,** you will just need your ID card. We also recommend bringing your national health certificate with you; it allows you to receive free emergency medical treatment if needed. If you are from **outside the EU,** you will need to bring a passport. Passports must be valid for at least six more months from the date of your entry into Italy. We also recommend making photocopies and virtual copies of all your important documents in

Planning Your Trip

case anything gets lost or stolen. Scan the documents and email them to yourself, or save them onto a USB drive, or both.

If you plan on renting a car, you will need a driver's license and a credit card. Most companies require at least two years of driving experience, and the credit card must be under the same name as the driver's license. You may also want to print out driving or walking directions to your hotels, or at least the hotel where you'll be staying your first night. If you plan on sleeping in Venice, be sure to find out in advance which *vaporetto* (public water bus) stop is closest to your hotel, and print out precise walking instructions.

If you've booked any e-tickets or rented your car online, print out the confirmation letter. Some companies require just the code you were sent; others require the actual printed ticket/voucher, especially if there is a barcode on it. If you are flying with low-cost companies like Ryanair or EasyJet, carefully read about their online check-in process and luggage limitations, which can be very strict, and print out any required documentation.

Local Money and Credit Cards

Like the rest of the EU, prices in Italy are in euros. As of May 2018, €1 was worth about $1.14 or £0.74, though you should check the rates yourself before traveling. Venice is a city of tourists, and it is quite easy to find a place to exchange money; there are exchange offices (*Cambio*, in Italian) in the train station, the airport, and the city center. In Verona you can exchange money in the airport and at the central train station. When exchanging money, in Italy or in your home country, ask for bills no bigger than €50. €100 bills are hard to break, and €500 bills, which are very rare, will arouse suspicion.

If you have an international credit card (a very useful item; contact your bank for more information.) you can also simply withdraw money in the local currency from ATMs across Italy. This has become an increasingly popular solution for tourists, as most exchange places offer poor exchange rates and charge a high additional handling fee. Withdrawing cash from the ATM also saves visitors from the need to travel with large amounts of cash. Though these cards do save a great deal of hassle, they are also notorious for the high commissions charged by the banks, both for the withdrawals and for the conversion from dollars/pounds to euros, so do check in advance what those might be. We also recommend notifying your bank before you leave the country that you will be using your card abroad.

Some travelers forget to do so, and their cards get blocked, because the bank thinks the card was stolen and is being being used fraudulently.

If you are planning to use your US credit card in Italy (not just for withdrawing money but also for paying in hotels and restaurants), you should know that many businesses only accept Visa and MasterCard. American Express and Diners are far less common in Italy, and may be declined in some small restaurants and shops. Lastly, note that US credit cards and European credit cards have different security systems. While the new standard in Europe is cards with microchips (and PIN code), many cards in the US still rely on magnetic strips. Though most machines in Italy can read both types of cards, some machines, especially automatic machines (such as ticket selling machines in train stations and gas machines at gas stations), might not be able to read your card if it has no microchip. Also, if you have a PIN for your card that consists of numbers and letters, contact your bank and replace it. ATM machines in Italy can only read cards with a four- or five-digit PINs.

Fraud

Two of the most common frauds involve counterfeit bills or coins and identity theft. The probability that you will be given a counterfeit €20, or even €100, bill is extremely low. This trick is mostly used in stores when trying to scam owners. Counterfeit coins, however, can sometimes be found in markets; check the €2 coin you're given as change to make sure it really is a €2 coin and not an old 500-lire coin. The two look very similar, but the lire is obviously now worth nothing. Identity theft happens when thieves attach small cameras to ATMs to steal PINs (and your money). Simply cover your hand with your other hand, your wallet, or a scarf while entering the PIN to avoid any problems.

Another thing to watch out for is people who stop you on the street and ask you to sign various petitions, usually "against drugs," "against poverty," or "for the children." These are obviously not real campaigns, and even though they may be quite persistent, we highly recommend you avoid giving them your signature.

Crime

Venice, Verona, Lake Garda and the Dolomites are very calm areas, and even though there is, naturally, some criminal activity, tourists very rarely feel unsafe. The biggest hassle is pickpockets, and the items most at risk are your wallet, your camera and your smartphone. A little common sense will go a long way toward avoiding unpleasant events. Never leave your phone or camera unattended or in a half-open bag, especially when you are on the *vaporetto* (in Venice), on the bus (in Verona), or at a crowded tourist sight. Don't carry all of your money in one bag, so that even if you do get targeted, you won't lose $600. If your hotel has a reliable safe, leave some of your money there. Always keep your hand on your bag, and never put your wallet in your pocket or in the outer or side pockets of your backpack or purse, where it can be pulled out without you even noticing. We promise you that the pickpockets in Venice could teach Fagin, Oliver twist and the rest of the crew a trick or two.

Even more importantly, don't put your documents and your cash in the same wallet; that way, if your wallet does happen to get stolen, you will still have your passport and other documents, and your vacation won't be ruined. Write down the emergency number of your credit card company so you can call immediately if your credit card is stolen. For obvious reasons, don't keep that piece of paper in your wallet. Instead, hide it, together with an emergency 100-euro bill, in some unlikely place. If you do get robbed, you will need to file a complaint at the police station, so they can help you get new documents and for insurance purposes. Try to do this as quickly as possible, as some banks and insurance companies insist that you lodge a complaint within the first twenty-four hours of the robbery.

Insurance

Consider taking out some kind of travel and luggage insurance. There are several options available, and a quick search online will yield affordable results. If you plan on taking part in any physical activities while on vacation, if you are pregnant, or if you suffer from any medical conditions, good travel insurance becomes an even better idea.

Emergency Numbers and Medical Emergencies

Call 113 or 112 from any phone to reach the police.

Call 118 for an ambulance.

If you need a pharmacy, hospital or any other shop or service, call 1254. This will put you in touch with an information service, where an operator will help you find whatever you are looking for. Alternatively, use the Italian yellow pages website: www.paginegialle.it

Medical Assistance

There are a number of private clinics in Venice, but finding an English-speaking doctor can be difficult. If you have travel insurance, don't forget to contact your insurance company before going to any hospital or clinic. Most insurance companies will provide you with the name of a specific English-speaking doctor they work with, and won't necessarily cover the expenses at other clinics.

If there is an emergency, go directly to the hospital; you won't be turned away, even if you don't have insurance. **VENICE'S** main hospital is SS. Giovanni e Paolo Hospital (Castello 6777, Campo Santi Giovanni e Paolo. *Vaporetto* stop: Ospedale. Tel: 041.529.4111, www.aulss3.veneto.it). Alternatively, take a cab from Piazzale Roma straight to the hospital in Mestre (10 minutes from Venice). The Mestre Hospital can be found on Via Paccagnella 11, Mestre. Tel: 041.9657111.

In **VERONA**, go to the AOUI Hospital in Piazzale Aristide Stefani 1. Tel: 045.812.1111, www.ospedaleuniverona.it.

In **LAKE GARDA,** there are temporary clinics (Assistenza Sanitaria, or Guardia Medica, in Italian) that operate in the high season (mid-June—Late August) and are open for tourists, too. In **Torri del Benaco,** go to the town clinic on Via Gardesana 50, Tel: 045.722.5528, open daily, 8:30—10:30; In **Brenzone sul Garda,** go to the town clinic in Via XX Settembre 15, Tel: 045.658.9570, open Monday—Thursday, 11:00—12:30; In **Castelletto di Brenzone** go to the clinic on Via Amerigo Vespucci 3, Tel: 045.743.0494, open Friday—Sunday, 11:00—12:30; in **Malcesine** go to the small hospital on Via Gardesana 37 (Loc. Val di Sogno), Tel: 045.658.9356, open daily 14:30—16:00; in **Garda**, go to the clinic on Via Colombo 2 (first floor), Cell: 320.669.1261, open daily 13:00—15:00; in **Bardolino** go to the clinic on Via Gardesana dell'Acqua 9, Tel: 045.621.3108, open daily 15:30—17:30; in **Tremosine** go to the clinic on Via Monsignore Giacomo Zanini 95, Tel: 0365.917.071, open Tuesday & Thursday, 9:00—14:00, Wednesday 16:00—19:00; in **Salo'** go to the clinic on Via Montessori 6 (Località Due Pini), Tel: 0365.521.032, open Monday, Tuesday and Friday, 12:30—12:30 and Wednesday—Thursday, 15:00—17:00; in **Toscolano-Maderno** go to the clinic on Via Verdi 3, Cell: 333.721.1453, open Monday, Tuesday and Friday 14:00—18:00 and Wednesday—Thursday 9:00—13:00, Weekends 9:00—12:00; in **Sirmione**, go to the clinic in Piazza Virgilio 35, Cell: 348.5817.703, open daily 9:00—14:00. Off-season, or in case of a serious emergency, go to the aforementioned hospital in Verona (20 minutes from the lake). In the

DOLOMITES, go to the Santa Chiara Hospital in **Trento**—Largo Medaglie D'oro 9, Trento, Tel: 0461.903111, www.apss.tn.it/presidio-ospedaliero-s.chiara

We also highly recommend bringing some basic medicines with you—ear and eye drops, pain killers, antacid, vitamins, and, of course, whatever prescription drugs you require. (Bring extra, just in case.) There are numerous pharmacies in Venice, but they won't necessarily carry the specific medicines you are used to, and trying to translate the name, or finding out the local equivalent of the medicine you need when you are ill, can be quite a hassle.

Calling Home and Using the Internet While in Italy

Aside from the well-known apps and programs you can use on your computer or smartphone to call home, such as Skype, FaceTime or WhatsApp, you can also buy a local SIM card to use during your travels. This is an especially good idea if you plan on staying for a week or more in Italy, and if you plan on using navigation apps such as Google Maps or Waze. Keep the SIM after you return home, and use it for your next trip to Italy. It should remain functional for two to five years.

A local SIM card will work with your phone as long as you have a GSM-compatible, unlocked phone—which means it will work in Europe—and your phone allows the use of SIM cards other than the original one. If you don't have such a phone, you can get one in Italy for a very reasonable fee. An Italian SIM card costs around €10 and is already charged with that amount. You can add more money and activate an Internet service that will allow you to use your phone and the Internet during your entire trip in Italy for a very low fee. You will need an ID or passport to buy a SIM card, as the shop must make a photocopy for legal reasons. Normally, your phone will be activated within 24 hours or less. You can buy a SIM card at the airport, at the Santa Lucia train station in Venice, or at any of the main cell phone operators' shops (try WIND, TIM or VODAFONE). These can be found on the main streets in both Venice and Verona. Make sure you buy a SIM card from an authorized shop only. Ask for *ricaricabile*, which means pay-as-you-go, and ask the shop to activate the cheapest Internet offer they have, which usually works out at around €9 per month. Be sure to remember to deactivate the service when you leave Italy. If you are using your own phone and your own non-Italian SIM card, make sure you deactivate international data roaming, which can be very costly.

Planning Your Trip

Packing and Luggage

The two best pieces of advice we could give you regarding packing are: keep it light and make sure to pack essential items you won't be able to find abroad.

Essential items: Your list of essential items may change, based on your specific needs and the ages of your kids, especially if you are traveling with babies, but it usually includes an extra pair of glasses (especially if you are the driver), music for the car (if you plan on renting a car, and you have younger children), any special foods you may need (specific baby formula which may not be available in Italy, kosher food, gluten-free food, etc.), vitamins, and any medicine that you use regularly (assume you won't find it in Italy) or that you might require. A transformer (adaptor plug) is important too. Note that the European electrical system is different than the American and British system (220 volts). In fact, you may want a few adaptor plugs, since you will likely be traveling with at least two phones and one computer.

Knowing what to pack when traveling with kids can be stressful. Since the exact list of what you need greatly varies depending on the age of your children, we recommend learning from the experience of other parents and Googling "what to pack kids abroad" or "packing list abroad" to find **endless lists of suggestions online.** You'll find ideas that you hadn't even considered, from the best brand of backpacks to essential baby formula tips, from portable high seats and strollers to suitcase recommendations, from baby wipes suggestions to space-saving ideas.

Keeping it light: It's natural to over-pack, but the truth is, if you can hardly lift your suitcase when you're still at home, you certainly won't manage (easily) to carry it to the train and to your hotel. You should know that most train stations and under 3 star hotels in Italy don't have elevators, so you will have to lift your suitcase constantly.

Before packing, check the weight allowance for luggage on your flight. Most companies allow you to bring one suitcase that weighs up to 20 kg (we've tried and the answer is no, they won't let you bring two bags weighing 10 kg each). You may also bring a handbag that is no bigger than 55 cm x 40 cm x 20 cm (some companies also limit the handbag weight to 8 or 10 kg).

Low-cost companies (like Ryanair and Easyjet) are VERY strict about letting you take only one item on board. They are also very strict about the weight and measurements of your handbag, and they actually do measure it before they let you on the flight. You won't be able to get on the plane with a handbag and a personal bag, plastic bag, camera bag, computer bag, or anything else (except for the duty-free shopping you bought in the airport after the security check). Other companies are less strict, but they will require you pay for overweight luggage, which may be pricey (at the end of your trip, if you know you've bought too many souvenirs, consider popping by the post office and sending yourself a package instead of paying extra for your luggage).

Packing Extra Stuff for Activities and Fun

In addition to the usual packing, you will also need to bring accessories for the activities in this guide. They won't take up much space, but they are essential for carrying out the missions in the different itineraries. You'll need: Crayons; a notebook where kids can paint (preferably A4 size); another notebook for writing (a journal or notepad); and binoculars—this may seem like an excessive item, but it is absolutely not. It not only helps kids feel like detectives or spies but also helps them see things better. One of the reasons kids get so bored in churches is that they can't see; everything is too high or too far away. With binoculars, your little detective can see the dramatic expression on the saints' faces in the frescoes in Venice or check out the detail on the ceiling in Verona.

Additionally, we recommend packing some basic craft materials to help toddlers and young children survive long flights and car rides. Wikki stix, reusable stickers, Lego kits, an etch-a-sketch, glitter pens and colorful paper for origami are all useful. Tablets loaded with ebooks or audio books are also a big hit. If you plan on doing any crafts on the plane, take into consideration possible safety regulations, and know that you won't be able to bring liquid glue or scissors on board.

Getting into Italian Mode

Hours of operation

As time goes by, more shops and museums are adopting what is known as *orario continuato*, which means they are open all day long, but this is not yet the norm for Italian businesses. Many shops, especially in smaller towns but also in Venice and Verona, still operate according to traditional business hours.

Shops: Monday–Saturday, 10:00—13:00 and 15:00/16:00/17:00—19:00; Sunday, most shops are either closed or open in the morning only. Some shops are also closed on Monday morning (especially in Verona). In smaller towns, it is common to find that many shops and restaurants are closed for no apparent reason on a specific weekday, and that weekday changes from town to town (though it is usually Monday, Tuesday, or Wednesday).

Banks: Monday–Friday: 8:30–12:30/13:00/13:30 and 14:00–16:00.

Trains: There are very few trains after 22:00 and virtually no trains between midnight and 5:00 a.m., except for a few night trains.

Restaurants: Most restaurants are only open for lunch and dinner, usually between 12:00-14:30 and 19:00-21:30. It is rare to find a restaurant that will serve you outside these traditional mealtimes. Additionally, most restaurants in Italy are closed one day a week, and the closing day changes from restaurant to restaurant. The most common closing days (giorno di chiusura, in Italian) are Monday and Tuesday. In the off-season, many restaurants close for vacation in January, February, and a couple of weeks in August.

Museums: In Venice, most (but not all) museums are open daily. In Verona, most museums are closed Monday mornings. If you are traveling to other parts of Italy, know that in most cities museums are closed on Mondays. To be on the safe side, check the museum's website before visiting.

National Holidays

Everything, including museums, attractions, and most shops and restaurants, will be closed on: January 1 (New Year's Day); January 6 (Epiphany); Monday after Easter (Easter Monday); April 25 (Liberation Day); May 1 (International

Workers' Day); June 2 (Republic Day); August 15 (Assumption Day); November 1 (All Saints' Day); December 8 (Immaculate Conception Day); December 25 (Christmas); December 26 (St. Stephen's Day).

Traveling Off-Season and in August

August, though part of the high season, is a month when many Italians go on vacation. Although they often don't bother to mention it on their websites, some restaurants, markets, and shops may close for a week or two for what is known as *ferie*, or vacation holiday. This is most common during the second and third weeks of August. If you are traveling during that period, it might be a good idea to double-check whether a place is open before making your way there.

When traveling off-season, from November to April, you run the risk of finding quite a few places, especially restaurants, but in some cases even attractions and museums, closed or with reduced hours of operation. Specifically, many shops close down for the winter break, which lasts from the third week of December until January 7. Certain tourist attractions may close down completely in January and February and reopen in mid-March. Double-check everything to be on the safe side. This is yet another advantage of having a local SIM; you can always call before driving somewhere, avoiding the disappointment of finding closed doors.

Understanding Italian Phone Numbers

Home and office telephone numbers have an area code, followed by the number. Rome's area code, for example, is 06, Milan's is 02, and Venice's is 041. Whether you call a number from within Italy or from abroad, you have to dial the full area code, including the zero at the beginning (unlike area codes in other countries, where you remove the zero when calling from abroad). **Cell phone numbers** begin with 3. For example: 338.2222222 or 329.4444444, etc. Calling a cell phone is more expensive than calling a landline.

Understanding Addresses in Venice

The address system in Venice is different from other cities in Italy, and has to do with the city's unique structure. It is also very hard to navigate, and even if you are given the most precise address possible, it is still very likely that you will get lost. Venice is built like a crazy maze, and navigating it is a skill which can take a lifetime (or two …) to master.

24
Getting into Italian Mode

The most basic thing you should know is that Venice is divided into six wards, or neighborhoods (*sestieri* in Italian). There are three wards on one side of the Grand Canal, and three on the other side. The six wards are: San Marco, Cannaregio, Dorsoduro, Santa Croce, Castello and San Polo. A typical address in Venice will include the name of the ward, followed by the house number. For example: Hotel Ciao, San Marco 3427. This indicates that Hotel Ciao is located within the San Marco ward, at number 3427. However, unless you are using a GPS, there is no way of knowing exactly where number 3427 is located within the large perimeter of San Marco ward. For this reason, most locals add a second piece of information, indicating the specific *calle* (street, in Venetian lingo) on which the hotel is located, or at least the nearest *campo* (town square). With that extra piece of information, the address is: Hotel Ciao, Calle dei Genti, San Marco 3427. This means that you have to locate Calle dei Genti within the San Marco ward, and somewhere along that street you will find the hotel you are looking for. Since Venetians are aware of just how impossible their system is, they usually add some more information when possible, and tell you the nearest *vaporetto* stop or the nearest church (both serve as an anchor point for starting your navigation).

As you can imagine, navigating the streets of Venice without a very good map or GPS is somewhat of an impossible mission. The map in this guide and even the map provided by the tourist information can only give you a general indication of the layout of the city and the main *calli* and *campi*. The tourist office map is actually sufficient for finding the largest sights in town (Piazza San Marco, the Rialto Bridge, the Accademia, etc.), but isn't enough if you want to locate any specific restaurants or hotels. We usually use the GPS on our phone (and bring an extra battery, since the GPS will leave your phone empty in no time), but there are traditional paper maps, too. If you want to invest in a serious road map, then buy a book called *Calli, Campielli e Canali*. It lists all the streets, the tiniest alleys, and all the canals and bridges in an easy-to-follow manner, and is very useful. Alternatively, pick up a good map of the city (such as the one published by the Italian Touring Club) at a newsstand. This should be enough for standard navigation. It is also worth mentioning that throughout the historic center you will find signs indicating the way to Piazza San Marco, the Rialto Bridge or the Santa Lucia train station. That, together with the constant stream of people making their way to these focal points, will help you know in which general direction to proceed.

One last piece of useful information has to do with the peculiar nomenclature in Venice. While everywhere else in Italy a street is called *via*, and a town square is called a *piazza*, in Venice the locals have come up with very different terminology, which is useful to learn in advance:

Ca': The abbreviated term for *palazzo* (usually indicating an important building).

Calle: the Venetian word for *via*, meaning street.

Campo: the local name for *piazza*. Remember, in Venice there is only one piazza and that's Piazza San Marco. All the other town squares are known as *campo* (or *campiello*—a little town square). Most *campi* (the plural form of campo) are named after the church around which they are built.

Canale: a large canal

Fondamenta: a quay, a road along the water

Ramo: a street branching from a larger street

Riva: the roads along the Grand Canal or the lagoon.

Salizzada: a wider street

Ponte: bridge

Understanding Addresses in Verona and the Rest of Italy

Venice aside, addresses in Italy always include the name of the street (*via* in Italian), the name of the town, and the province in which the town is located. For example: Hotel Ciao, Via Marconi 4, Negrar (Verona). In this case, Hotel Ciao is located on Marconi Street, in the town of Negrar, which is in the province of Verona. The reason the province is added to the address is to avoid confusion, since there are many towns with the same name all over Italy. This is also helpful to remember when you are setting your GPS. Note that the province is named after its largest town, but that doesn't mean that everything will be close to that town. The province of Verona, for example, consists of the city of Verona and 97 other towns and villages, some of which are quite far from Verona itself. If booking a hotel, never rely exclusively on the address provided to determine whether the hotel is close enough to the city center; we recommend always consulting Google Maps, too.

Getting into Italian Mode

Most addresses are similar to the example reported above, but in some cases, especially when looking for hotels, *agriturismi* (B&Bs on farms in the countryside) and restaurants that are located in the countryside, you will find addresses like this:

Agriturismo Buongiorno

Via Puccini 14

Loc. San Terme

Verona

Loc. stands for *località*, and it simply means a suburb or small village that technically is part of the town but is physically located outside the town itself. If you don't have a car, you will have a very difficult time reaching these places. Another type of address you may encounter is:

Agriturismo Ciao Bella

Pod. Marche

Verona

Pod. stands for *podere*, which means a farm or ranch, and in this example, the farm is located near Verona (but not actually in Verona). A *podere* will always be in the countryside. Typically this address belongs to a ranch, a rural *agriturismo*, or even a remote restaurant. If you book an *agriturismo* or dinner in such a place, see if they can give you their GPS coordinates, which will make navigation much easier.

Driving, Parking, and Renting a Car

Driving in Italy

Though you don't need a car in Venice (or Verona, for that matter, as it is quite small), you might decide to rent a car to visit other parts of northern Italy. If you are an EU citizen, your driver's license is valid in Italy, and you need no other documentation. If you are traveling from the United States or Canada, you need to obtain an International Driving Permit before leaving for Italy. Driving in Italy is just like driving in any other country. Don't be intimidated by stories of horrifying and insane Italian drivers; for the most part, they are not true.

> **Tip:** You've heard the saying 'when in Rome, do as the Romans do', and this is especially true when picking a rental car. It is tempting to pick the largest vehicle on offer so everyone has room and the backseat isn't a battlefield. But remember, you won't be driving on American, Australian or British roads. Italian cars are small for a reason—Italian roads are small. Unless you stay on the autostrada, you'll often be navigating narrow roads and sharing them with motorcyclists and bicyclists. Parking a very large car will also quickly become an issue. For these reasons, we recommend choosing a medium sized car with a powerful engine.

The Italian road system is fairly easy to navigate. There are two kinds of highways in Italy: free and toll. Those with a toll are called *autostrada*, and they are marked with green road signs. The free roads have different names (SP, SR, SS, etc.) but are always marked with blue road signs. When traveling in northern Italy, it is likely that you will choose to use the *autostrade* most of the time. Traveling on the small country roads takes a lot more time, and what you save on tolls you spend on gas. Ideally, take the *autostrada* from one destination or region to the other, but once you reach the destination itself, switch to the smaller country roads, to enjoy the scenery.

If you are traveling with younger kids, by law they are required to sit in **child car seats or booster seats.** Children under 36kg (80 pounds) or under 150 centimeters (4.9 feet) can choose between a booster seat and a child car seat; children under 18 kg must have a child car seat. Book these

28
Driving, Parking, and Renting a Car

in advance when renting a car, or buy one when you reach Italy and then take it home with you; they are really not that expensive.

Drinking and driving: The maximum amount of alcohol permitted in your blood while driving is 0.5 mg/ml (the precise number of glasses you can drink before you reach that level depends on your body weight). This is especially relevant if you plan on doing any wine tasting in the many delightful little vineyards of the Valpolicella and Prosecco hills during your trip.

What are ZTLs and Why Should They Be Avoided?

Limited traffic zones (in Italian, *zona traffico limitato* – ZTLs) are an issue that many tourists aren't aware of. They should be, however, as ZTLs are the main reason tourists are fined when traveling in Italy. Most towns in Italy protect their historical centers, which is where most of the attractions are, by defining them as ZTLs where only residents can drive or park. There is a security camera at the entrance to any ZTL that registers your vehicle number and sends you or your rental company notification of a fine, which, together with handling fees charged by the rental company, is about €100.

Stories about tourists getting confused, entering the same ZTL three times in less than 10 minutes, and being fined each time are more common than you'd think. Our best advice is to simply avoid driving in cities. Most town centers, including Verona, are so small that you don't really need a car anyway. If arriving by car, park in a park lot outside the *centro storico* and walk or take a bus to the center. You will usually find very accessible car parks, especially in touristy towns (see details in the various itineraries). What does a ZTL sign look like? A white circle surrounded by a red ring and next to it another sign saying ZTL (or *zona traffico limitato*).

Renting a Car in Italy

The major rental companies in Italy are Avis, Europcar, Sixt, and Hertz. In Venice, they all have offices at the airport, and a number of companies keep offices at Piazzale Roma, too. We suggest looking into all four before booking a car. You can rent a car in Italy if you are over 21 and have had a license for more than two years. Some companies require only one year of experience. When renting a car, you have to present personal identification (a passport or an ID card for EU citizens) and a credit card, though not a debit card. The name of the person renting the car must be

Driving, Parking, and Renting a Car

on both; for example, you can't rent a car with Mr. Smith's license and pay with Mrs. Smith's credit card. There are a number of insurance options, but we recommend taking the most comprehensive. Regardless of the type of insurance you have, mark every scratch and bump on the car. Some insurance deals claim to be all-inclusive, but the small print can reveal that damage to things like mirrors, the underside of the car, or the wheels is not covered.

You should know that most cars in Italy have a manual transmission (stick). If you don't feel comfortable driving such a car, make sure you specifically order a model you are comfortable with. Cars that run on diesel will save you money. Always fill the gas tank when returning the car; you will be charged extra if the company has to fill it for you. You will also be charged extra for returning the car dirty; you don't have to take it to the car wash; just make sure it's acceptably clean. Charges can also be incurred for returning the car at a different office than the one where you picked it up, handling any fines or tickets you receive, and renting accessories such as a GPS, snow chains, or baby seats.

GPS units are very useful and we highly recommend using them with this guide for a number of reasons. First, they are far more convenient to use than maps (phone apps like Waze are excellent, but will use up your battery and internet minutes very quickly; bring a car charger and choose an adequate internet plan if you plan on navigating with your phone). Second, signs in Italy are often hard to understand or follow. It is not unusual to find a tiny sign indicating the exit to the town you need just a few meters before the exit itself. Signs on regular country roads (i.e., not *autostrada*) are often quite small and can't be easily seen from afar. On rural roads, which are also very poorly illuminated, it is highly unlikely that you will be able to see any of the signs at all if driving after dark. A GPS will save you the hassle of having to play detective and indicate when and where to turn. If you plan on renting a car with a GPS for a week or more, it's probably cheaper to buy your own GPS, as long as it has recently updated European maps on it. You can walk into any of the three largest chain stores for electronics in Italy—Mediaworld, Euronics, or Unieuro—and buy a GPS that includes all world maps for about €100 and then take it back home with you. You can also buy a GPS at home and bring it with you.

Snow chains are required by law if traveling between mid-November and mid-April in most regions in Italy. Rental companies never seem to mention this, but if you are stopped by the police and don't have snow chains or winter tires, you are the one who will have to pay a hefty fine, not the rental company. One last thing: Try not to fill your car with gas on Sunday. There

Driving, Parking, and Renting a Car

is usually no one manning gas stations on Sunday, so you will have to use the automatic machine; it isn't complicated at all, but may be a problem if you don't have exact change.

Parking

Parking spaces marked with white lines or no lines at all mean parking is free. That is, of course, unless there is a sign prohibiting parking in that area. Blue lines mean you have to pay for parking: Look for the parking meters around the parking lot, decide how long you will stay, and put the appropriate amount of change in the machine. Take the receipt the machine prints out and put it facing out, on the dashboard of your car, near the steering wheel. Yellow lines mean you can't park there; these spaces are reserved for those with permits. To find out more about parking in Venice and Verona, see below.

Moving Around on Public Transportation

Trains

Trains are an excellent way to move around and reach the main towns. Venice's main train station is **Venezia Santa Lucia,** and Verona's is **Verona Porta Nuova**.

The two main train companies that operate from Venezia Santa Lucia and Verona are **Trenitalia** and **Italo**. Trenitalia is Italy's national train company, and as such it covers the entire country, going to every province and small town. Italo, on the other hand, is a relatively new and privately owned company that connects only the major cities in Italy, such as Rome, Florence, Venice, Turin, Bologna, and Napoli.

Buying a Ticket for a Trenitalia Train

The Trenitalia trains can be divided into two categories: regular trains, known as regional or IC trains, and high-speed trains, which are collectively known as Freccia trains. The high-speed Freccia trains connect major cities—like Rome, Milan, or Florence—but not small towns (those can only be reached on the IC or regional trains). Freccia tickets are more expensive and they are for a specific time and seat. Regional trains, on the other hand, have no reserved seating, and the only limitation is that you must use your ticket on the same day that you bought it.

To buy a ticket in the train station, go to the ticket office (*Biglietteria* in Italian) or use the self-service machines. The self-service machines are easy to use, and you can select a menu in English, too. But before you start, take a look at the pictures at the top of the machine; some only have a picture of a credit card, which means they don't accept cash. When purchasing a ticket from the self-service machines, you will be given the option to purchase first-class tickets on regional trains. On Freccia trains, first class is more comfortable, but on regional trains, there is no difference whatsoever between first class and second class (except for the price...). So, on regional trains, it makes sense to choose the second-class option and save the money.

Moving Around on Public Transportation

> **Tip:** If you are traveling a short distance, usually under 80 km, say from Venice to Mestre or Treviso, you can buy a generic "up to X km" ticket at a newspaper stand, instead of waiting in line at the ticket office. Just make sure this ticket covers the right distance. Ask the vendor, "Va bene per X?" meaning, "Is this ticket okay for reaching X?" In the Venice train station there is a newsstand next to Track 3, and two more stands outside the station itself.

Whichever ticket you buy, always validate it in one of the little white-and-green machines near the tracks before getting on the train. A ticket is valid for six hours from the time it is validated. A non-validated ticket can lead to a hefty fine.

Buying a Ticket for an Italo Train

Italo offers only one kind of train, the standard Italo train, but the cars are divided into various categories with various seating plans—there are "smart tickets" that can be bought in advance for a considerable discount, XL seats, seats with a screen (cinema service), and more. To find out about the various seating options and to review Italo's many (convenient!) offers, consult their website: www.italotreno.it.

Finding Your Way in the Train Station

With the exception of Venice and Verona, most of the train stations you'll come across are rather small and easy to navigate. Tracks are called *binari* (singular *binario*), and in every station you will find screens or electronic boards listing the departing trains (*partenze*) and the arriving trains (*arrivi*). It can happen that when you go to look for your train on the departures board, the board lists a different destination than what is on your ticket. Let's say, for example, that you've just bought a ticket to go to from Venice to Treviso. Your ticket says "Treviso" and you were told at the ticket office that the train will leave at 16:00. Yet, when you check the departures (*partenze*) board to find out which track (*binario*) your train is leaving from, you don't see a train leaving for Treviso at 16:00, there's only a train to Udine. Don't be alarmed. The station that appears on the departures board is the final destination, and most regional trains (and some high speed trains) make several stops along the way. It is very likely that the stop you need to reach isn't the final destination of the train, which is why it doesn't appear on the board. Simply walk to the track and check the more detailed board on the

Moving Around on Public Transportation

track itself. It will list all the stops along the route. If you are still unsure, simply ask the station staff.

Taxis & Ride-sharing Apps

Taxis in Italy are expensive, and can't be stopped in the street—you have to call and order a car by phone. A taxi can be a good way to get from the airport to your hotel, but don't rely on using taxis as a substitute for a rental car. Popular ride-sharing apps such as Über are not common in Italy, and can only be found in the largest cities, such as Rome and Milan.

Getting to Venice

By Airplane

Venice has its own airport, the Marco Polo Airport, which is located about seven kilometers from the city center. It isn't very large, but it is convenient, and many national and international flights land here. The airport has a detailed website where you can read more about the various airlines that fly here, as well as parking in the airport and other services: www.veniceairport.it.

To get from the airport to the city center, you will need to take a water taxi (about €120) or use the services of the **Alilaguna** company, which operates a private *vaporetto* (water bus) that connects the airport with Venice. The public *vaporetto* system does not cover the airport. The Alilaguna tickets cost €14 one-way and €27 for a round trip, and you may board with one suitcase and one handbag. Extra luggage will be charged separately (about €3 per bag). Please note that in high season, the boats **from Venice to the airport** can be very, very crowded; leave an ample margin for possible delays or you might risk missing your flight. Alternatively, if you don't want to arrive by water, take a bus or a regular taxi from the airport to Piazzale Roma (a taxi will cost €40 to €50). From Piazzale Roma, proceed on the public *vaporetto* lines.

By Train

Trains from all over Italy arrive at Venice's main train station, Venezia Santa Lucia. The station has been expanded in recent years, and today you will find, among other things, the ticket office for Trenitalia trains, the ticket office for Italo trains, a small tourist information office operated by Venezia Unica, and a luggage deposit room where you can leave your bags. Right outside the train station you will find the stop for many of the *vaporetto* lines. Almost every *vaporetto* line in town makes a stop at Santa Lucia (the train station *vaporetto* stop is marked on most maps as: Ferrovia).

By Car

Venice is built on the water, so driving is obviously out of the question. The farthest point you can get to with your car is one of parking lots offered to visitors. From that point on, you can walk, take a boat, or use the public *vaporetto* system. The two best-known parking lots in Venice are located in

Piazzale Roma (www.avmspa.it) and in Tronchetto (www.veniceparking.it). Both are very large and well-connected to Venice itself (by the public *vaporetto* system), which means you can get directly to town from the parking lot without having to get a water taxi; both are fairly expensive—about €25 per day. Note that some parking lots calculate a day from the time of your arrival until midnight, not 24 full hours. You can usually book a spot in advance online and save up to 50% on the cost.

Other parking options are available. If you don't necessarily want to park in Venice itself, you can park in the large parking lot in front of the **Mestre** train station (in Viale Stazione 10, right next to the Best Western Hotel Bologna). If you come on a weekday, you might pay as little as €10 a day, though prices change in high season and on weekends. Consult their website to find out more and book in advance: www.sabait.it. To reach Venice from this parking lot, simply cross the street, enter the Mestre train station, and take the regional train to Venezia Santa Lucia.

Another option is parking at the **Venice Airport Parking** Lot. Prices at the airport are much more reasonable than the lots in Piazzale Roma and Tronchetto, and you can pay as little as €4.50 a day if you book a spot in advance. The main issue, however, is getting from the airport to the city center, which, as we've explained earlier, can be fairly expensive. If you plan on parking for just one day, then choosing the airport parking lot doesn't make much sense. But if you plan on spending a number of days in town, or even a week, then the airport lot is absolutely worth considering. Book your spot online in advance to cut costs, and find out more here: www.veniceairport.it.

Getting to Verona

By train

If you are planning a day trip to Verona from Venice, you will most likely take the train. Trains leave every 15 to 45 minutes (depending on the hour of the day). With the Freccia trains, you will be in Verona within 80 minutes. With the regional trains, your trip will take about 2.5 hours.

By plane

Verona isn't just a fun destination for a day trip. It is also a major center in Veneto, prides itself on its own airport (Verona Villafranca Airport), and offers excellent connections to several cities. When searching for a convenient flight to Italy, it is worth considering flying to Verona instead of

Venice, if you find a good deal. Verona's airport is located right outside the city, and is connected to the main train station via shuttle bus, which runs every 20 minutes (between 5:30 and 23:00).

By car

The easiest way to reach Verona is by car. The reason is that Verona's train station, unlike most other towns, is somewhat far away from the town center and has to be reached by bus. With a car, on the other hand, you can park at one of the centrally located parking lots, which are just two minutes (on foot) away from the main sights. Use your GPS to navigate your way to the town center (take care not to go into any ZTLs) and park at **Parcheggio Cittadella** (located in Piazza Cittadella, just 200 meters from the Arena), where you will find a small street-level parking lot and a very large underground parking lot; or at the **Arena Parcheggio** (Via M. Bentegodi 8), which is also quite conveniently located and close to the Arena. Note that parking in Verona is quite expensive (about €16 for 24 hours).

Getting to Lake Garda

By train

The main train station in Lake Garda is located in **Peschiera del Garda,** at the southern part of the lake. If you are traveling by public transportation, you can take a train here from Venice or Verona, and then continue by bus to the various towns around the lake, using the services of the local bus company, ATV (Azienda Trasporti Verona); find out more here: www.atv.verona.it.

By bus

You can reach Lake Garda with an extra-urban bus from Verona. There are several lines connecting the city with Sirmione, Malcesine and Riva del Garda. Additionally, in April through October, you can buy a combination ticket for the Malcesine cable car (Funivia di Malcesine; see the Lake Garda itinerary for full details) and a daily bus pass for a reduced fee. Consult the aforementioned ATV website to learn more.

By car

The easiest way to reach Lake Garda is by car. For a detailed review of driving and parking in that area, see the Lake Garda chapter.

Getting to the Dolomites

It is possible to tour the Dolomites without a car, though it isn't the most comfortable way to move around that region, in our opinion. A car gives you the freedom to visit lakes, nature reserves, and agriturismi that are off the beaten path, as well as setting your own independent schedule.

If you prefer moving around with public transportation, you can take the train with Trenitalia to one of the two main cities here: Trento (in the Trentino province) or Bolzano (in the Alto Adige province). From there, continue by bus to the various towns and valleys you wish to visit. To find more about the bus lines that operate in this area, consult the Trentino Bus Service (www.ttesercizio.it) and the Alto-Adige bus service (www.altoadigebus.com) websites.

Moving around in Venice

The two most common ways to move around in Venice are by foot and by the **public vaporetto system** (which is operated by ACTV – www.actv.it). The *vaporetti* are basically water buses, and they connect various points in the city as well as some of the main islands in the lagoon (Lido, Murano, Burano, and others). A single fare on the *vaporetto* is quite expensive at €7.50, which means that buying a 24-, 36- or 72-hour pass, or a weekly pass, instead of a few single tickets, makes much more sense. The pass grants you access to the entire vaporetto system (excluding the private Alilaguna *vaporetto* to the airport); you will receive an electronic ticket, and you must validate it with the electronic machines by the piers every time you board a *vaporetto*.

If you plan on staying in town for four or five days, buy the weekly ticket, it's a better deal than buying two three-day tickets. Substantial discounts for senior citizens, children and people under 28 are also available, consult the Rolling Venice website to learn about the right vaporetto ticket for your family: www.veneziaunica.it/en/content/rolling-venice.

Note that children under 6 usually don't have to pay at all; confirm this at the ticket office.

The *vaporetto* system may seem complicated at first, but it is actually quite easy to navigate, especially if you are used to metro, tube and underground railway systems. The *vaporetti* leave from small piers. The *vaporetto* line is clearly marked on top, and often the pier is divided into two separate

Getting into Italian Mode

sections—one for each direction. The two most important lines for tourists are *vaporetto* lines 1 and 2. These cross the Grand Canal and stop at the top tourist sights (Line 1 is the slowest, because it makes more stops enroute). You can pick up a map of all the lines and their timetables at the ticket office, including the night vaporetti. Note that *vaporetti* have different timetables in high season and off-season, to match the influx of tourists. Aside from the *vaporetti*, you will quickly discover that walking is the most common way to get around. And it's a great way to discover the city's hidden corners.

If you need to cross from one side of the Grand Canal to the other, you can do so by using the **traghetti**. This is a secret that locals would like to keep to themselves. Basically, there are only four bridges that connect the two sides of the Grand Canal, so if you want to get from one side to the other, you have to walk quite a distance. The *traghetti* are gondolas that will help you cross from one side to the other for a modest fee (€1.50). There are quite a few *traghetti* crossings, but they have limited operating hours, usually from 8:00—13:00. The main ones are: from San Stefano to San Toma; from the Ferrovia to San Simeon; from Riva del Carbon to Riva del Vin; from San Samuele to Ca' Rezzonico, and from Santa Sofia to Pescheria.

Staying in Venice

Types of lodging in Venice

As you might expect in a city visited by over 20 million tourists a year, Venice offers quite a selection of lodging. There are hundreds of hotels, B&Bs, apartments and resorts, and the variety can be confusing.

Hotels are a popular choice. Many are located in renovated medieval or Renaissance town houses that have been remodeled to accommodate guests. This means that on the one hand, you will enjoy a truly authentic sojourn, in a *palazzo* that was probably erected 200 or 300 or even 500 years ago, and often still boasts original fixtures. On the other hand, this means that modern amenities might be lacking, elevators will be a rare sight, and in many cases the Wi-Fi will be weak, because medieval walls are very thick.

If you are interested in a specific lodging option, know that in Venice, booking in advance is the key to securing the hotel you want, since many of the better venues in town are booked solid months in advance. Booking can be done directly through the hotel, or through websites such as www.booking.com, www.expedia.com, www.venere.com, www.skyscanner.com, www.hotel.com, and www.hotelpricebot.com (a website that compares the prices on various websites and helps you choose the best one). These websites often offer very competitive deals, even lower than the prices offered by the hotel websites, but if you need to modify your booking, it might be difficult—read their terms.

B&Bs are another popular choice. They offer the comfort of a simple hotel, but in a much more accessible price range. You can find several choices on the aforementioned websites, and on specific bed and breakfast websites such as www.bed-and-breakfast.it.

Renting a small apartment can be very convenient, especially if you are traveling as a family. We would recommend consulting websites such as Airbnb, obviously, but also www.homeaway.com, www.homeinitaly.com, www.housetrip.com, www.flipkey.com, www.viewsonevenice.com and www.venicerentapartments.com to find the best options. We also highly recommend checking the reviews of other travelers on websites such as TripAdvisor and Booking.com before you book.

If renting an apartment, be sure to ask what the price includes to avoid unpleasant surprises. Is there a minimum number of nights? Does the price include all cleaning charges? Will you be charged separately for electricity, gas, or heating? Does the price include a weekly change of linen and use of the laundry room and Wi-Fi? Is the apartment properly furnished and adequate for daily cooking and living? This last question is especially important if you plan on shopping in local markets and cooking for yourself most nights.

Where to stay

Picking a location to stay in Venice requires a basic understanding of how the city is built and how to move around it. This seems important enough for us to review in detail, to help you make the most informed decision.

In or outside Venice?

The first decision you should make is whether you are going to stay in or outside Venice. Many travelers on a budget choose to stay outside of Venice, because in the summer, hotel prices in the city can be high. These travelers usually end up booking a room in Mestre, which is technically a different city, but from a practical point of view it is a suburb of Venice. Other travelers might book a room in a different town altogether (such as Treviso, 30 minutes away). So before we discuss staying in Venice itself, let's discuss the alternatives:

Outside Venice: Mestre

Mestre is the last stop on land before Venice and is only 15 minutes away. There are some cheap options in Mestre, and some not-so-cheap options (hotels such as the Best Western and the Trieste are priced similarly to hotels in Venice). Personally, we don't recommend that Mestre be your first choice, for a number of reasons. The first and most important reason is ambiance. Venice is an incredibly beautiful city. Certain parts of it, and we don't use this word lightly, are awe-inspiring. Mestre, on the other hand, is industrial and fairly unappealing. Certain sections, especially those around the train station, can be unpleasant. It's important to note this, because if you've been dreaming of a special Venetian getaway, then spending your nights in a hotel in Mestre is going to be a big letdown. We would only come here if we found a very good deal that made up for the location and the commute.

Staying in Venice

The second issue that should be taken into consideration is getting to and from Venice. That's easy enough from Mestre, but you should know that if you are planning any late nights (after 23:00), you won't be able to return to your hotel in Mestre using public transportation. Instead, you'll need to get a taxi from Piazzale Roma, and not only are these expensive, but there are also not that many of them. If you do decide to book a room or an apartment in Mestre, we recommend choosing one of the many hotels in the area around the train station (the Best Western, located right in front of the Mestre station, is a good choice), and avoiding the hotels that tout themselves as being "just five minutes from Venice by bus." The reason is simple—it is very easy to reach Venice from Mestre by train. The bus, on the other hand, can get incredibly crowded and messy in high season.

Outside Venice: Surrounding towns

Some travelers choose to stay in other towns in the area and travel to Venice every day and evening. The most popular choices are the towns located along the railway line, up to Treviso. In our opinion, this is a reasonable option only if you've found a very good deal on a hotel that is within a five-minute walk from the train station in a town that is no more than 30 minutes from Venice. The Continental Hotel in Treviso is a good example: Treviso is 30 minutes from Venice, and the hotel itself is no more than 200 meters from the Treviso train station. Anything farther won't be as convenient, and won't justify the time you'll have to spend commuting back and forth and the money you'll have to spend on train tickets. Also, don't forget to check the train schedule in advance on www.trenitalia.com; you may discover that in certain hours of the day, there are hardly any trains departing from the town you are sleeping in to Venice.

Outside Venice: Family Resorts

For families, another option is staying in a resort or a bed and breakfast in the countryside (agriturismo), driving daily to Venice with your rental car, and parking each morning in Piazzale Roma or Tronchetto. There are some fantastic family resorts within a 25 kilometer radius from Venice, and we would recommend this option if you are in Venice as part of a longer trip, and you plan on spending just a couple of days in town with your kids and then moving on to other destinations in northern Italy. In that case, a family-friendly resort with a pool will justify the hassle and cost of the the daily drive.

Staying in Venice

In Venice

Staying in Venice itself is the best option, in our opinion. There are hundreds of hotels, B&Bs and apartments in Venice, and if you book in advance, it is very likely that you will find something to your taste and within your budget. Staying in Venice lets you enjoy and really get to know the town. There's something magical about wandering the streets of Venice at night, walking along the canals, crossing the little bridges lit only by moonlight and the occasional street lamp, and seeing the city at play. At night, when the hustle and bustle of the tourist-flooded streets calms down, you can see another face of Venice. Not having to leave to commute to Mestre or some other town means you can enjoy your evening without needing to constantly check your watch. Dinner can be followed by ice cream on a little *campo*, and then just walking around and exploring, for no reason or purpose, enjoying yourselves and forgetting the rest of the world exists.

If you decide to stay in Venice itself, choose your hotel based on three main factors: **location, closeness to the vaporetto stops**, and **ambiance**. While ambiance is a subjective matter and depends on your personal taste, location and closeness to the *vaporetto* are two much more technical details. As mentioned previously, mainland Venice is divided into six wards: San Marco, Cannaregio and Castello on one side of the canal, and San Polo, Santa Croce and Dorsoduro on the other side of the canal. Giudecca Island is across the lagoon from Piazza San Marco, and farther away (between 15 minutes and an hour) are the islands like Lido, Murano, Burano, and Torcello. Each of these locations offers a different kind of stay. If you want to be in the very heart of Venice, where most shops, events and museums are concentrated, choose a hotel in the San Marco neighborhood. If you want an area that is quieter than tourist-heavy San Marco, but still lively, choose Dorsoduro (the main draws here are the Accademia Gallery and the Guggenheim Collection). San Polo is another reasonable option.

Cannaregio, Castello, and Santa Croce wards may be too far away from the main sights to be considered a first choice, but they offer plenty of charming hotels that are somewhat off the beaten track. Choose one of these neighborhoods if you are hunting for a bargain hotel and don't mind spending 15-20 minutes on the *vaporetto* commuting each day. The area around the Santa Lucia train station isn't recommended, unless you are looking for a cheap one- or two-star hotel.

Staying in Venice

> **Tip:** It's worth remembering that moving around in Venice is a very slow business. Because of the way the city is built, expect everything to take about double the time it would take if you were traveling by land in another city.

Choosing a hotel on one of the islands off the mainland, such as Murano, Burano, and Lido has its charms, but when traveling with kids it may not the best idea, as you will be far from the sights and spend a great deal of time commuting (Burano is more than an hour from Venice!). If you do specifically want one of the islands, we would suggest Lido; it's only 15 minutes by public *vaporetto* from the mainland, and offers many beaches to enjoy after a day of sightseeing.

Eating and Drinking in Venice, Verona, Lake Garda and the Dolomites

Venice's kitchen is influenced by its position, right on the sea. Fish and seafood are hugely important ingredients, while meat takes a secondary position on the menu (and in some restaurants it disappears altogether). Pasta dishes are very popular, but since this is northern Italy, rice (risotto) and polenta dishes can be found almost everywhere. **Verona's kitchen** is similar in many ways to the Venetian kitchen, with some modifications: The Veronese love their meat, and it is very common to find large platters of cold cuts for antipasto, and various grilled meats for lunch. The Veronese shy away from nothing—even horse meat is popular here, and if you are interested in trying it, ask for the famous *pastissada de caval*, a slow-cooked horse stew enriched with Valpolicella wine and spices. In **Lake Garda** you will find the usual classic pasta dishes (see below) as well as fresh fish from the lake. In the **Dolomites**, the German and Austrian influence is very noticeable, with beer, sauerkraut (fermented cabbage), and sausages served everywhere.

Breakfast, Lunch and Dinner

The three main meals in Italy are *colazione, pranzo,* and *cena. Colazione*, or breakfast, is usually eaten in a bar. In Italy, that isn't a place that serves alcohol, but rather a venue that serves coffee and snacks in the morning and sandwiches later in the day. Italian breakfast is very limited, and unless you are staying at a good hotel that is accustomed to working with international tourists and serves a full breakfast buffet, you might be surprised to find that the traditional Italian *colazione* consists of nothing more than a cappuccino, a brioche, and some marmalade or Nutella to spread on a piece of toast.

Pranzo, or lunch, is usually served between 12:30 and 14:00. You will find very few, if any, restaurants that serve lunch later than 14:30. Cena, or dinner, is served between 19:30—21:30. With the exception of pizzerias, most places won't seat you at a table after 21:30, unless they run two dinner turns (one at 19:30 and one at 21:30—this often happens in the most popular restaurants in Venice).

Eating and Drinking

Unless you buy a sandwich to go or sit down for a light lunch in a bar, you will usually eat in a *ristorante*, a *trattoria*, or an *osteria*. A *Ristorante* is the more high-end, serious dining option—stylish and reserved, with prices to match. *Osterie* and *trattorie* are more homey; they cost less and have a more casual atmosphere, but they can also be huge discoveries, as they often offer excellent, authentic food. To enjoy the best that Venice has to offer, we suggest mixing things up, and trying out both homey *trattorie* and upscale, sophisticated *ristoranti*.

Whichever restaurant you choose, whether it is a neighborhood diner or a 3-star extravaganza, remember that most restaurants are closed one day a week, even in high season. Whenever possible, we have inserted the relevant info in the guide, but for other places not mentioned in this book we recommend you call to see when they are closed.

What should we order?

Breakfast

If you ask for *un caffè*, you'll get an espresso. Alternatively, ask for a *cappuccino* or a *caffè latte*, which is closer to the Starbucks version of coffee, with a lot of milk. Note that if you ask for a *latte* (the popular American term), you will simply get a glass of milk and a perplexed look. You can also try a *macchiato*, which is an espresso with a touch of milk foam. Our personal recommendation for the hot summer months is to ask for a *shakerato* (pronounced "shekerato"), a refreshing cold coffee shaken with ice cubes. If you want it sweetened, make sure you ask for it *con zucchero*. Accompany that with a brioche or *cornetto* (the Italian version of a croissant); there are plenty to choose from, and they will all be on display, together with a small selection of savory sandwiches. If you eat standing up by the bar, as most Italians do, you will be charged less than if you sit down at a table and order. If it's been a long day of sightseeing and you need an afternoon pick-me-up, you can always ask for *un caffè corretto*, which is an espresso "corrected" with a shot of grappa, sambuca or some other liqueur.

Lunch and Dinner

A traditional Italian meal starts with an *antipasto*, which is a selection of meats, cheeses, and other little bites that will awaken your appetite. The *primo*, or first dish, usually follows and is most typically pasta, soup, or a *risotto*. Next is the *secondo*, or main dish, which usually consists of meat or fish. The *secondo* can be served with a *contorno*, or side dish, usually

Eating and Drinking

vegetables, roasted potatoes, or French fries, and is followed by a *dolce*, or dessert and a coffee (*espresso* or a *macchiato*, an Italian will never ever order a *cappuccino* after a meal). At dinnertime, this is occasionally followed by an *ammazzacaffe*, also known as *digestivo*. This is a liqueur, like limoncello, to help you digest. Of course, each course is accompanied by wine, whether it's the house wine or your choice of a bottle, and water.

Clearly, you won't be able to order this much food every time you sit down to eat. What most Italians do is choose a *primo* or a *secondo* and add something small that can be shared, like an *antipasto*, a *contorno*, or even just a dessert. Whatever your order, bread and water will be brought to the table. Bread is free, included in the price of the *coperto* (see below), while water is charged separately. You can ask for still water (*naturale*) or carbonated/ fizzy water (*frizzante*). If you ask for tap water, you will receive a perplexed and judgmental look.

When eating in a *trattoria* or *osteria*, you will be asked if you want the house wine to go with your food. The house wine is usually very good, and ordering a carafe will nicely complement your meal. (The rule of thumb is simple: Red wine with meat and most pasta dishes; white wine with fish and seafood). If you are curious to try something new, or if there's a chance you will be drinking more than a glass or two each, it may be better to order a bottle, instead. A bottle of your choice will cost a little extra, but it will also allow you to enjoy something special, rather than settling for whatever the restaurant has on hand at the moment. A good, entry-level bottle should cost up to 25 euro. More complex wines will be more expensive. For more wine tips and suggestions, see below, under "Italian Wines".

Antipasti

Venice is famous for its seafood, and one of the best ways to discover the full selection is by trying various *antipasti*. Unlike the restaurants in Milan, Florence or Rome, or even Verona, where the *antipasti* will often be a plate of cold cuts and cheeses, most Venetian restaurants pride themselves on a wide selection of seafood-based *antipasti* (vegetarian and meat-based options are far more limited). The two most popular *antipasti* are *sarde in saor* (sweet and sour sardines) and *baccala mantecato* (creamed cod, usually served with polenta). Mixed antipasti plates of steamed or raw seafood are also very popular. These might include everything from tuna carpaccio to raw langoustines (*scampi crudi*), a selection of *gamberi* (shrimp), *cozze* (mussels), *vongole* (clams), grilled or boiled tiny octopuses (*moscardini*), spider crabs (*granseola*, typical of Venice), and other seasonal seafood. *Pepata di cozze* (sautéed mussels in tomato sauce), *capesante gratinate* (creamed scallops), and *moeche fritte* (fried crabs), are also popular.

Primo

On the menu for the *primo* (the first dish) you will usually find either pasta with a seafood based sauce, or a risotto. In **Venice**, the stars of the *primi* section are *pasta e fagioli* (a traditional Veneto style stew, made with a meaty broth, pasta and beans, which is quite popular in Verona, too), *spaghetti alle vongole* (spaghetti with clams), *spaghetti alle seppie* (black spaghetti, prepared with cuttlefish ink), *spaghetti allo scoglio* (spaghetti with a mix of clams and shrimp and tomato sauce), *bigoli in salsa* (a thick maccheroni-like pasta typical of Venice, served with a traditional anchovy and sautéed onion sauce), *risotto ai frutti di mare* (seafood risotto), and *risotto agli asparagi* (available in season only—a risotto made with fresh asparagus). You will usually (but not always) find a selection of non-seafood options, too, such as ravioli, gnocchi, lasagna, pasta with tomato sauce, and more.

In **Verona** the choice also includes many meat-based *primi*. Some of the better-known dishes are *risi e bisi* (a rice and pea dish), gnocchi served with various condiments, pumpkin-filled tortellini, anything with polenta, and the famous *risotto all'amarone* (a classic risotto cooked with rich-tasting Amarone wine). In **Lake Garda** you will find the usual popular italian pasta dishes—penne all'arrabbiata sauce (arrabiata means angry, and this sauce is nice and spicy); spaghetti all'amatriciana (tomato sauce, guanciale, and pecorino Romano cheese); spaghetti alla carbonara (made with egg yolks, pecorino cheese and black pepper); tortellini with porcini mushrooms;

ravioli in butter and sage sauce, and more. In the **Dolomites**, expect to find *canederli* (boiled dumplings with a spinach or ham filling; knodel in German); pasta with a variety of sauces; wurstel with polenta; ravioli with poppy seeds; tagliatelle with mushrooms, and more.

Secondo

For the main dish, the *secondo*, you will normally be given a choice of fish- or meat-based dishes. (Once again, the fish-based selection is much wider in most restaurants in Venice. Check the menu before sitting down for your meal, to make sure there is something that matches your preferences.) Those who are ready to sample more delicacies of the sea will enjoy an abundant selection of fresh grilled fish and seafood, such as *coda di rospo* (monkfish), *anguilla* (eel), *branzino* (sea bass), *orata* (sea bream), or *scampi* (langoustines). *Seppia alla Veneziana,* also known as *seppie al nero* (cuttlefish in black ink sauce, served with polenta) is a very popular option, as is *frittura mista*, a mixed deep-fried platter (which usually consists of calamari, shrimp and *scampi*, often still in their shells). *Baccala mantecato*, mentioned earlier in the *antipasti* section, is also eaten as a secondo (the size of the portion is simply larger). Meat lovers will want to try the most famous Venetian dish, *fegato alla Veneziana* (veal liver cooked in sauce and served with polenta). Other popular options are *spezzatino* (beef stew), *osso buco* (braised veal shank) steaks and grilled meats.

In **Verona**, try the aforementioned *pastissada de caval* (horse stew), *bollito con la peara* (veal cooked with spices, bread, cheese, and bone marrow), and grilled meats. In the **Dolomites**, try the locally made sausages (wurstel or salsiccia), *Gulasch* (a Hungarian beef stew popular in this area, too); *spezzatino con i mirtilli rossi* (game stew, served with a blueberry marmalade); and the most popular cold cut in this region—Speck (a dry cured and slightly smoked ham).

Contorno

For the side dish, the *contorno*, you will often find *patate al forno* (oven-baked potatoes), *patatine fritte* (French fries), *fagioli* (white beans), *spinaci* (spinach), *ceci* (chickpeas), *verdure alle brace/alla griglia* (roasted/grilled vegetables), *insalata mista/insalata verde* (a simple salad, though you should know that the Italian definition of a salad is very limited, usually involving little more than lettuce, a few other green leaves, and a couple of lonesome cherry tomatoes).

Pizza

Pizza is, of course, a hugely popular choice for many Italians. A meal in a pizzeria is much cheaper than a dinner in a *trattoria*, and can be just as enjoyable. We recommend choosing a pizzeria that advertises itself with the magic words *forno a legna* (real wood-burning stove). In Venice there is no shortage of popular pizzerias. For an authentic flavor, try Pier Dickens pizzeria in lively Campo Santa Margherita. For a pizza with a view, try Ristorante-Pizzeria Alvise, right next to the Fondamente Nove *vaporetto* stop. In Verona, Lake Garda and the Dolomites, the choices of good pizzerias are endless.

Vegetarian

If you are a vegetarian, there are a few precautions you should take when visiting restaurants in Venice, or Italy, for that matter. First, you should know that most (but not all) soups are made with meat or chicken stock. If you are unsure about the contents of a dish, just ask: "*Sono vegetariano, c'e' carne o pesce?*" (Pronounced, "Sono vegetariano, che carne o peshe?"). The Italian idea of vegetarianism can be difficult, however, and while most waiters have no trouble telling you if there's meat in the dish, they often don't think it's a problem if there's chicken broth in it, or lard, or gelatine, or any other animal by-products. More than once we were assured that a certain dish was vegetarian, but on further investigation we found small pieces of salami in the sauce, or noticed that the broth had a distinct meaty flavor. When we confronted the waiter with our findings, he answered, slightly offended, "There's just a little bit—only for the taste!"

You should also know that most hard cheeses are produced with *caglio* (rennet, produced from cows). Some cheesemakers offer a cheese made with *caglio vegetale,* suitable for vegetarians. Vegetarians should also avoid anything containing *strutto* and *lardo*, both of which mean lard. It might seem strange, but *strutto* is sometimes found in breads, *focaccias*, and pastries. The safest choices for vegetarians are pizzas, pasta dishes (risottos tend to be trickier, because of the stock used in preparing them) and, naturally, salads.

In **Venice**, the most popular vegetarian restaurant is La Zucca, on Santa Croce 1762 (five minutes by foot from the Natural History museum). Tel: 041.524.1570, www.lazucca.it. Open Monday-Saturday, 12:30–14:30 & 19:00-22:30; Sunday closed. In **Verona**, you will find a variety of vegetarian and vegan dishes at Ristorante Flora, Stradone Scipione Maffei 8, Verona. Tel: 045.800.6300, www.ristoranteflora.it. Open daily, 12:30-14:30 & 19:00-22:30.

Desserts

Italians have a talent for salty baked goods—their *focaccias* and *schiacciatas* are famous the world over. Italian desserts, on the other hand, tend to be a little disappointing, as they often suffer from lack of imagination, and are sometimes rather heavy. With the exception of a real *ristorante*, desserts are typically weak and not homemade. If they do make their desserts in-house, they will usually make a point of explicitly stating *dolci fatti in casa* (homemade dessert) on the menu. Look around and check out the desserts served to others in the restaurant. If they don't seem that tempting, skip them and head for a *gelato* or *granita* instead.

Aperitivo

An *aperitivo* is a light snack and cocktail consumed before dinner, much like the Spanish tapas or the French aperitif. The *aperitivo* is popular all over Italy, but in Venice it is a culture unto itself. Here, taverns and restaurants open early and offer a large selection of snacks and canapés (all on display at the counter), together with various local wines and popular cocktails. To make the most of your *aperitivo*, do as the locals do: Order a Spritz (the most popular cocktail on the menu, made with bubbly Prosecco and a shot of slightly bitter Aperol or Campari), add two to five *cicheti* from the selection at the bar (a *cicheto* typically costs between €1.5 and €2.5) and then sip and munch away, standing up, with the rest of the merry Italians.

Your *aperitivo* can consist of just a short visit at one *bacaro* (a tavern that serves the traditional Venetian *aperitivo*) before dinner, or can be expanded into a tour of two or three popular *bacari*, sampling various local delicacies in tiny portions in each tavern, and enjoying an inexpensive and diverse meal on the go. The selection on offer changes from *bacaro* to *bacaro*, but most include the following staples in their *aperitivo* buffet: *baccala mantecato*; *sarde in saor*; polpette (meatballs, usually deep-fried); tiny sandwiches; canapès; slices of cheese or ham; mozzarella in *carrozza* (coated and deep-fried mozzarella); and a selection of *crostini* with inventive toppings, everything from Gorgonzola and nuts to ricotta, pumpkin and pistachios to salmon, mustard and sautéed artichokes.

Tipping and the *Coperto*

To request the bill at the end of your meal simply ask the waiter for "*il conto per favore,*" pronounced as it is written. Once this is done, the issue of tipping arises. Restaurants in Italy charge what is called *coperto*, which means a fixed fee for "opening the table." Contrary to what many tourists believe, it has nothing to do with how much bread you eat or whether you ask for water. In Venice the *coperto* is often higher than in other cities and ranges between €1 and €3 per person. Michelin-starred restaurants and other famous venues will easily double that fee. Water is always charged separately. Since restaurants charge a *coperto*, tipping isn't mandatory. You may want to leave a 10% tip at the end of a dinner, but only do this if you were especially pleased with the service, as it is not obligatory. Tipping in taxis, hotels, etc. is up to you. Doing so will be appreciated, but it isn't considered a faux pas if you don't do it. The one case in which tipping may be a good idea is when someone goes out of their way to help you, in which case a tip is the best way to show your appreciation.

Wine

There are many books dedicated to the complex and fascinating subject of Italian wines, so it goes without saying that any introduction we give here is only meant as a very general primer. However, seeing as Italian wines are world-famous, and since you will surely sample a number of Veneto's fine wines during your travels, it would be foolish not to provide a general summary of the local wine industry. Venice, Verona and Lake Garda are located in the Veneto region, which is one of the most important wine-producing regions in Italy. The best-known wines produced in this area are Valpolicella, Amarone, Prosecco, Soave, and Bardolino. In the Dolomites, the wines to try are Cabernet Sauvignon, Lagrein, Müller-Thurgau, Teroldego, and the Gewürztraminer.

Amarone di Valpolicella (often simply referred to as Amarone) is a rich and powerful red, and is considered one of the most prestigious wines in all of Italy. It is full-bodied and complex, and is made with a mix of Corvina, Rondinella and other permitted grape varieties. Try it with a good steak, and you will fall under its spell.

Bardolino is a light red wine produced around the town of Bardolino, on the eastern shores of Lake Garda. It is a light and simple wine, very drinkable, and fun for an aperitivo.

Eating and Drinking

Soave is one of the best-known and loved white wines in Italy. Fresh, smooth, straw-colored, and fruity, it's perfect for an aperitivo or with a seafood-based meal. It is produced in the province of Verona using a blend of Garganega, Trebbiano di Soave and Chardonnay grapes. Since there is such a huge selection of Soave wines available, we recommend you stick to tasting and buying Soave Superiore DOC wines, to a guarantee a good level of quality.

Valpolicella is a fruity and perfumed red wine. It is one of the best and most popular choices in the region, and an excellent go-to wine when touring Veneto. There are different categories and classes to Valpolicella, including Valpolicella Classico DOC, Valpolicella Classico Superiore, and Valpolicella Ripasso, each of which is made according to different techniques that confer a somewhat different taste. Generally speaking, you can't go wrong with a Valpolicella Ripasso, or a Valpolicella Superiore.

Prosecco is the best-known sparkling wine in Italy. It is prepared with Glera grapes, and since 2009 it has been regulated, which means that today you can find Prosecco DOC wines with guaranteed quality. Prosecco wines differ based on their level of foaminess and sweetness. The drier version is known as Brut, while the sweet is referred to as Dolce. A good in-between choice is Extra-Dry Prosecco. In Venice, you will often enjoy a glass of bubbly Prosecco on its own, or as one of the two main ingredients of the famous Bellini cocktail.

Wine Classification

All Italian wines adhere to a classification system set by the government. This system protects local production, so that a wine from the North of Italy, for example, won't be able to advertise itself as a Chianti (a wine from Tuscany), and a wine produced near Florence won't be marketed as a Valpolicella. This system ensures that certain quality standards are followed, and divides wines into four major categories:

Vino da Tavola, or table wine, is the simplest wine available. Don't bother to waste your time with it.

IGT stands for *indicazione geografica tipica*, and defines wine that comes from a specific geographic location. Though it's not the highest classification, there are some excellent wines in this category. Ironically, in recent years many important producers who refused to adapt their wine-making recipes to the government guidelines could no longer call their wine DOC and were forced to define it IGT.

Eating and Drinking

DOC, *denominazione d'origine controllata*, means you are guaranteed a product of a certain quality, from a specific area, made according to specific guidelines.

DOCG, *denominazione d'origine controllata e garantita*, marks the highest-quality wines.

The best way to learn more about Italian wines is, quite simply, to drink them. In Italy, wine isn't considered a snooty hobby reserved for the rich; it's a way of life and a popular traditional passion. Most Italians grow up with wine on their family dinner tables, and develop a palate from an early age. Many, and not necessarily just foodies, are well-informed about good products. Don't be afraid to experiment and order a bottle at a restaurant. Stick to the aforementioned local wines, and you can't go wrong. A bottle of red goes well with meat (try: Amarone, Valpolicella, Cabernet Sauvignon), and a bottle of white is excellent with fish or seafood (try: Soave, Lugana, or any white wine from the neighboring Friuli region).

Choosing the "right" wine is, in many cases, simply a question of taste. Top marks and high prices are often used as proof of a wine's quality, but both factors can be misleading. Your taste may be different from that of a noted wine critic, and some excellent wines simply go unnoticed, which doesn't mean you should exclude them from your tasting list. Prices, too, can offer guidance, but they are not an automatic guarantee of taste. You will be surprised at the reasonably priced, quality finds you might come across in the local enoteca, or at one of the large supermarkets, which usually have a respectable selection of excellent wines priced under €25. But it actually shouldn't be surprising that the selection is so appealing here; this is, after all, where most Italians go to do their shopping and pick up a bottle or two for their party or family dinner.

Booking in Advance

If there is a specific restaurant you want to try, we highly recommend booking a day or two in advance. With hotels, the situation is much trickier. Venice is busy almost year-round, but during the summer months it is packed to the rafters, and the most popular hotels are booked solid months in advance. Start your research early to guarantee the room you want.

Verona isn't as busy as Venice, but in high season it can be hard to find openings at both restaurants and hotels. Advanced reservations are highly recommended here, too.

Eating and Drinking

Italian Manners

Italians take manners very seriously. They pride themselves on their *buona educazione* (proper education), and appreciate it when others play by the same rules. It's considered rude, for instance, to ask for something without first saying "Excuse me" (*scusi*, pronounced "skuzi"). Starting a conversation with *scusi* and ending it with *grazie tante* ("Thank you very much"; note that the word is pronounced graziE, not graziA, as many tourists mistakenly say) will leave a good impression and help you get better service at hotels, restaurants, and attractions. The polite way to say "Goodbye" is *arrivederci*, while the polite way to say "Hello" when arriving somewhere is *buongiorno* or *buonasera*, depending on whether it's day (*giorno*) or night (*sera*). Of course, like anywhere, a smile goes a long way.

That said, we have to admit that no matter how polite a tourist may be, service in Italy can be lacking at times. Though the majority of Italians are friendly and welcoming, be prepared for the occasional annoyed waiter or shopkeeper. If it makes any difference, know that it's usually not personal; salesmen and waiters are often short with locals as well as foreigners (to many of the local businesses, a foreigner is anyone that didn't grow up on the same street and go to the same kindergarten as them). Sometimes you may get the feeling that Italians get better service, and occasionally you'll be right. Often, however, it's not because you are being discriminated against, it's simply due to the language barrier. Many Italians don't speak English very well and keep their sentences as short as possible to avoid embarrassment.

Lastly, it is worth mentioning that Italians are very attentive to fashion and style, and usually prefer to dress up rather than down. Take a look around any given centrally located *piazza* on a Saturday night, and you will immediately understand what we are talking about. The women are all in skimpy dresses, 6-inch heels and perfectly done hair, and the men walk around in chic jackets and pricey shoes. This means that even though most Italian restaurants have a far more relaxed dress code than that of their French counterparts, they do welcome slightly more elegant attire. You will probably feel more welcome (and get better service) if you dress the part.

Traveling with Kids

There is much to say about travelling with kids, and some books are dedicated entirely to this subject. We'd like to offer a few general tips we've found helpful.

Slow down

When traveling with children, time must be a flexible concept. You want to see as much as you can, but everything takes longer with kids (especially younger ones). Unless you plan on becoming the family sergeant and rushing everyone along all day, accept that you won't be able to see every single thing there is to see in Venice or the rest of the region. Focus on fewer attractions and really enjoy the ride. If there's anything we can learn from the Italians, it's the charm of taking things slowly. Decide on a reasonable number of sights and attractions (no more than three a day, for the most part); we promise you will still have a great time and won't feel like you are missing out on anything, and the added bonus is that getting from place to place will be a fun adventure, not a hysterical race against the clock.

Enjoy the fact that you are together and that you are on vacation

It seems so obvious, but sometimes we forget that the best vacation memories aren't of the exact view you saw from the bell tower in Venice, or the artwork in the Doge's Palace. The best memories are more personal, like the time a pigeon tried to steal dad's pizza, or when you got lost in Venice and accidentally came across that amazing mask shop, or the day you went to the farm in the Dolomites and made friends with a goat named Francesca. In other words, this vacation is also your chance to just enjoy your family, create special memories, and laugh together.

Combine serious activities, like museums, with fun activities

Balance your days by combining sightseeing with fun activities your kids will enjoy, like bike riding, going to the beach, horseback tours, or visiting an amusement park. If you spend the morning touring a botanical garden and castle, spend the afternoon doing something more active or relaxed. After visiting the Palazzo Ducale in Venice, don't rush off to see another museum. Instead, do something fun, like climbing up the Campanile, running around at the Giardini Biennale, booking a gondola rowing lesson or a mask-making workshop, or even going to the beach on Lido island. Stop for lunch and ice cream, and then squeeze in one more sight you want to see.

Budget for your comfort in advance

This may seem like a small tip, but it can make a huge difference in your trip. Taking the whole family abroad for a vacation is expensive, and it's natural to try to save money whenever possible. But it is easy to cut the wrong corners when you are away from home. In our experience, paying a little extra money for the right things can save you a lot of stress and hassle, and when you have small children that can be priceless. For example: It is possible to find free parking in Verona or Lake Garda at some distance from the center, and walk or take the bus, thus saving the money you would have spent on a parking lot. But in the summer, when the days are hot and long, dragging children across the city also has its price. Booking tickets in advance is another example. Yes, it will cost more, but it will also save you the time and grief of standing in a long line with the children, and starting your tour with everyone already tired and cranky from the long wait. These little extras don't add up to much in the end, yet the difference they make to your day is important.

Get kids of all ages (from toddlers to teens) involved

Before you visit a museum, try to read about the work or the artists' lives in advance—kids usually enjoy looking out for works by artists whose names they recognize. If they know what they are seeing, and know a few details about the painters and the city it will make their visit more meaningful and logical. If possible, encourage your children to read up or watch YouTube videos about the places you are going to visit. Mark the sights on the map, and figure out together how far they are about to travel. Ask if there are any special places that THEY are interested in seeing (and then insert these places into your itinerary).

Set aside a budget for buying knick-knacks

What may seem like useless rubbish to adults may mean a great deal to a seven year-old boy or girl, who loves to fill pockets with "treasures". For the price of just one dinner at a restaurant (about 25-35 euro), you can budget an entire week of knick-knack shopping, including the little prizes kids get for completing the missions in this guide.

Give kids some economic freedom

Give your kids a few daily euro to budget their own purchases. Younger children adore having "a lot of money" (i.e., lots of coins in their very own purse; lots of ten-cent coins are much better than just one 1-euro coin, of course...). Older kids love the sense of independence and maturity that comes from having their own money and deciding where to spend it.

Encourage kids to communicate

Most Italians love kids, and they can't get enough of sweet kids trying to speak Italian. Most children will enjoy the attention and affection they will receive if they try to be communicative and friendly. This is another good reason to have them learn, in advance, how to say a few basic Italian words and phrases, like "Hello", "Thank you", "Excuse me", "Goodbye", "Where is…?", "How much does it cost?", "My name is…", "I am X years old" etc.

Get your child a cheap camera

Whether it be a basic digital camera, or the new generation Polaroid cameras (which print on inkless paper your digital photos), there are several inexpensive options on the market. A child with his own camera (assuming he is interested in taking his own photos) will feel more independent and be more interested in his surroundings. Yes, it might slow you down sometimes, especially when he wants to take yet another photo of that tower (which won't be that different from the 50 photos that came before it), but it's worth it. Your child's photos can be used to update the family's digital travel blog (see more on that under "Travelling with Tenagers and Older Children") or for his own cool travel diary, where he can also glue ticket stubs, postcards and other colorful mementos. Of course, you should also carry your own camera, but once you get home, try to incorporate a few of the photos your children shot into the family album. They will be very proud.

Use games to combat boredom while standing in line

Ten out of ten scientists will tell you that kids don't like standing in line. You will find tips on how to avoid the lines in the itineraries themselves, especially in Venice, but when you do find yourself stuck in a line, use that time to master activities that don't require moving. For example, before leaving for your trip, watch YouTube videos that demonstrate yo-yo tricks. Then, while standing in line, pull out a yo-yo and let the kids practice the tricks. Do the same with magic tricks that don't require much moving. Braid your child's hair in unique styles or, if you are brave, do some face painting for the toddlers. Play games like "I Spy" or "Guess What Famous Person I Am Thinking Of (21 questions; yes or no only)". With grade-schoolers, ask "What would you do if …." questions and insert some funny or gross hypothetical questions (What's worse, being eaten by a vampire or a zombie?). If you don't mind people staring, you can play a game of "Guess that Word" (Dad writes a word on Mom's back with his finger, Mom writes the same word on the first child's back, who in turn writes it on the second child's back, etc.). You can also carry games around to pass the time, anything from PSP to Etch-a-Sketch. Soap bubbles are another popular activity for toddlers. Encourage your kids to make friendship bracelets, take pictures of their surroundings with their cameras, or check out how far away they can see with their binoculars.

Traveling with Teenagers and Older Children

Traveling with teenagers can be challenging, but it is also a fantastic opportunity to experience new things together.

Try to offer adult-like experiences, that have a wow factor. Most teenagers will appreciate these and be happy to later brag to their friends about what they've seen and done. Half a day at a thermal spa, a speedboat tour in Sirmione, rides up the best funivie (cable cars) in the Dolomites, half a day at the water parks in Jesolo or Canevaworld, working on their tan at private beaches like Baia delle Sirene in Lake Garda, late night picnics by the water, surfing lessons, tours of the Ferrari, Lamborghini and Ducati museums, horse riding lessons in the Alps and shopping excursions in Venice and Verona are all fantastic things to try and enjoy together.

Give your teenagers (and pre-teens) some responsibilities. Many teenagers will benefit from playing a more active role in the trip, though not all teenagers will be comfortable with this additional responsibility. Consider your teenager's personality, and if this will make him/her feel stressed or ruin his/her vacation, don't do it.

Use technology to your advantage. Technology is a huge part of the average teenager's life; you can get teenagers to download travel apps to their smartphones that will help you during the trip (most of them are free). Here is a partial list of apps and the ways your teenager can use them to make your trip successful (you can find more by Googling "cool travel apps", "travel apps kids", and "Italy apps").

1. Encourage teenagers to take photos of their surroundings and live blog their experience on photo sharing websites such as Instagram, Tumblr or even Pinterest. They might just discover they have a natural talent and will draw the attention of new fans.

2. Instead of fighting and having to nag your teenagers about packing, get them to manage their own packing with an app, like Triplist. This app is also very useful for building the entire itinerary.

3. Appoint your teenagers Head Navigators, using apps like Google Maps and Waze. This is not only a good way to get them involved and responsible, it's also the easiest way to plan your itinerary and not get lost in town. Many teenagers and even pre-teens turn out to be quite savvy and resourceful when it's up to them to decide where to go and how to get there, instead of being led passively from one point to the other.

4. Ask your teenagers and pre-teens to search for extra information on the places you plan on visiting, using anything from Wikipedia to apps like Triposo (which works offline, too).

5. In their capacity as Official Translators, ask kids and teenagers to help with translating menus or instructions using Google Translator.

6. Choose your hotel together with your kids, and read together reviews on websites such as TripAdvisor, Hotels.com, Booking.com, and Trivago.

7. If they want, teenagers can learn some basic useful phrases with the popular Tourist: Language Learn & Speak app.

8. Ask your teenager to download a currency convertor and appoint them as the Official Treasurer of the family, helping you figure out what is and isn't a good deal and how much things really cost.

Tip: If you plan on booking a special activity, always ask in advance whether it is appropriate for your family. Make sure, for example, that a riding tour/lesson is offered in English, and is suitable for younger children and inexperienced riders before booking it, and make sure your travel insurance covers any extreme sports and riding tours. Take into consideration any health issues before booking activities like quad tours, hikes, rafting, bike rides, extreme sports, and more. Also, you may want to consult with your doctor before making plans to visit any thermal baths (which are very popular in Italy); thermal water has medicinal properties, and some doctors do not recommend those with health concerns or children younger than 12 to enter them.

Travelling with Toddlers and Younger Children

It is easy to get toddlers excited about your trip, because just about everything will be new to them: the airplane and trains (both major hits among the toddler community), the tall buildings and the motorcycles everywhere, the pizza and the castles. Show them pictures of what they are about to see to prepare them and create anticipation.

Wherever you go, don't forget to add several breaks to your itinerary, especially in Venice (you will find a special box about gardens and playgrounds in the Venice Itinerary). Make sure you pack plenty of surprises, such as travel size board games, and tablets with games and books on them, stickers, coloring pages, activity books and crayons. Binoculars, walkie talkies, and a loved toy from back home are always useful options. Finally, use the special activity section at the ends of each chapter to find the best attractions to balance out your itinerary.

Tip: Looking for the perfect book to read with your kids during your vacation? Try our popular Riddle Books! **The Great Book of Animal Riddles** is specifically designed to intrigue young readers with fun new facts and beautiful pictures of wild animals. Find out who is stronger: a grizzly bear or a tiger; whether some turtles really breathe through their behinds; which animal is even faster than the cheetah; how ants communicate with each other; and whether koalas really have fingerprints. Visit us at www.bankierbooks.com to find out more, and to receive a **free gift** with every purchase.

… How to Build a Trip

How to Build a Trip
Using the Suggested Itineraries in this book

Here are a few examples of trips you could build based on the seven chapters in this guide. For more suggestions, consult the additional sample itineraries in the Lake Garda and Venice chapters, too.

Sample Itinerary N. 1

Family of four: Two children, ages 6 and 10.

Looking for: Some nature, a little bit of art, a couple of children's activities, and some low-key, relaxing fun.

Duration: Family has one week in northern Italy.

Sleeping: The family will choose two focal points (Venice for two nights, and Lake Garda for the rest of the week) and rent an apartment or book a room for each.

Days	Itinerary
Day 1	Venice, including Piazza San Marco, the Campanile, the Rialto, Scuola San Rocco, take a gondola ride.
Day 2	Spend the morning in Venice, then drive to Jesolo and spend the rest of the day there.
Day 3	Lake Garda—visit Gardaland and Sirmione.
Day 4	Lake Garda—visit the Parco Natura Viva zoo and Safari, Malcesine, and Riva del Garda.
Day 5	Lake Garda and Sigurta park, or Merano (see Dolomites chapter).
Day 6	Lake Molveno (see Day Trips from Lake Garda chapter).
Day 7	Verona and the Nicolis Car Museum (see Day Trips from Lake Garda chapter).

How to Build a Trip

Sample Itinerary N. 2

Family of four: Two children, ages 8 and 13.

Looking for: A lot of active fun, no more than a two or three museums, beautiful views, good food, some unique activities.

Duration: Family has six days in northern Italy.

Sleeping: The family will choose two focal points (Lake Garda for most nights, except for perhaps one night in the Dolomites).

Days	Itinerary
Day 1	Venice, focus on the "must see" sights, mainly Piazza San Marco, the Campanile, Rialto Bridge and a mask shop. Book a rowing lesson or a kayak tour in advance.
Day 2	Lake garda—Sirmione + boat tour + adventure park. Eat by the lake, on the promenade in Salo' or Maderno.
Day 3	Lake Garda—visit Gardaland and / or Canevaworld.
Day 4	Visit the Varone waterfall and do some watersports near Riva del Garda, or visit Lake Tenno and the airplane museum in Trento.
Day 5	The Dolomites - Hike at the Gilfenklamm Canyon, visit Dobbiaco and Lake Braies.
Day 6	Lake Garda and Malcesine, spend some time at the beach.
Day 7	Visit Verona and the nearby adventure park or water park (see Verona itinerary) or the Ferrari museum.

How to Build a Trip

Sample Itinerary N. 3

Family of four: Two children, ages 11 and 14.

Looking for: Some nature and light hiking, seeing the highlights in Venice, just relaxing and having a lot of fun in lake Garda.

Duration: Family has one week in northern Italy.

Sleeping: The family will choose two focal points (Venice for two nights, and lake Garda for the rest of the week).

Days	Itinerary
Day 1 & 2	Venice—follow the suggested itinerary in the Venice chapter
Day 3	Gardaland during the day, Verona in the evening (stroll around, see Juliet's house, have dinner at a good restaurant near the famous Roman Arena in Piazza Bra).
Day 4	Lake Garda—Sirmione, Malcesine, Riva del Garda, Salò.
Day 5	The Dolomites—Ortisei and an adventure park, or Canazei, the zipline, and Pass Pordoi.
Day 6	The Dolomites—Alpe di Siusi + a special activity there: either a carriage ride across the meadows, or a hike with alpacas. Spend the afternoon in one of the recommended lakes in the Dolomites chapter.
Day 7	Lake Garda + the Ferrari Museum

64
How to Build a Trip

Sample Itinerary N. 4:

Family of four: Two children, ages 15 and 17.

Looking for: Art and history, a couple of easy family hikes with excellent views, some time by the beach, some unique activities.

Duration: Family has one week in northern Italy.

Sleeping: The family will choose two or three focal points (Venice for two nights, and lake Garda for the rest of the week.

Days	Itinerary
Day 1	Venice—Piazza San Marco, the Doge's Palace, a gondola ride (or gondola rowing lesson), cicheti at the Rialto bridge.
Day 2	Venice—Basilica I Frari, Scuola San Rocco, Guggenheim Collection, family dinner in the Dorsoduro neighborhood or on Lido island, by the beach.
Day 3	Verona (Juliet's house, Sant'Anastasia, panoramic view from Castel San Pietro), followed by a visit to the Ferrari Museum.
Day 4	Lake Garda—Sirmione + boat tour, Malcesine, Baia delle Sirene.
Day 5 & 6	The Dolomites—follow one or two of the ten suggested itineraries in the Dolomites chapter.
Day 7	Lake Garda—one of the amusement parks (Gardaland or Canevaworld) and some free time at the beach.

VENICE

Venice

A City of Mysteries

The glorious Venice you see today, with its ornate displays of art and architecture, began as a ragtag collection of people desperately fleeing wars. After the Roman empire collapsed, parts of what is now Italy were relentlessly raided by Barbarian tribes, forcing people to escape their homes and find a new, safer place to live. A lagoon might seem like a strange place to settle, but it was not uncharted territory for those early arrivals, and the Barbarians were a serious inspiration to get creative. Torcello was the first area in the lagoon to be inhabited, on March 25, 421, and the first settlers were soon joined by many others.

How Trade Fueled Venice's Rise

In the sixth century, Venice was part of the Byzantine Empire, but as it became more successful economically, the local merchants became uncomfortable with the idea of being ruled (and taxed…) by an outside force. The Venetian drive for independence led them to elect their own ruler, the Doge, and conduct the city's affairs with greater independence. The Ducassy of Venice was founded in 697, and it soon became an economic hub. The city grew wealthier through international and local trade, and was also involved in financing the some of the Crusades. This allowed the Venetians to control some of the most coveted routes in the Mediterranean, increasing the city's profile and generating great wealth for all those involved. In some respects, Venice filled the vacancy on the Mediterranean stage created when the Roman Empire fell. The Venetians established themselves as far away as Greece and Cyprus with bases that served as informal embassies and trade centers. In fact, you'll notice that Mercury, the god of trade, and Neptune, the god of the sea, show up often in symbolic artwork representing Venice.

In the Middle Ages, the Venetian lagoon was a busy port, with ships arriving and setting sail in armed groups known as 'taxegia'. Naturally, such wealth drew more than just merchants; what pirate could resist all that loot passing through one part of the sea? In addition to fighting against neighboring cities (such as Genoa, Pisa and Amalfi), the Venetian fleet waged a constant war against the pirates, especially those who were backed by the Turkish Sultans. Luckily, the Venetian fleet was state of the art for its time—the Arsenale (Venice's shipyard, see self-guided walking tour for details) was at one point the biggest industrial enterprise in Europe. Stronger than ever, Venice furthered its dominance of the land and ruled over several other cities and towns in Italy. During the height of its power, the Venetian republic (the Serenissima) controlled large sections of the Veneto region, and even today you will see the Venetian winged lion in Verona, Bergamo, Vincenza, and other Italian cities.

As Venice grew power became less consolidated, and with time the role of the Doge became more ceremonial. The real decision-making power rested in the Maggior Consiglio, the Great Council, which was like a parliament comprised of the city's most elite merchant families. Venetians valued ancestry and family connections highly, and they kept a registry book of all the marriages and deaths of the powerful noble dynasties. It was known as the 'Golden Book', and it was a real who's who of Venetian patrician families. Only people from families listed in this book could hold office or obtain the best political and trade positions.

Enemies, Disasters and the Downfall of Venetian Trade

Success breeds jealousy and enemies, and in the 1500s, Venice faced increasing competition. Pirates posed a constant threat to the city's merchant fleet, and the royal courts in Aragon (today's Spain), France and Milan grew restless as Venice amassed power, wealth and land. The papacy was a very political office back then, and even Pope Julius II was losing patience with Venice's independence, especially with the city's stubborn refusal to allow pope-appointed clergy members to be elected to the Venetian senate, which thwarted his efforts to influence local politics.

In 1508 Venice's enemies developed an alliance called the League of Cambrai, for the express purpose of bringing Venice down. Soon the battles went from competing over trade routes to actual combat. Luckily for Venice, the league members were so focused on their own individual gain that they were prone to conflict between themselves, and some clever and conniving diplomacy eventually brought the League of Cambrai down. But political savviness was not enough. Strong enemies, such as Portugal, the Turks, and to a lesser extent Genova, were a growing threat as they constantly expanded their trade routes. Portuguese sailor Vasco da Gama's famous 1497 voyage quite literally changed the map, as did the discovery of America. (Christopher Columbus traveled under the auspices of the Spanish king, but originally he was a merchant from Genova.)

Venice's decline began to snowball in the 1570s. First the Serenissima lost Cyprus, a major trade hub, in a war with the Turks, and then a particularly violent episode of the plague (black death) cut down almost a third of the city's population. Other European forces continued to plot against the republic, deadly weather destroyed the city's crops, and twice fire ripped through the Doge's palace. Soon, Venetian currency, which had once been accepted around the Mediterranean, collapsed. The void was quickly filled up by the competitors who sprang into action—the city of Marseilles developed a large port, giving France a boost in power. In Tuscany, Livorno, under the guidance of the Medici family, began to develop more trade. And the Spanish, Portuguese and even the English launched successful international trade routes that the weakened Venetians could no longer compete with.

As Venice lost status and confidence, the city's elite began to shift their focus from sea trade to real estate, and people became less civic-minded. Even the council shrunk. But as trade declined in Venice, the arts bloomed to fill the void. Society became more hedonistic, and theater, literary salons, book publishing and wild, decadent masquerade balls became increasingly popular. The party came to an end with the arrival of Napoleon's army in March of 1797. The last doge stepped down from his office without any real resistance, which upset many Venetians and earned him a harsh judgement from history. Venice was annexed to the Austrian Empire as part of a deal Napoleon cut, and later played an important part in the Risorgimento revolution (the Italian fight for independence), until Venice was finally freed, and joined the new Italian kingdom in 1866. Eventually, Italy became a republic, and Venice remained as part of the new nation state.

New Visions of Venice

In the 1970s, young Venetians began to leave the city in search of new opportunities. Factories were closing in the city, and an influx of wealthy tourists drove prices up, making Venice a harder place to live in. Today, Venice's prime challenges are a declining population and a rising sea level. The number of Venetians has dwindled significantly (there are only 56,000 residents in the city, compared with more than 22 million tourists a year). Locals are working to create a balance where Venice's glorious past is celebrated, while the city finds a way to exist as a modern and vibrant place to live, too.

Through all the changes and centuries, Venice has remained a magnet and an inspiration for all types of creative people, from artists and writers to actors, musicians and thinkers. The city has been a muse even to those who have never visited it—Shakespeare set The Merchant of Venice and Othello here, without having ever set foot in Venice himself. When you walk here, following the footsteps of Lord Byron, Thomas Mann, Charles Dickens, Henry James, Claude Monet, Cole Porter, and Sigmund Freud, among others, it is easy to see the draw. Hopefully, Beautiful *Venezia* will work its magic on you, too...

How Venice Was Built & the Acqualta

The physical building of Venice is an incredible achievement unknown to many travelers. While the lagoon has been inhabited since ancient times, the land on which Venice is built is man-made. The entire city—not merely the buildings—is basically an artificial island held above the water by pillars of oak that were driven into the rock bed of the lagoon. Because the wood was not exposed to oxygen, it petrified instead of rotting. A layer of wood was then built on the pillars, and that was topped with stone blocks. In some areas, additional islands were created by draining the water and adding rocks and rubble. The sheer scope of the building is as incredible as everything else about Venice—the city today consists of 177 canals weaving around 118 islands linked by 416 bridges. The Rialto Bridge alone is supported by 12,000 wooden pillars.

Venice faces many challenges today, too, and keeping it afloat, given the rising sea level, is an endless task requiring some serious engineering creativity. Flooding and erosion are constant threats, as is the **Acqualta.** This famous phenomenon happens during a peak high tide, when the water rises higher than normal high tide levels, partially flooding Venice and other areas along the northern Adriatic. The acqualta is determined by a number of factors, including the moon and the strength of the winds. The shape of the Adriatic Sea, and particularly of the Venetian Lagoon, are contributing factors.

The Venetians have learned to live with constant flooding, and they are well prepared for them. Many homes have special rubber blocks to keep water from coming in through the doors and windows, and hardware stores keep an ample supply of wading boots and other flood supplies. If you are visiting Venice in the winter, be aware that you might experience some flooding, but don't panic. It only lasts for a few hours; then the tide goes out and the water recedes. Fashionable flood boots aside, the city has also developed a long-term solution to cope with the threat of sinking Venice and the serious hazard of flooding (the famous flood of 1966 buried the city under nearly two meters of water). MOSE is a system of flood barrier gates designed to hold back the rising water. It's a highly controversial project, that is still debated by many.

Planning A Family Visit to Venice

Venice is overflowing with beautiful sights, incredible art, exciting attractions ... and more than 22 million other visitors. In our opinion,

72
Venice

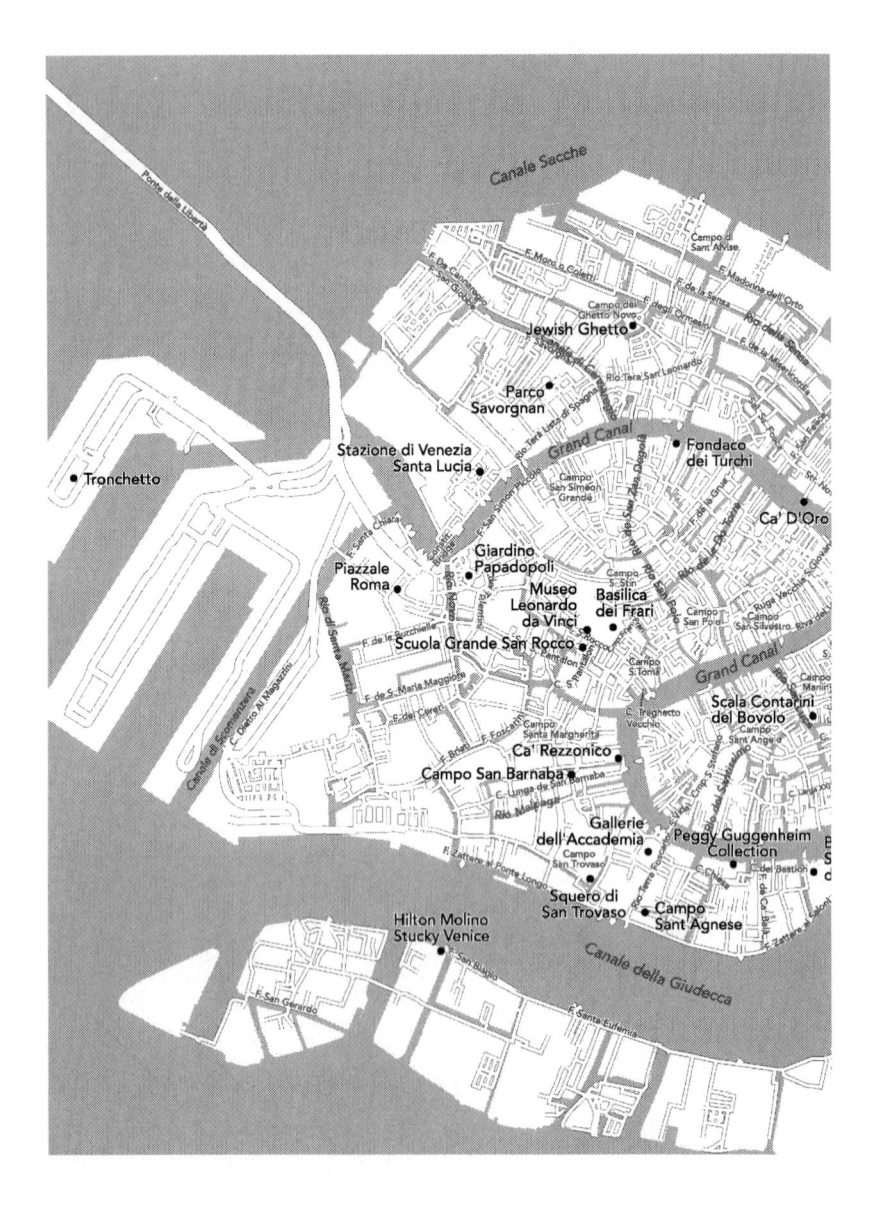

73
Venice

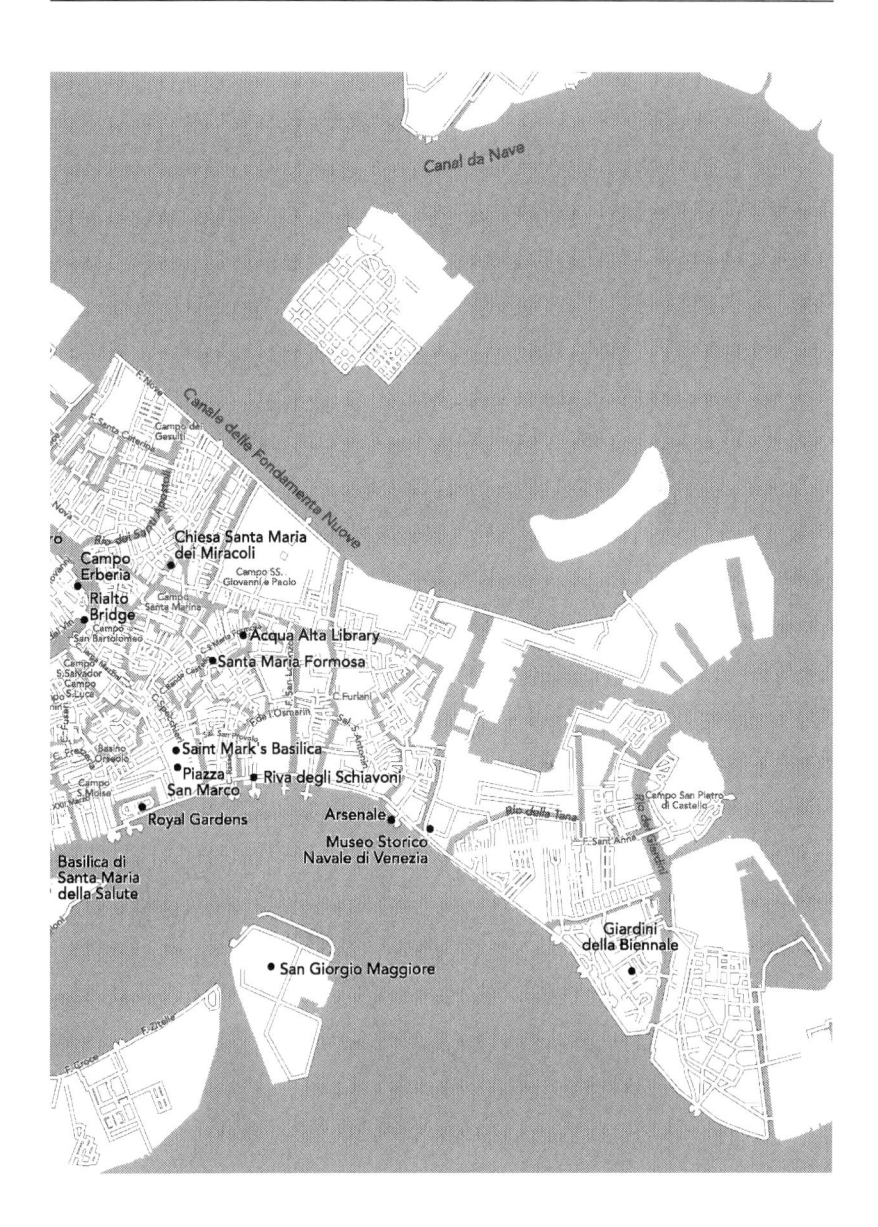

Venice isn't a city where you can hit the important sights by just winging it and making plans on the spot. Preparing a detailed plan before you arrive is the secret to leaving Venice with everyone in your family feeling content that they saw and did the most important things to them. Because Venice is such a maze of hidden alleys and tiny bridges, you should also factor in the time it will take you to find your way through them, and, better yet, to amble aimlessly discovering and exploring hidden treasures. A smart plan that includes a schedule for visiting the highlights and time for wandering is the ideal way to balance your trip and keep everyone happy.

Deciding Which Churches and Museums to Visit

More than 20 attractions in Venice are listed as "must see" spots across the internet, on blog posts and websites such as Tripadvisor. But time is limited, and so is the kids' patience. So how do you choose where to spend your day (and money)? The first rule of thumb to remember is that in Italy, many churches feature artwork as spectacular as any museum. In fact, you would miss much of Italy's greatest art if you only looked for it in museums. In Venice, go for the churches with a serious wow factor—the Basilica of Saint Mark (Basilica di San Marco) is unforgettable with its golden mosaics, and the Basilica dei Frari, the Gesuiti (Chiesa di Santa Maria Assunta detta I Gesuiti) and the dazzling School of Saint Rocco (Scuola Grande di San Rocco) are all profoundly beautiful. Whenever possible, try to visit in the morning, when the children are at their most patient. Like always, encourage the kids to read in advance about the main works of art on display in the churches that you will visit (thank you, Wikipedia!). When you arrive, they will be excited to look for pieces that they recognize, by artists they know something about.

Combination Tickets, the Venezia Unica Card, and Reductions for Families

If you plan on visiting a number of museums in Venice, consider purchasing one of the Venezia Unica city combo-passes. These give you access to a varying number of attractions (depending on the pass you choose), for a reduced price. Some of the tickets give you discounts at shops and restaurants across the city, too, as well as free use of Wi-Fi. There are more than a dozen different passes to choose from, but before you purchase any sort of ticket, double check the specific museums you want to visit—it is very likely that your child may enter for free, or for a reduced fee, regardless of the Venezia card.

Remember that children under 6 years old are entitled to use the vaporetto for free (and young adults under 28 pay a reduced fee). Additionally, the Civic Museums of Venice (Musei Civici) offer free admission for children ages 5 or under; the churches that belong to the Chorus Association (see full list here: www.veneziaunica.it/en/content/chorus-churches) offer free admission for children who are 10 or under; the Querini Stampalia Foundation offers free admission for those under 18; and the museums on Piazza San Marco offer a special reduced ticket for families of two adults and at least one child (ages 6 to 14). To maximize your savings, read through the three walking itineraries in this chapter; whenever possible, we mention whether kids receive any reductions. Then, review the available offers on the Venezia Unica website to decide whether you'll need a Venezia Unica combo-pass, just a vaporetto pass, or none of the above. Consult: www.veneziaunica.it. **Please note:** Some museums may require to see a valid ID, to confirm your children's ages if you ask for any reductions.

How to Build a Family-Friendly Itinerary in Venice, and How to Use the Suggested Self-Guided Walking Tours in this Chapter

To help our readers devise their perfect vacation, this chapter outlines all of Venice's main sights and attractions in **geographical order,** and **organizes them into three detailed self-guided walking tours.** The **first tour** takes you from Venice's only train station, Santa Lucia–Ferrovia, all the way to Piazza San Marco. The **second tour** leads you from Piazza San Marco to Venice's intriguing Arsenale area. The **third tour** explores Venice's best known and best loved islands: Murano, Burano, Torcello and Lido.

The information on these self-guided walking tours is enough to easily fill a week on sightseeing in Venice, should you decide to do so. However, because most families won't visit every single attraction in the city, and will only follow certain parts of our suggested walking tours, we have added a second feature, to make things easier: Below, you will find **three sample itineraries (A, B and C).** Each of these sample itineraries uses the information detailed in the self-guided tours to create a family-friendly vacation in the city.

> **Tip:** Venice has hundreds of bridges, so walking around with a stroller really isn't recommended. If possible, opt for a baby sling or a structured baby carrier that puts the baby's weight on your hips instead of your shoulders. If that's impossible, consider a light-weight jogging stroller that you can easily lift up the stairs.

SAMPLE ITINERARY A: Family with Three Children (Ages 2, 4 and 7), Two Days in Venice

Day 1: Take Vaporetto (water bus) Line 2 from the Santa Lucia train station straight to **Piazza San Marco**. (This will take about 20 minutes. Line 1 does the same path, but it stops more and takes much longer, so kids may lose patience by the time you get there.) The famous **Rialto Bridge** is located between the train station and the piazza, so you can make a pit stop there for ice cream, shopping and photos, but be aware it can get extremely busy in high season.

Get off the Vaporetto at Piazza San Marco and take a moment to admire it; you will quickly understand one why this is one of the most famous town squares in the world. There are a number of attractions here: Take the elevator up the **Campanile** (Bell Tower) for a spectacular view over Venice and the lagoon. A visit to the **Palazzo Ducale** (Doge's palace) will impress tweens and teens, but may be too much for most toddlers. We do recommend that whatever your kids' ages are, you go into **Basilica di San Marco** for a quick visit. The queue moves along quickly, and entry is free, so don't miss this incredible attraction (see walking tour N. 2 for full details).

From Piazza San Marco walk along **Riva Degli Schiavoni** (the waterfront promenade, lined with souvenir stands) until you reach the **Arsenale**. Both the **Ship Museum** (Padiglione delle Navi) and the **Naval Museum** (Museo Storico Navale, currently closed for renovations) are here and are likely to intrigue even the littlest little ones. Continue walking along the promenade until you reach the **Public Gardens** (the vaporetto stop is Giardini-Biennale) for some free play-time at the park. Alternatively, skip the gardens and take the 15-minute vaporetto ride to the **Island of Lido** (see walking tour N. 3) for some beach time so the kids can relax, splash in the water, and enjoy a cone of delicious ice cream.

Day 2: Seeing Venice with children won't be like taking a tour with your university art history class, but you don't want to miss out Venice's

amazing art even if not everyone in your family will appreciate it in the same way. **San Rocco Scuola** and the **Frari Basilica** are two must-sees, and mercifully they are right around the corner from each other and from an attraction for the children—the **Leonardo da Vinci Exhibition,** dedicated to his ingenious machines. (This is one of two da Vinci museums in town.)

After those three sights, walk to the famous **Accademia Bridge** (in front of the **Accademia Museum** and vaporetto stop) and climb it to admire the stunning view of the **Basilica della Salute** and the Grand Canal. It's only another five-minute walk to the **Gondola Garage** at **San Trovaso Squero.** (See walking tour N. 1.) In the mornings, you can usually see people working on the gondolas, which is sure to entertain those kids who love all things transportation. This is also a great area for a lunch break. If you want to stay in Venice, the **Natural History Museum** is a fun option, or you can take the vaporetto to one of the quieter islands such as **Burano** or **Torcello** and let the children explore.

Museum Tours for Families

Museums can be difficult for children, but there may be a solution—the Civic Museum Foundation of Venice offers a program called Museums for Families (on demand, book in advance) so kids can enjoy special tours and activities to bring the art to life on their scale. The participating museums include: The Doge's Palace, Museo Correr, Ca Rezzonico, Ca Pesaro, Natural History Museum, the Glass Museum, and others. The activities at the Doge's Palace (Palazzo Ducale) are especially interesting—they offer a fun mystery-themed tour where the children use clues and an activity book to explore the palace and learn its history. Kids can also participate in a two-and-a-half-hour workshop including games and crafts, or they can go on a 'lion hunt' searching for Venice's symbol in the various rooms. For more information, see: www.visitmuve.it/en/educational-services/for-families.

SAMPLE ITINERARY B: Family with Three Children (Ages 6, 8 and 10), Two Days in Venice

Day 1: The previous itinerary can work well for this age-group, too, with some modifications. From the Santa Lucia train station, take the vaporetto along the **Grand Canal** to the **Rialto Bridge** to explore the vibrant fish market as well as the many shops in this area (including the Hard Rock Cafe). Campo Erberia and Campo San Giacometto, in front of the Rialto, are excellent places to sit with an oversize gelato cone watching the world—and the gondolas—go by. (For the best gelato shops in this area, see 'Eating in Venice' at the end of this chapter).

From the Rialto proceed by foot to **Piazza San Marco,** where you can see the stunning **Basilica di San Marco** and take the elevator up to the top of the **Campanile** (Bell Tower). Check out the **Doge's Palace,** then ride the vaporetto across the canal to the **Basilica della Salute,** one of the most beautiful churches in Venice, and the **Accademia**. The streets around the Accademia are fun to explore and are buzzing with interesting shops. For your day's grand finale, take a sunset gondola ride. (Book in advance if you want the full show, including a serenata. If you don't want the seranta, just hop on one of the dozens of gondolas in the canal.)

Day 2: Visit the **Leonardo da Vinci Museum** at Campo San Barnaba, near the Accademia. (This is the second Da Vinci museum in town; the first one is near the Frari Church.) Next, consider a special activity such as a **gondola rowing lesson** or a **mask making lesson,** both of which should be booked in advance (see the list of special activities at the end of this chapter). That should give everyone a good appetite, so for lunch you could eat at a real Venetian *bacaro* (tavern) at the cool Campo San Barnaba. Then either visit the **Natural History Museum,** or have a stroll through **Ca Rezzonico House-Museum** to see how Venetian patrician families once lived (for more details on both, see walking tour N. 1). Alternatively, stop by the famous **Frari Basilica,** and don't skip **San Rocco Scuola's** dramatic Tintoretto-decorated ceilings and halls. Take the time to roam around, discovering the magic hiding in every corner and alley of Venice. The real beauty of this city is stumbling across unexpected and interesting finds at every turn. There are also several beautiful mask shops in this area (such as Marega; see itinerary for details).

SAMPLE ITINERARY C: Family with Three Children (Ages 13, 15 and 17), Two days in Venice

Day 1: With teenagers, you can mix things up a bit and include dazzling sights that younger children would not appreciate. (Your teens will be pleased about how good it all looks on their Instagram accounts.) Take the vaporetto to the Rialto Bridge, visit the market, have espressos by the canal and a snack at a popular *cicheti* bar such as Naranzaria or Bancogiro. Then take a short walk (10 minutes) to the small but beautiful **Santa Maria dei Miracoli** church. Discover the little vintage shops in this area, and try to squeeze in a visit to the **Church of Santi Giovanni e Paolo** (next to Scuola di San Marco and the hospital, where ambulance boats park). The world-famous **Libreria Acqua Alta,** a bookshop right on the water (Castello 5176, open daily), is another must-see in this area, with dozens of books stacked inside a Gondola, and an endless selection of old postcards and posters to choose from. You'll find many intriguing boutiques and mask shops nearby, too. Follow the lacework of laneways in the direction of Piazza San Marco to connect to the **Merceria**—Venice's most famous shopping street. Once you reach Piazza San Marco, take the elevator up the **Campanile** (Bell Tower) for top views, visit the stunning **Basilica di San Marco,** and tour the **Palazzo Ducale** (Doge's Palace), with or without a guided tour. Then treat your teens to a grown up evening by taking the vaporetto to the

Hilton Hotel near the Giudecca for **sunset non-alcoholic cocktails** at the **Skyroof Bar,** one of the best spots in Venice to enjoy a spectacular view. If you don't want to go that far, you can enjoy beverages at the Danieli Hotel terrace. This is one of the most exclusive addresses in town, and the once-in-a-lifetime view over the Grand Canal will justify the sometimes snooty service and 20-euro drinks.

Day 2: Book a special activity such as a gondola rowing lesson or cooking class in the morning, and then visit the **Guggenheim Collection** and the Dorsoduro neighborhood which is brimming with interesting studios and boutiques. In the afternoon, don't miss the **Frari Basilica** and the **San Rocco Scuola.** At least a couple of hours before sunset, take the vaporetto to visit the colorful island of Burano (one hour away) for some easy-going fun, or Murano (15 minutes away) for a glass blowing demonstration. Ca d'Oro and Ca' Rezzonico are also worth a tour, if you have the extra time.

Parks of Venice

After visiting museums and churches where they have to be quiet and not touch things, your kids are going to need a break. Luckily, Venice has a few parks where children can run around, climb, swing and relax.

Giardini Reali: This small park is just 50 meters from Piazza San Marco, right in front of the San Marco Giardinetti vaporetto stop. Gondola makers once worked right here, but today it is full of flowers and benches. There's no playground, but there is a little fish pond (and a public toilet).

Giardini della Biennale & Sant'Elena: If your kids want a place to pretend battle after seeing the Arsenale, this park is conveniently located by the Giardini and Sant'Elena vaporetto stops. This is the largest park in Venice, and the kids can enjoy the playground and see how many sculptures they can find among the shrubbery while the parents refuel themselves with something from Caffe' Paradiso. If you visit during the Biennale (Venice's biennial international art exhibition), you'll find that access is limited as this park fills up with stands and art on display.

Parco Savorgnan: This is a shady, relaxing park near the train station and the Jewish ghetto. It's ideal on a hot day, and it is walking distance from Ca d'Oro and the Guglie vaporetto stop. The main entrance to the park is right off the Guglie bridge (Ponte delle Guglie).

I Giardini Papadopoli: It's right off Ponte dei Tolentini and two minutes from Piazzale Roma, so it is a perfect spot for a break after you visit San Rocco, the Leonardo de Vinci museum, or Dei Frari Basilica (five minutes away by foot).

Campo di Sant'Agnese: This is near the Accademia, and while it is a large town square, not a park, it's a great spot to let the kids run around being kids. (In fact, this is where many Venetian kids come to play soccer.) Find it by walking from the Accademia toward Zattere.

Top 10 Family Activities in Venice

1. Ride along the Grand Canal in a vaporetto (water bus).
2. Climb to the top of the Campanile (Bell Tower) in Piazza San Marco to enjoy the incredible view.
3. Learn how to become a real Venetian gondolier with a gondola rowing lesson.
4. Marvel at the stunning, gold covered Basilica di San Marco.
5. Create your own Venetian work of art at a mask making class.
6. Chill at the Rialto Bridge and watch the fishmongers at the market.
7. Admire the jaw-dropping art at the Scuola di San Rocco and the Frari Basilica.
8. Enjoy a hands-on tour of the Leonardo da Vinci Museums.
9. Explore the boats at the Naval Museum and Shipyard at the Arsenale.
10. Step back in time to see fossils, birds and bears at the Natural History Museum.

THREE SELF-GUIDED WALKING TOURS IN VENICE

SELF GUIDED WALKING TOUR N. 1: From Santa Lucia Train Station (Ferrovia) to Piazza San Marco

Featuring: the Natural History Museum, Ca d'Oro, Campo San Barnaba, the Rialto Bridge and Market, the Accademia Museum, the Peggy Guggenheim Collection, the Frari Basilica, Scuola di San Rocco, and the Leonardo da Vinci Science Museum

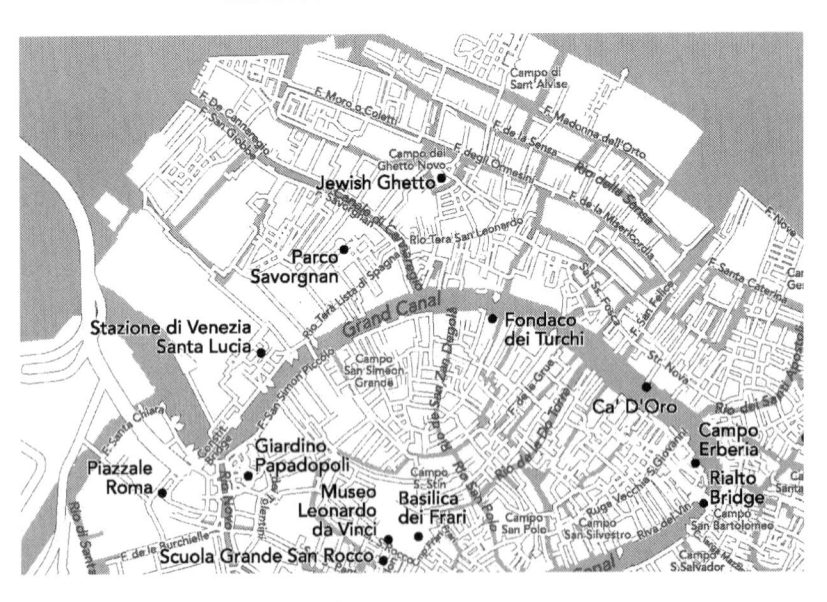

Our day in Venice starts at the Santa Lucia Ferrovia train station. As soon as you walk down the stairs, the magic of Venice is revealed—the turquoise dome of San Simenon's church is in front of you, and the Grand Canal buzzing with people, porters, gondolas and boats, is right there. Venice really does make a dazzling first impression!

> **Tip:** As of 2016, The Venice tourist information office is operated by a **Venezia Unica,** a private operator. There's a Venezia Unica office inside the train station (near track number 2), and a larger office immediately outside the station. There are also offices in Piazza San Marco 71, Piazzale Roma (the main parking lot in town) and the Marco Polo airport. All offices are open daily, 8:30-19:00.

Before you begin your tour, take care of the logistics. If you have any luggage, leave it at the luggage office in the station, next to track number 1 (open daily until 23:00, they will make a photocopy of your passport for security reasons) or at the small newsstand outside the station marked 'deposito bagagli' (please note that they close **much earlier,** ask before you leave your bags).

Then, based on the number of museums you plan to visit, purchase either a vaporetto pass or one of the comprehensive Venezia Unica cards. If you decide which museums you want to visit in advance, you can save some money by picking the right discount card and the right vaporetto pass. With your tickets ready and your bags in storage, you are ready to take on the city!

There are five vaporetto docks in front of the train station—A, B, C, D, and E—each serving different vaporetto lines. The two main vaporetto lines running along the Grand Canal are 1 and 2. Line 1 offers a leisurely trip and makes more stops en route, while Line 2 connects the main sights in town (the Rialto Bridge and Piazza San Marco, mainly).

As the vaporetto slowly makes its way along, you will enjoy a front seat view of the **Grand Canal,** affectionately known as one of the most beautiful "streets" in the world. It doesn't take much to let your mind float back in time and imagine what this vibrant canal was like hundreds of years ago, during Venice's heyday: Instead of tourists taking pictures with their ipads, these streets were roamed by merchants from every corner of the earth, noblemen in velvet clothes, stern clergymen leading religious processions, and noisy fishermen returning from the Rialto market.

As the vaporetto makes its way you will be treated to stunning examples of Venetian architecture. Centuries ago, many of these *palazzi* (or Ca' in the Venetian dialect) were the mansions of the most powerful Venetian noble families. As gorgeous as they are on the outside, the inside is sometimes even more dazzling, with silk-lined walls, ornate tapestries, gold gilding, silverware, porcelain ornaments, and, of course, huge Murano glass chandeliers. In a sense, the dramatic and opulent internal décor made up for the restrictions imposed by the republic. The strict and very religious Venetian senate governed many details of daily life, from clothing and jewelry to food and ceremonies, and forbade ostentatious behavior. One 1562 law even declared that only one type of roasted meat and one type of boiled meat may be served at weddings, and certain fish and 'exotic' fowl were outlawed.

As you continue along the canal, your vaporetto will pass the Casino' stop (where Venice's historic gambling house still stands and operates). On your right, you will see the Byzantine-looking **Fondaco dei Turchi,** also known in English as the Turk's Inn. Venice was a city of merchants, and all those international traders needed a place to stay. But the Venetian officials were suspicious of foreign guests. They were particularly concerned about the Turkish merchants, and confined them to this one building, allowing them to leave only at certain times. At night, 25 lanterns were kept lit, and the guards on duty would watch for any suspicious activity or espionage attempts. (Don't worry—today Venice hotels are considerably more relaxed about the hours guests keep.) Although the Venetian Republic ended in 1797, Turkish merchants continued to use the building for another 40 years. Today it houses the Natural History Museum of Venice.

NATURAL HISTORY MUSEUM OF VENICE

Getting there: Get off at the S. Stae vaporetto stop and backtrack to enter the museum through the back entrance. (Don't get off at the previous vaporetto stop, since there are no bridges here and you can't cross the canal to reach the museum's front entrance.)

Venice's Natural History Museum is a popular attraction for families. It's small, and the English version of the signage is certainly lacking, but it is one of the top attractions for kids in town, and an ideal stop to make if you encounter the occasional summer storm. When you buy your tickets, ask for a guidebook in English at the ticket office.

Venice

Mission: An interesting sculpture hangs at the entrance of the museum. Can you tell what it is?

The first room features mostly fossils, and the next room offers the chance to actually touch some dinosaur fossils, which will surely impress younger kids, and they'll love telling people about the experience.

Mission: Can you find the skull of an animal with huge front teeth in one of the rooms? See if you can guess what animal it is before checking the sign!

You might find the next room fascinating, horrifying or both, depending on your perspective. It is filled with taxidermied animals brought back by Venetian explorers who traveled to "exotic" destinations long ago.

Mission 1: This room also features two crocodiles and a real mummy. Can you find the mummy? How old do you think that person was?

Mission 2: Sauropode eggs from Mongolia are somewhere in these rooms. Can you find them?

The next room might be creepy for small children, but it will probably intrigue some of the older ones. It is filled with animals with deformities—taxidermied specimens that is.

Mission 1: Find the turtle with two heads!

Mission 2: Find the scariest fish, the one you would least want to meet at sea—or swimming next to your gondola in Venice—and take a selfie with it.

The interactive room at the end of the tour offers cool touch screens that the kids can operate to learn how various animals move. 🕙 Natural History Museum, Santa Croce 1730. Tel: 041.275.0206, www.msn.visitmuve.it. Open November—May 31, Tuesday—Friday, 9:00—17:00 (last entry at 16:00); Saturday—Sunday, 10:00—18:00. Monday closed; June 1—October 31, Tuesday—Sunday, 10:00—18:00. Monday closed. Special activities for kids are available on demand, book here: www.msn.visitmuve.it/it/attivita/per-la-famiglia/on-demand. Children under 5 enter for free, under 14 pay a reduced fee.

CA D'ORO

Getting there: Take vaporetto Line 1, and get off at the Ca d'Oro stop.

After the Natural History Museum, board the vaporetto and continue along the Grand Canal to Ca d'Oro. On your right, you will see San Stae, a Baroque church that boasts an exterior decorated with intricately designed statues. Shortly after that Ca d'Oro will appear on your left.

Ca d'Oro is one the most famous palazzi on the Grand Canal. Its façade was once decorated with golden gilding, but the name, which means 'the golden house,' has outlasted the gilding. One of Venice's most prominent families, the Contarinis, had the house built in the 1420s, and in 1894 Baron Giorgio Franchetti purchased it to be used as a gallery to exhibit his large art collection. Ca d'Oro was donated to the government in 1916, and today it is a public gallery. Adults will be enthralled by the artwork it contains, but children will probably find this attraction far less engaging. 🕐 Ca' d'Oro, Cannaregio 3932 (Strada Nuova). Tel: 041.520.0345, www.cadoro.org. Open Monday, 9:00—14:00; Tuesday—Sunday, 9:00—19:00. Last entry 30 minutes before closing. Children under 18 enter for free (you may be required to show an ID).

RIALTO BRIDGE

Getting there: Take either vaporetto Line 1 or 2 and get off at the Rialto stop. To first visit the market, get off at the previous stop—Rialto Mercato.

The Rialto Bridge is as much as symbol of Venice as Piazza San Marco. The structure you see before you today is not the first bridge at this location—Antonio Ponte designed this one, in 1588. Before that, the bridge was made of wood and could be pulled open to let larger boats pass as they sailed along the Grand Canal, heavy with spices and goods, to the open sea.

The streets around the Rialto are in ways the heart of the city, and certainly the best place to get some shopping done. If you go in the morning you can explore the vibrant fish and vegetable market, buy fresh fruit, and even see the sea gulls that wage a constant battle here, hoping to win a bite to eat. Watch out, they mean business! The small *campo* by the bridge is the perfect place to stop for some gelato with a view and watch the gondolas glide by.

> **Tip:** Did you know? Gelato and ice cream aren't exactly the same thing. Both are made with milk, cream and sugar, but ice cream contains egg yolks, which are cooked to create a rich tasting custard. The ice cream is then churned at a high speed, which introduces a lot of air into the mixture, and increases its volume. Gelato, on the other hand, traditionally does not contain egg yolks, and it is churned at a lower speed, keeping it smoother, denser, and creamier. If you'd like to taste the difference for yourself, check our top gelato shop recommendations at the end of this itinerary!

PALAZZO (SCALA) CONTARINI DEL BOVOLO

Getting there: The Scala del Bovolo is located on San Marco 4303, one block from Campo Manin. It can be difficult to find—try using Google maps to navigate your way.

Known as the 'Bovolo' (snail shell in Venetian dialect) because of its dramatic exterior spiral staircase, this unique building is within a walking distance from the Rialto Bridge and is worth the effort it takes to find it. Architect Giovanni Candi built this palazzo in the 15th century for the rich and powerful Contarini family (from which no fewer than eight of Venice's *Dogi* emerged), and architect Giorgio Spavento added the dramatic staircase later. Many Gothic buildings had exterior staircases, but few of them have survived, making this palazzo a rare example, which is perhaps why Hollywood director Orson Welles chose it as one of the locations for his film Othello (1952). From here, walk back to the Grand Canal, and get back on the vaporetto going in the direction of San Toma'. Some of the most beautiful palazzi in Venice can be found along this section, such as the delightful Palazzo Barbarigo (on your right), adorned with golden mosaics. 🕓 Scala Contarini del Bovolo, San Marco 4303. Tel: 041.309.6605, www.scalacontarinidelbovolo.com. Open daily, 10:00–13:30 & 14:00–18:00. Last entry 30 minutes before closing. Children under 12 enter for free, under 18 pay a reduced fee.

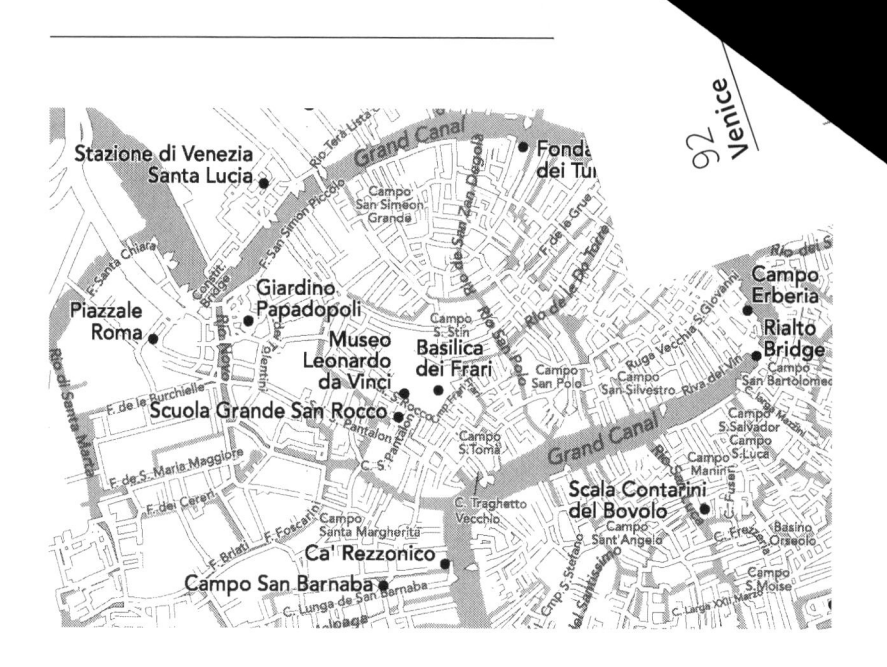

BASILICA DI SANTA MARIA GLORIOSA DEI FRARI

Getting there: Get off at the San Toma vaporetto stop and proceed on foot.

Often referred to simply as 'I Frari', this Franciscan basilica is a must-see in Venice. And while churches might not be a popular attraction for small children (or even teenagers), the Frari is impressive enough to merit a visit. It is awesome in the original sense of the word, and as large as it may seem today (102 meters long!), when it was built in the 13th century it was even larger, as it was just one part of an entire complex that included a monastery, too.

The basilica is shaped like the Greek letter tau, a symbol of the Franciscan order. The simple, classic Gothic exterior hides an incredibly rich artistic interior—Titian's massive masterpiece *The Assumption* awaits you at the altar, and his stunning *Pesaro Madonna* is on the north wall of the nave. In fact, the great painter is buried here, alongside prolific composer Claudio Monteverdi and many of the city's rulers. Other important works on display are Donatello's figure of St. John the Baptist, Pittoni's *Hagar in the Desert* and works by Giovanni Bellini, Antonio Rizzo, Alessandro Vittoria and many others. ◷ Basilica I Frari, San Polo 3072. Tel: 041.2728.611, www.

basilicadeifrari.it. Open Monday—Saturday, 9:00—18:00 (last entry 17:30). Sundays, 13:00—18:00. Children under 11 enter for free, under 18 pay a reduced fee.

●●●●●●●●●●●●●●●●●●●●●●●●●●●●●●●●●●●●●●●

Mission 1: Somewhere in this church hides a tomb decorated with angels with wings. Can you find it?

Mission 2: How many choir stalls are there in this church?

Mission 3: It's time to take out your detective binoculars! Can you find a work of art featuring a man with a beard, dressed in a long black cape, holding an open book?

●●●●●●●●●●●●●●●●●●●●●●●●●●●●●●●●●●●●●●●

Leonardo da Vinci Machine Museum (Campo San Rocco)

You don't have to go very far to get to the next stop on this itinerary; the Leonardo da Vinci Exhibition (museum) is right behind the Frari Basilica. This is one of two Leonardo da Vinci museums in Venice. (The other, which is on Campo San Barnaba, is discussed later in this chapter.) This exhibition isn't large, but for most children it is a great opportunity to get introduced to the genius of da Vinci in a friendly, hands-on environment.

The exhibition takes you through 60 functioning machines built according to da Vinci's plans. Older kids will be fascinated by the insight into his process and the mechanics involved, and younger kids will be delighted to learn that they can touch and operate the models. The museum also includes some displays on his artwork and anatomical studies. 🕒 Da Vinci Museum, Campo San Rocco, San Polo 3052. Tel: 041. 887.6815, www.davincimuseum.it. Open April 1—October 31, daily, 10:00—18:30; November—March 31, daily, 10:30—17:30. Children under 6 enter for free. Under 18 pay a reduced fee.

SCUOLA DI SAN ROCCO

Getting there: The Scuola is on the same square as the Leonardo da Vinci Museum—walk around the large palazzo to reach the front entrance.

To modern visitors, the concept of the Venetian Scuola (school) may be hard to explain, but for the inhabitants of Renaissance Venice, this was a central cultural institution, a hybrid of sorts between a religious order, art studio, and cultural meeting place that served the city's rich families. The scuole began in the 13th century and flourished until the Republic of Venice (the Serenissima) fell in 1797.

The scuole promoted values similar to those of a religious order—community, charity and penance—but were meant for lay people. In many respects, this was a gentlemen's club, with substantial political and financial power. Quite a lot of money passed through these schools, and one of the popular ways for the powerful members to demonstrate their deep pockets was through funding incredible works of art, that only the truly affluent could afford.

The Great Scuola of San Rocco, built in 1478 and dedicated to Saint Roch, is the most stunning example of this intriguing Venetian institution to survive. (There are four additional schools that can be visited in the city. All four are very special, but not quite as impressive as San Rocco. Find out more at the tourist office.) Some of the greatest painters in town, including Titian and Giorgione, were invited to participate in the decoration of this edifice, but the real star here was Tintoretto, who in 1564 created the dazzling, heavily ornate ceiling, that earned the Scuola di San Rocco the nickname 'Venice's Sistine Chapel'. 🕒 Scuola di San Rocco, Campo San Rocco, San Polo 3052. Tel:041.52.34.864, www.scuolagrandesanrocco.org.

Open daily, 9:30—17:30, last entry at 17:00. Children under 18 enter for free, if they are accompanied by at least one adult.

● ●

Mission 1: Using the mirrors provided (you'll find them on the tables) or your binoculars, examine the scenes on the ceiling and describe the one you think is the most beautiful. Why is this one your favorite?

Mission 2: Can you find a painting with more than three angels in it?

● ●

MAREGA MASK SHOP

Getting there: The shop is located on Calle del Scaleter, near the Frari Church.

Carnival masks are a fun symbol of Venice, so why not pay a visit to one of the best mask shops in the city? Marega has a gorgeous selection, and if you are looking for a hand-made, distinctive souvenir of Venice this is a good place to find it. Otherwise, you can simply admire the craftsmanship and the masks that every year are used for Venice's world-famous carnival masquerade balls. To learn more about the colorful carnival, check our 'Special Events in Venice' section at the end of this chapter. %% San Polo 2940. Tel: 041. 717.966, www.marega.it. (There's a second location on Fondamenta de l'Osmarin 4968.)

Tip: Every self respecting mask shop in the city boasts a selection of traditional Venetian Masks, too. The mask with a long beak, for example, is called the plague doctor mask. In the 14th century, doctors would wear these masks when examining patients, and filled the beak with herbs, which they believed protected them from catching the black plague. Ready to find out more? Check out the Kids' Corner at the end of this chapter!

CA' REZZONICO

Getting there: Take vaporetto line 1 toward Piazza San Marco and get off at the Ca' Rezzonico stop.

The classically designed Ca' Rezzonico is Venice's most famous house-museum: Here you can visit the home of a powerful 18th century patrician family to see how they lived. The Rezzonico family was incredibly powerful and influential—Carlo Rezzonico became Pope Clement XIII, and several other members of the family served in key positions in the Venetian Republic. The house today remains just as it once was, and as you tour the rooms, it's fun to imagine the hushed conversations, dramatic exchanges and political plots that were woven between these frescoed walls. Over the years, this sumptuous *palazzo* hosted many illustrious guests, including composer Cole Porter and painter Robert Barrett Browning (son of the poets Robert Browning and Elizabeth Barrett Browning). 🕐 Ca' Rezzonico, Dorsoduro 3136. Tel: 041.427.30892, www.carezzonico.visitmuve.it. For special activities call: 0412.700370. Open November 1—March 31, Wednesday—Monday, 10:00—17:00 (last entry at 16:00), Tuesday closed; April 1—October 31, Wednesday—Monday, 10:00-18:00 (last entry at 17:00), Tuesday closed. Children 5 years old and under enter for free; 6-14 pay a reduced fee.

Right by the palazzo sits one of the most delightful town squares in Venice, **Campo San Barnaba.** You might get a slight sense of déjà vu here, but don't panic. It is familiar because it was a location in Steven Spielberg's film *Indiana Jones and the Last Crusade* (1989). This is a great area to stroll around and enjoy some window shopping at the many boutiques. There are a couple of good restaurants here (Oniga, Osteria dei Pugni, and Bitta—possibly the only restaurant in Venice that serves only meat and no fish). You can even buy some fruit to snack on from a floating greengrocer in the canal.

> **Tip:** The bridge off campo san Barnaba is known as the Ponte dei Pugni, or the boxing bridge, in Italian. This is where gondoliers would organize boxing matches, and because the bridge has no railings, the loser would end up in the water. Boxing matches were not the only way the gondoliers would compete. There were rowing competitions, agility competitions, and sometimes they even built extravagant human pyramids, to demonstrate their strength. For more fun facts, check out the Kids' Corners at the end of this chapter.

LEONARDO DA VINCI MUSEUM (CAMPO SAN BARNABA)

After so much time looking at but not touching beautiful artwork, children will be excited to visit the Leonardo da Vinci museum's interactive exhibits. They can try out replicas of da Vinci's inventive machines and see models of his ingenious glider and air screw (a sort of primitive helicopter). The cam hammer is especially fascinating; it is a form of hammer that is powered by a water mill. This invention was a real success and was used extensively during the Industrial Revolution. This is not a large museum, but it can inspire huge dreams, or at least inspire some creativity in little ones. 🕐 Leonardo da Vinci

Exhibition, Chiesa San Barnaba, Campo San Barnaba. Cell: 339.7985.464, www.leonardoavenezia.com. Open daily, 9:30—19:30. Children under 18 pay a reduced fee.

THE GALLERIE DELL'ACCADEMIA—ACCADEMIA MUSEUM

Getting there: Take vaporetto Line 1 or 2 and get off at the Accademia stop.

From San Barnaba take the vaporetto or simply walk to the **Accademia Bridge,** which is an iconic Venetian sight itself, and stands right in front of the museum. Art lovers won't want to miss this unique collection on the canal's south bank, which began as an art academy that nurtured Venice's incredible artistic tradition. The school thrived until Napoleon invaded Venice and shut it down, but even he realized its value and reopened it a decade later.

Today, the Gallerie dell'Accademia is a museum showcasing masterpieces by the most famous Venetian artists, including Titian, Giorgione, and Giovanni Bellini. Among the famous paintings here is Tintoretto's huge and once controversial Feast in Levi's House, a painting that led to him being tried by the Inquisition for heresy. Children probably won't enjoy these precious paintings as much as the da Vinci museum, but the museum is quite small and manageable, and with luck they will be busy dreaming of their own inventions while parents enjoy the art. ◉ Gallerie dell'Accademia, Campo della Carità (right off the Accademia Bridge), Dorsoduro 1050. Tel: 041.520.0345, www.gallerieaccademia.it. Open Monday, 8:15—14:00 (last entry at 13:00); Tuesday—Sunday, 8:15—19:15 (last entry at 18:15). Children under 18 enter for free.

> **Tip:** Has seeing the many gondolas in Venice inspired an interest in your family? Squero san Trovaso is a gondola garage where you can see the gondolieri building and repairing boats and gondolas in the mornings. The squero is located just two minutes away from the Accademia (Fondamenta Bonlini 1097). Sadly, tours are available only to groups of 25 or more: www.veneziainbarca.it. Other squeri that can be visited (for a fee, book in advance, a minimum number of participants may be required) are Squero dei Rossi on Giudecca Island (www.costruzionegondoledeirossi.it/lo-squero.html) and Squero Vecio (www.squerovecio.wordpress.com) near the Scuola Grande San Marco and hospital.

Venice

Tip: If you want to enjoy a gelato with a view as beautiful as all the art you've seen, we recommend walking to the nearby promenade known as Zattere. It's a nice spot to enjoy a tasty Venetian gianduiotto, gaze at the blue lagoon, and watch the occasional fisherman at work.

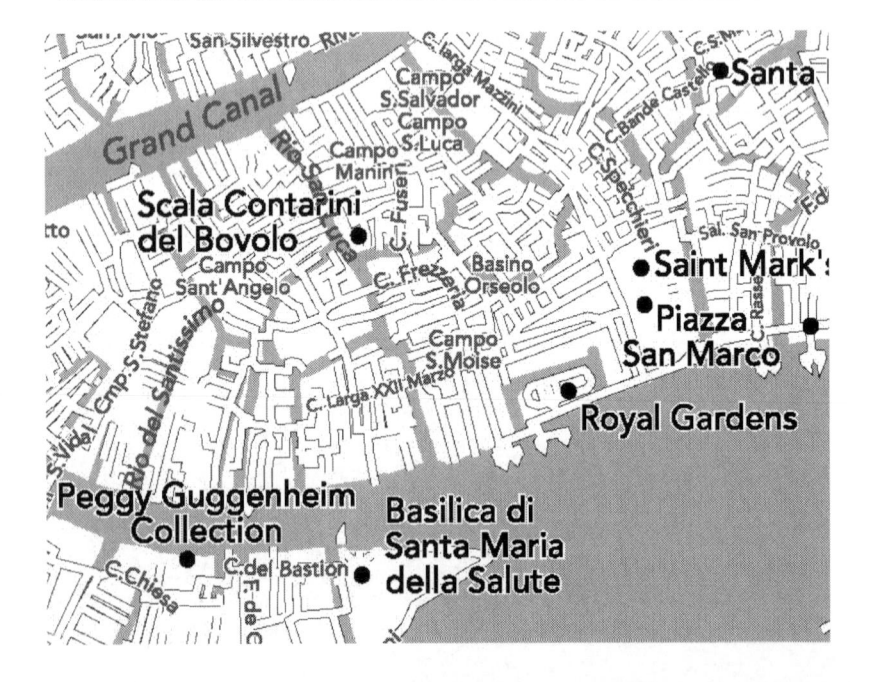

PEGGY GUGGENHEIM COLLECTION

Getting there: Take vaporetto Line 1 or 2, and get off either at the Accademia stop or the Salute stop. The Guggenheim collection is located halfway between the two.

Just five minutes (by foot) from the Accademia awaits one of the most important collections of contemporary art not just in Venice, but in all of Italy. The walk to the museum will put you in the right mood—the alleys leading to the Peggy Guggenheim Collection are filled with artists' studios and colorful boutiques. If you need some variety after seeing so much of the Renaissance, the Guggenheim museum will more than satisfy you with its collection of works from the leaders of different 20th century art movements including Surrealism, Cubism, Dadaism, and more. Picasso, Dali, Rothko, Pollock, Mondrian, Kandinsky, Marguerite, de Chirico, Magritte and Duchamp are among the big-name artists represented here.

To say Peggy Guggenheim was a socialite and art lover fails to capture the spirit of the woman who scorned the ordinary, pursued endless affairs, and rescued precious art from the claws of the Nazis. Born to a prominent Jewish family, she inherited a fortune after her father Benjamin Guggenheim died (he was one of the passengers aboard the infamous Titanic). She spent her 20s in Paris, reveling in the Bohemian art scene there, with friends such as Man Ray and Marcel Duchamp, and later married German painter Max Ernst, who she smuggled out of occupied France with other Jewish artists.

Guggenheim used her wealth to support artists and amassed a dazzling collection of artworks. As the Germans approached, she began purchasing art frantically to save it. The Louvre refused to accept her collect for safekeeping, and so, with her typical flair, she moved it to a friend's barn in the south of France before shipping it to New York, where she opened a gallery (and later discovered Jackson Pollock). When she turned 50, she moved to Venice and brought her extensive art collection with her. She moved into the historic Palazzo Venier, and in 1951 opened the doors to her museum (while still living in the building). Visitors could even go into her bathroom to view the art there. Her fashion sense was as fun and unconventional as you'd expect—today you can even buy replicas of her eyeglasses in the museum's gift shop.

The Guggenheim is a site that art lovers absolutely won't want to miss, but it can be a tricky stop with children. Luckily, on Sundays they organize fun workshops for kids including art labs and special tours. A saving grace for weekday visits is the museum's charming garden, which even features a few stone thrones and space to play. The museum's shop is well worth a visit, too. 🕒 Guggenheim Collection, Palazzo Venier dei Leoni, Fondamenta Venier, Dorsoduro 701. Tel: 041.2405.411, www.guggenheim-venice.it. Open Wednesday—Monday, 10:00—18:00 (last entry 17:30); Tuesday closed. Interesting guided tours (in English, too) are available, book in advance. The museum organizes activities and workshops for kids (4-10 years old) on Sunday afternoons, 15:00—16:30. All activities must be booked in advance no later than the previous Friday, call: 041.2405.444/401. Children under 10 enter for free, under 18 pay a reduced fee.

BASILICA DELLA SALUTE

Getting there: The Basilica is just a short walk from the Guggenheim collection, along Calle del Bastion. If you are arriving by vaporetto, take Line 1 or 2, and get off at the Salute stop.

The Basilica della Salute is truly striking, and its octagonal body and dramatic dome are a defining element of the Venetian skyline. You can easily walk here from the Guggenheim, but we actually prefer coming by vaporetto—the view of the Basilica from the Canal (and from the Accademia bridge) is incredible.

The basilica's name (salute means health) and location in the city hint at its intriguing origin as a plague church. In 1630, an episode of the plague (black death) struck Venice so violently that the city leaders decided to build a magnificent new basilica dedicated to the virgin Mary as a plea for divine protection. Architect Baldassare Longhena's design was selected from many proposals, the octagonal shape meant to resemble a crown in honor of Mary. The basilica's exterior is the star of this show, but if you have the time, the interior can also be visited; you will find works by Tintoretto, Titian and others in the six chapels surrounding the spacious nave.

> **Tip:** Did you know? When the plague (black death) swept across Europe, Venetians were determined to protect themselves. Anyone arriving to the city was kept in isolation for 40 days to make sure they did not spread the disease. 'Quarantine' comes from the Italian word for 40 (quaranta), and became a word in English, too.

It took more than 50 years to build the imposing edifice, so it was not exactly a quick fix for the plague, which killed nearly a third of the city's population. The location was chosen due to its relation to other key locations in Venice, particularly San Marco. An annual procession from San Marco to the basilica was a crucial part of the original vision for this church, and that procession is still held every November 21st and is known as the *Festa della Salute*. San Marco is just one vaporetto stop past the basilica, and that is where our next itinerary starts. 🕒 Basilica della Salute, www.basilicasalutevenezia.it. Open Monday—Saturday, 9:30—12:00 & 15:00—17:30; Sunday, 9:30—12:00 & 15:00—17:30. The sacrestia is open 10:00—12:00 & 15:00—17:00. Children under 10 enter for free.

The Art and Architecture of Venice

As a global trading port, Venice imported and exported more than merchandise—it was also where ideas and styles arrived from around the world. Strolling today along the city's canals offers a dazzling overview of different eras and artistic movements. The different looks weave together to create a fantastic tapestry of artistic style and color. Fashions in art and architecture from early trading partners of the new republic merged to create a unique new style we call Venetian Gothic.

Venice's largest church is also its best example of this: The Basilica di San Marco was heavily influenced by Byzantine art, and decorated with spoils of the crusades. The Doge's palace and the Ca d'Oro (see walking itinerary N. 1) are other good examples of Byzantine and Moorish influences. The 13th century was a turning point where Venice shifted its artistic focus from the east to Europe, creating a new, occidental look for buildings and piazzas. With the Renaissance, harmony reined in architecture, as can be seen with buildings such as Santa Maria dei Miracoli church. Andrea Palladio and Jacopo Sansovino are the two big names of Renaissance architecture in Venice (and beyond it), and you can see examples of both in the city.

As a global trading port, Venice imported and exported more than Sansovino designed the Libreria Marciana and was responsible for the redesign of Piazza San Marco; San Giorgio island has examples of Palladio's work. Baldassare Longhena, a leader of Baroque architecture, was the visionary behind the dazzling Basilica di Santa Maria della Salute and Ca' Pesaro.

The Venetian painting style has also left its mark. The city's churches are home to some unique artwork by the best-known Venetian artists, including Titian, Tintoretto, Carpaccio, and Bellini. In the 16th and 17th centuries, Venetian style eclipsed the dominant Mannerism style, putting color and emotion ahead of form and logic while earning Venice admiration from across Europe. Many of the most famous Venetian paintings can be admired at the Accademia Museum, and in the Doge's Palace.

# Venice

SELF-GUIDED WALKING TOUR N. 2: From Piazza San Marco to the Arsenale

Featuring: Piazza San Marco, Basilica di San Marco, the Campanile (bell tower), the clock tower, Palazzo Ducale (the doge's palace), Correr museum, Riva degli Schiavoni (waterfront promenade), Island of San Giorgio, the Arsenale, the Shipyard Pavilion, the Naval Museum, and the Jewish Ghetto

The famous Piazza San Marco is without a doubt the beating heart of the Venice, the center from which cultural, religious and political currents have pulsated for centuries. It is always buzzing with life, and where today tourists walk, noblemen and important traders once strode, stopping at their favorite cafés to debate art and politics and catch up on the latest gossip. Lined with exclusive boutiques and offering glorious views of the lagoon, this is a magical place where bands play on summer nights and people dance in the moonlight. Piazza San Marco is also the only "piazza" in Venice; all the other town squares are simply called 'campo'.

Piazza San Marco has starred in many movies and books, notably the memorable scene in the 1979 James Bond film *Moonraker* where 007 drives his amphibious gondola out of the canal and across the square. The piazza has also been the stage for centuries of religious and political events, parades, festivals and other high-profile events. There are six attractions to visit here: Palazzo Ducale (the Doge's palace), the Basilica of San Marco, the Clock Tower, the Bell Tower (Campanile), the Correr Museum and the Marciana Library. Exploring them all would fill up an entire day of sightseeing, which is why most families focus their attention on the two or three attractions that interest them the most.

BASILICA DI SAN MARCO

Getting there: From the Santa Lucia train station take vaporetto line 1 or 2 (much faster) and get off either at the San Marco Vallaresso or at the San Marco Giardinetti stops. Note that you cannot bring bags inside; leave your backpacks in the cloakroom in Ateneo San Basso (follow the signs).

Start your tour of the piazza at the massive Basilica di San Marco, one of the most famous churches in Italy. Much of the exterior is actually made of repurposed marble from Constantinople, a reminder of the role Venice played in the sack and fall of that great city. The Basilica was once adorned with many frescoes, but the only original one remaining today is in the lunette above the main doorway, and depicts St. Mark's body being brought to Venice. The four large bronze horses you see between the upper and lower sections of the façade are also spoils of the Fourth Crusade and the sacking of Constantinople.

Once you **enter the basilica,** it will be hard not to gasp. The interior stuns with an array of intricate decorations—colorful marble floors and columns frame over 4,500 square feet of gold mosaics and frescoes dating back to the 11th, 12th and 13th centuries.

●•••●•••●•••●•••●•••●•••●•••●•••●•••●•••●•••●•••●•••

Mission 1: When you enter, walk a few steps and turn around. Do you see a mosaic above the door with three people? Look at the man on the right. What color is his shirt? Red, green or blue?

Mission 2: Does this dazzling church remind you of a peacock? Well, there is one in here somewhere. Can you find him? Hint: Watch where you step!

●•••●•••●•••●•••●•••●•••●•••●•••●•••●•••●•••●•••●•••

The basilica is divided into a number of sections, including the Zen chapel on the right, the baptistery, and the Treasury (*il Tesoro*). Entry to the basilica itself is free, but there is a fee to visit the Treasury, which features some stunning artifacts by the city's best medieval goldsmiths.

The current basilica was built in 1063 on the site of a previous church and is dedicated to Venice's patron saint—St. Marco (Mark) who is said to be buried here, and the story of how his body was brought to Venice is one of the Venetian's favorite tales. According to them, two local merchants who traveled to Egypt in the 9th Century managed to smuggle Mark's remains out of Alexandria by covering them with herbs and pork to ensure the officers, who were Muslim, wouldn't look too closely at the crate. For a very long time, th Basilica was a work in progress that grew as the city's fortunes grew. The baptistry was added in the 14th century, and the Zen chapel only in the 16th century. 🕐 Basilica di San Marco, Piazza San Marco. Tel: 041.270.8311, www.basilicasanmarco.it. Open Monday—Saturday, 9:30—17:00 (last entry at 16:45); Sunday 14:00—16:30 (last entry 16:15). The museum and the Pala d'Oro inside the Basilica close half an hour earlier. Between April 1 and November 1 you can book (in advance, for a fee) a **"skip the line"** ticket for the Basilica and the Campanile (see next); find out more here: www.venetoinside.com.

After you leave the basilica, take the time to explore the piazza itself. The symbol of Venice is a winged lion, and the kids can become "lion hunters" and try to find as many as they can in the piazza and near the Basilica.

Mission: How many winged lions did you find? Take a selfie photo with your favorite one.

THE CLOCK TOWER

This clock tower, which was constructed between 1496 and 1499, does much more than tell the time. Based on a design by Mauro Carducci, it was built to show merchants what the conditions at sea were. It was positioned so it could be seen from afar, as a testament to Venice's great wealth, and features a complex mechanism that shows the movement of the sun and moon, which influences tides. If you happen to be in Piazza San Marco on the hour, have your binoculars handy. That is when you can see the two bronze figures known as the Mori come out of the tower to strike clock's bell. And if you are visiting Venice on the Feast of Epiphany (January 6th) or Ascension Day (the Thursday 40 days after Easter), you will be treated to this clock's most incredible feature: Three bronze Magi figures accompanied by an angel with a trumpet emerge from the clock and bow in front of Mary and the baby Jesus. If your children are amateur-engineers and loved seeing da Vinci's machines, you can delight them more by making an appointment (in advance) to see this feature up close. ⊙ Clock Tower, Piazza San Marco. www.torreorologio.visitmuve.it. The clock can be visited by appointment only, the visit isn't suitable for anyone who is claustrophobic, has a fear of heights, or for children under 6. To reach the clock, you will have to climb up a steep and narrow staircase of over 200 steps. Visits in English can booked for Monday—Wednesday at 10:00 or 11:00 or Thursday—Sunday at 14:00 or 15:00. Tours leave from Museo Correr.

THE CAMPANILE (BELL TOWER)

One of Venice's most notable symbols, the campanile towers above Piazza San Marco at more than 98 meters (323 feet) in height. This is a highly recommended attractions for families, and don't worry, you can take an elevator up! A weather vane statue of the archangel Gabriel at the top of the marble belfry was included to be a pragmatic help for sailors. The Campanile boasts five different bells, and each served a different purpose. The Marangona is the largest of the five, and it marked the beginning and the end of the workday. The Trotteria bell rang to hurry people up (in fact, its name comes from the verb 'to trot'). The Nona bell rings at 12:00, and the Mezza Terza bell was used to announce the meetings of the Venetian Senate. Finally, the Renghiera or Maleficio bell was used to announce executions.

Venice

The tower's position is hardly incidental—this spot has held some form of watch tower since Roman times. The current tower was created in the 16th Century but required major renovation after dramatically collapsing in 1902. Miraculously, no one was killed by the falling tower, and almost as miraculously, the city council managed to have it rebuilt in a matter of weeks. 🕒 Il Campanile, Piazza San Marco. May 1—September 4, 8:30—21:00. Off season the tower usually closes down earlier, check the website for details. In case of very bad weather, the tower will close down even in high season. Children pay a reduced entry fee. Please note: Between April and November you can book (in advance, for a fee) a "skip the line" ticket for the Campanile (and the San Marco Basilica), find out more here: www.venetoinside.com.

● ● ·· ● ● ·· ● ● ·· ● ● ·· ● ● ·· ● ● ·· ● ● ·· ● ● ·· ● ● ·· ● ● ·· ● ● ·· ● ● ·· ● ● ··

Mission 1: It's time to take out your detective binoculars—how many windows you can you spot on the Campanile?

Mission 2: Use your binoculars to get a good look at the very top of the bell tower. What creature is perched there? An owl, an angel or a lion?

Mission 3: Climb to the top of the tower to see how many famous Venice structures you can spot. While you are there, can you guess where Galileo Galilei stood when he visited this tower? The famous scientist came to Venice to demonstrate the telescope he invented to the city's ruler, Doge Antonio Priuli.

● ● ·· ● ● ·· ● ● ·· ● ● ·· ● ● ·· ● ● ·· ● ● ·· ● ● ·· ● ● ·· ● ● ·· ● ● ·· ● ● ·· ● ● ··

> **Tip:** If your family isn't inclined to wait in the sometimes very long line to climb the tower, and you haven't booked the 'skip the line' ticket in advance, you can try the bell tower at the church at San Giorgio Island across the canal, instead. The views are almost as good, and the line is shorter.

DOGE'S PALACE (PALAZZO DUCALE)

The Doge was Venice's ruler, a unique position that was invented by the early inhabitants of the Venetian lagoon. The Doge's palace has a complex history, and the elaborate structure in Piazza San Marco is not the first one. It all started in the 9th century, when Doge Angelo Partecipazio decided to relocate his palace from the island of Malamocco to what is now the Rialto. After only a century there, the palace was destroyed by fire. Doge Sebastiano Ziani moved his office to the current location, transforming Piazza San Marco with the Byzantine fortress he constructed.

Over time the doge's role become more ceremonial and less military, and this change is reflected by the current palace that was built during the 14th and 15th centuries. This legendary residence, which served over 80 dogi for over 600 years, remains today one of the main tourist attractions in town. It has been damaged by fire and restored more than once since then, and while much irreplaceable art was lost, the palazzo today is astonishingly lavish. History-loving families should consider booking one of the guided tours of the palace (see tech info below for details). These tours will take you to hidden corners and give you an in-depth look into the secrets and treasures of the Doge's residence.

Who Was the Doge?

The Doge wasn't a hereditary king or a religious figure. In fact, he was much weaker than the senate that effectively ruled the city. But the doge was a figurehead with tremendous influence nonetheless, and he played an important cultural role in the Serenissima Republic. The Doge was a ceremonial leader elected by a council of the city's noble families in a process similar to how popes are elected in the Catholic church. Representatives from the richest and most powerful families met in a hall and weren't allowed to leave until they agreed upon a new Doge who they felt would serve Venice best without regard to their own interests (wink, wink...). The coronation process was just as elaborate—the newly elected Doge was taken to Basilica di San Marco and dressed in special clothing covered with gems. Then a grand procession of religious groups and officials dressed in red began, while the members of the senate and council wore purple. Children marched in the procession dressed as angels, while people carried religious relics or played silver trumpets.

The main role of the doge was to perform in and lead various ceremonies such as the annual Marriage of the Sea. (During which the he symbolically wed the city of Venice with the sea, to represent its importance to the Venetian life.) While technically, Doges served for life, many of the early ones didn't fare that well. Some unpopular Doges were deposed and exiled, and a couple were murdered. Doge Pietro IV Candiano was locked into his palace with his son while it burned. His successor abdicated to become a hermit. When a Doge died of natural causes, he was dressed entirely in gold (even his slippers were gold!) and buried in a full state funeral at the Santi Giovanni e Paolo Church, where several funerary monuments built for the most important Dogi can still be seen today.

Venice

Before you enter the Palazzo Ducale (through the side entrance) take the time to admire the main entrance, which once served noblemen and clergy, kings and queens. The magnificent marble staircase is topped with statues of Mars and Neptune by Sansovino.

Mission: Two large statues sit at the base of Staircase: One is Atlas holding the world on his shoulders. Can you guess who the other is? Hint–his strength is described in mythology, and there is a famous myth about him killing two snakes when he was only baby...

The tour of Palazzo Ducale begins in the Doge's personal apartments. These rooms once held incredible pieces of furniture, but today it is the detailed artwork that impresses visitors. One very important piece of furniture remains: the doge's throne. It faces the sea to honor Venice's relationship with the water. The rooms on the second floor are even more impressive: The Hall of Four Doors features paintings by Tintoretto in golden frames in the ceiling panels, and the Hall of the Senate—the Oval Office of the Venetian Republic—is especially glorious, with its golden stucco and beautiful artwork. The furniture here is original, and it's easy to imagine the members of the senate sitting on these very seats, 500 years ago, as they debated Venice's international relations.

The Hall of the Council of Ten is next, and it is less dazzling but just as historically significant. The Council was created in 1310 and with time became the most feared and most secretive institution in Venice—a sort of 15th century CIA or Homeland Security, that even had its own secret police force. Like so many other formal roles in the Venetian republic, the members who were elected to this office could not decline the position (nor did they receive pay for their work). This room contains a wooden box that was the downfall of many Venetians—people could anonymously report crimes by writing the details on paper and putting the paper into the mouth of the lion on the top of the box. To discourage malicious false reports, anyone found to make such a report was tortured and jailed.

Venice

●•··●•··●•··●•··●•··●•··●•··●•··●•··●•··●•··●•··●•··

Mission: In one of these rooms there's a beautiful painting of the goddess Juno throwing gold coins. Can you find it? Hint: look up!

●•··●•··●•··●•··●•··●•··●•··●•··●•··●•··●•··●•··●•··

In the **Armory**, which occupies the next two halls, you will see the arms of the Council of Ten from the 15th century. This supply of weapons, shields and helmets was kept on hand in case the state faced an emergency.

●•··●•··●•··●•··●•··●•··●•··●•··●•··●•··●•··●•··●•··

Mission: Can you find a cannon, a two-handed sword, and an armor for animals in this room? Look at all the different helmets in this room. Which is your favorite and why?

●•··●•··●•··●•··●•··●•··●•··●•··●•··●•··●•··●•··●•··

Next, head downstairs to the Hall of the Great Council, which is spectacular enough to make you sigh. This massive, intensely and ornately decorated room is 54 meters long by 24 meters wide with 12-meter-high ceilings, and the 300-member council met here to run the republic. The artwork you see today by Tintoretto and Veronese was created when the hall was restored after a fire in 1577. Tintoretto's impressive Coronation of the Virgin hangs at the far end of the room, commanding attention and admiration. It may be hard to imagine, but this hall was once even more impressively decorated, but sadly the fire destroyed many priceless pieces by Titian, Bellini, Tintoretto, Veronese, and other greats.

From here, you can walk down to the bottom floor of the Palazzo, and visit the prison cells, though this might be too scary for young children (the corridors are narrow, humid and dark). Once you exit the palace, don't forget to make another stop to see the famous **Bridge of Sighs.** To reach it, walk from the Doge's palace along the Riva degli Schiavoni promenade, and once you get on the first bridge, turn your head left. That small white travertine stone bridge that protrudes from the Doge's Palace is the Bridge of Sighs.

The bridge was named for the sighs of prisoners crossing it on the way from their trial in the palace to the prison cells. Many realized they would not survive to walk back across it to freedom because the cells were so damp and musty prisoners often succumbed to illness and died there. As they walked and sighed, some prisoners took one last glimpse of beautiful Venice, and if they were lucky, threw a last letter through the tiny window to their family members who waited in a gondola below the bridge. 🕐 Palazzo Ducale (the Doge's Palace), Piazza San Marco, enter through the Porta del Frumento, Piazzetta San Marco. Open April 1—October 31, daily, 8:30—19:00 (last entry at 18:00); November 1—March 31, daily 8:30—17:30 (last entry 16:30). Special daily guided tours are available for an additional fee; book in advance here: 041.4273.0892. Combo tickets available—the **Piazza San Marco** ticket costs 20 euro and grants you entry to the Palazzo Ducale, Museo Correr and the Archeological Museum. Children under 5 enter for free, under 15 pay a reduced fee. The combo ticket can be purchased **online in advance,** thus allowing you to skip the long line. Find out more here: www.palazzoducale.visitmuve.it/en/pianifica-la-tua-visita/tickets. Note: Depending on which other museums you wish to visit in addition to Palazzo Ducale, one of the Venezia Unica comprehensive passes may be a better deal than the Piazza San Marco ticket; check both before you make your purchase.

LIBRERIA MARCIANA

This impressive library sits on the western side of Piazza San Marco, directly across from the Doge's Palace. It was designed in 1537 by architect Jacopo Sansovino, holds some of the oldest existing manuscripts in Italy, and it is widely considered one of the most beautiful libraries in the country. Sansovino never got to see the completed edifice (he died while it was being built) and the project hit difficulty after difficulty, including a partial collapse and the arrest of one of the architects involved. The library won't interest most children, but book-loving teenagers might enjoy taking a peek inside this beautiful space, especially if you've already bought the Piazza San Marco Combo ticket. 🕐 Libreria Marciana, Piazza San Marco. Open 10:00—19:00, off season until 16:00.

CORRER MUSEUM

The last sight to see on Piazza San Marco offers a fascinating glimpse into the lives of ancient Venetians with a collection of artefacts including coins, armor, model ships and artwork. It is directly opposite the Basilica, and older children are more likely to appreciate this museum than younger ones. For history buffs, the Correr museum offers several surprises. ◉Correr Museum, Piazza San Marco. Enter through Piazza San Marco 52 (near caffe' Florian). Tel: 041.240.5211, www.correr.visitmuve.it. April 1—October 31, 10:00—19:00 (last entry 18:00). November 1—March 31, 10:00—17:00 (last entry at 16:00).

> **Tip:** One of the main parking areas for gondolas is right next to the Correr Museum on a wide waterway known as Bacino Orseolo. From the museum, turn onto Calle Salvadago, and Fondamenta Orseolo and the Bacino will be on the right, 150 meters from Piazza San Marco.

RIVA DEGLI SCHIAVONI

Now that you've seen the famous Piazza San Marco, it's time to stretch your legs on Venice's best loved promenade, Riva Degli Schiavoni. (This will also lead you to the Arsenale.) Today, the promenade is filled with touristy restaurants and tacky souvenir vendors, but in the past, it was brimming with merchants from all over the world, who tempted the locals with exotic commodities – spices, creams, strange new foods, arrows and amour, and more.

Along the way, you will pass the glorious **Hotel Danieli,** and if you are traveling with teenagers, it's worth stopping here for a drink on the exclusive rooftop terrace bar so you can take in the dazzling views. (Prepare your heart and wallet for the hefty price tag—cocktails are 20 euro.) If you do enter this hotel, you'll be walking in the footsteps of famous visitors including Charles Dickens, Honore de Balzac, Marcel Proust, Jean Cocteau, Gabriele d'Annunzio, Woody Allen, and Steven Spielberg among others.

If you have any fans of Antonio Vivaldi in your family, watch for Santa Maria Della Pieta (in front of the San Zaccaria vaporetto stop), a church and school built in 1346 that also served as an orphanage and music conservatory where the great Vivaldi taught. The ceiling is decorated with lovely frescoes by Tiepolo, and the revolving door behind the building was where desperate parents could leave their babies anonymously. A sign outside in Latin warns of severe fines for anyone abandoning a child they were capable of providing for.

THE ISLAND OF SAN GIORGIO

Getting there: Take the vaporetto (line 2) from Piazza San Marco one stop across the canal to San Giorgio.

A lot of history sits on this small but significant island across the San Marco Basin from Piazza San Marco. The first Renaissance building in Venice was Michelozzo Michelozzi's library here, which can still be visited today. It was followed in 1559 by Andrea Palladio's Benedictine abbey, church and cloister. San Giorgio became an important religious center until the Republic of Venice fell and the Austrian army took over. Its revival began in 1951 when Count Vittorio Cini purchased the island in memory of his late son Giorgio. It became a cultural quarter with a theater, art exhibitions, a beautiful garden, and other cultural events. For art lovers, this is a must see, but for families, there is far less to do here. One interesting spot is the church's *campanile* (bell tower) that offers lovely views and is a reasonably good alternative to the bell tower in Piazza San Marco if the line there is too long. ◉ San Giorgio Maggiore. Open April—October, 9:00—19:00; November—March, 8:30—18:00. Last entry 20 minutes before closing. Sundays, entry is suspended when mass is celebrated (10:40—12:00).

THE ARSENALE

Getting there: From Piazza San Marco, walk along Riva degli Schiavoni until you reach the Arsenale (10 minutes by foot). Alternatively, take the vaporetto and get off at the Arsenale stop.

Today's Arsenale reveals little of its glorious past. During Venice's heyday, this was a massive collection of shipyards and armories that were at the heart of the city's military and economic power. Back then, Venice ruled the sea and dominated the trade routes. Competition was fierce, and the Arsenale was Venice's secret weapon.

Today, the Arsenale is much smaller, and the Italian navy owns it. It welcomes visitors to the beautiful **Shipyard (Pavilione delle Navi)**, where you can see some cool ship models, and the interesting **Naval Museum**, which is very popular with families, but is currently **closed** for renovation. (Hopefully it will open again in 2018 or 2019.) The rest of the Arsenale is military property, and access to most areas is restricted. Our second self-guided walking tour ends here. From the Arsenale you can take the vaporetto to Lido island (see next itinerary), or return to the Train station and visit the Jewish Ghetto (see box below). ☯ Shipyard-Pavilione delle Navi, Arsenale, Castello 2162, Rio della Tana. Tel: 041.2441399. www.visitmuve.it. Open 8:45—17:00 (last entry 16:30). Children under 5 enter for free, under 14 pay a reduced fee. The northern part of the Arsenale is open to the public can be visited free of charge, daily, 9:00—18:00.

More about the Arsenale

The Arsenale was founded in 1104 on two islands that locals called 'the twins', and spread across 110 acres. The term 'arsenale' comes from the Arabic word 'darsena', which means 'house of industry'. In many ways, the Arsenale was centuries ahead of its time: Long before the Industrial Revolution, workers here were assembling prefabricated parts rather than custom building each ship. Inside two miles of ramparts, this early version of an assembly line style production system, meant that they could produce up to 100 galley ships in two months, which gave Venice a massive advantage in both trade and warfare.

The Arsenale was a major economic hub in itself, employing an array of workers including ship builders and carpenters, rope makers, seamstresses to sew the sails, iron smiths and chefs, who cooked and served food to the workers. Those who worked at the Arsenale were known as arsenalotti, and they collectively wielded enough power to ensure fair working conditions. Even the Doge dared not oppose this union! The Venetians took tremendous pride in their city, and in the Arsenale in particular, which translated into respect for the arsenalotti. The arsenalotti also made weapons such as catapults and guns to fend off pirates and ensure Venice's military might. Some of the bombarding devices made at the Arsenale were given intimidating names such as 'The Lion' and 'No More Words', and at one point, even the famous Galileo Galilei was involved in the operation—he advised about ballistics manufacture, keeping the Venetian military at the cutting edge.

If you have some extra time, make your way back to the train station to visit the **Jewish Ghetto**. Though not a popular sight for families, the Jewish Ghetto in Venice is an important part of the city's history, and is included on most of the Venezia Unica passes. The Ghetto is located five minutes by foot from Santa Lucia: From the station walk along Rio Tera Lista di Spagna, cross the Guglie bridge, and turn left, where you will see the narrow entry lading to the Ghetto Campo. The Jewish community in Venice is one of the oldest in the Europe, and the Ghetto in which you are now standing is in fact the first in the world. For hundreds of years, Jews were allowed to visit Venice and trade with the locals, but they were prohibited from purchasing land or homes, and more than once were forcefully expelled during periods of religious fervor. In 1516 the Consiglio proposed a new compromise, designating a specific area in the city for the Jewish community to reside in (the ancient foundry, geto in Italian, from which the word "ghetto" probably comes). However, several limitations were set: Men and women had to wear special red and yellow markings on their clothes to indicate their religion; they were not allowed to mix with the Christian population; they were not allowed to leave the Ghetto at night (armed guards were placed at the entry); and the professions that Jews could practice were strictly limited by law, consisting essentially of trade, medicine and moneylending. Since they were not allowed to leave the Ghetto, this is the only area in Venice in which you will see "skyscrapers," tall buildings that were hastily built to provide housing for the growing population.

Despite various attacks and restrictions, the Jewish community grew and thrived, and even produced several scholars and writers of international fame. When Napoleon conquered Venice in 1797 he ended this forced segregation, allowing Jews to live wherever they wanted. Following the unification of Italy, Italian Jews were finally emancipated. During World War II, over 200 Jews were deported from Venice to Auschwitz and other concentration camps. Today the Jewish community is very small (less than 500 people, most of whom live outside the Ghetto) but vibrant. The main sights worth visiting here are the museum, which is tiny but holds an important collection of Judaica objects and textiles, and the ancient synagogues. The best way to complete your visit is by joining a guided tour (book in advance, find out more here: www.museoebraico.it.)

SELF GUIDED WALKING TOUR N. 3: The Islands of Venice—Lido, Mutrano, Burano and Torcello

Ready for some island hopping, Venetian style? In addition to mainland Venice, where most of the tourist attractions are concentrated, there are a number of interesting, smaller islands to discover. Each island has its own distinct feel; collectively, these islands offer something for everyone from beach fun to history to nature to art. The most interesting and best-suited islands for families are listed below.

> **Tip:** Expect to spend plenty of time on boats getting from one island to the next. The Vaporetto from Venice to Lido takes 15 minutes. The vaporetto from Venice to Murano takes about 10 minutes; from Murano to Burano, nearly an hour. From Burano to Torcello, an additional 10 minutes. From Torcello back to Venice, just over an hour. The islands can be toured autonomously (using the public vaporetti) or, if you prefer, you can book an organized tour with a local operator and spend half a day seeing the islands. The advantage of a guided tour is that you won't need to take care of any logistics; the disadvantage is that the excursion can feel rushed. To book a tour, check one of these: Alilaguna (www.alilaguna.it), Viator (www.viator.com/venice) and Isola di Burano (www.isoladiburano.venetoinside.com).

LIDO

Getting there: To reach Lido, take vaporetto 5.1 or 5.2 from the Santa Lucia train station (Ferrovia) and get off at the Santa Elisabetta vaporetto stop. From Giardini (the park near the Arsenale) you can also take line 6.

Water is everywhere you look in Venice, but if you want to get in and go swimming, you have one option—Lido. Just 15 minutes away by vaporetto, this large island offers many beaches for families to relax, hike and enjoy a swim. You can even find secluded nature reserves that are quiet and not at all crowded. (If you visit the reserves, bring water, walking sandals, sunscreen and plenty of insect and tick repellent, just to be on the safe side.)

Viale Santa Elisabetta is the Lido's main street, and you can continue down this road from the vaporetto stop until you reach the roundabout. The road on your right, Viale Marconi, leads to the more exclusive and expensive beaches run by the top hotels. The road to the left leads to the popular beaches, including some that are free, such as San Nicolo Beach, Murazzi, and Alberoni. Paradise beach, on Via Klinger, is another great option for families (www.spiaggiaparadiso.it). It's a pleasant 15 to 20-minute walk to reach most beaches, or you can rent bikes on the island (there's a shop on Viale Santa Elisabetta, right by the newsstand) and explore them all.

> **Tip:** Lido offers parks and playgrounds for the kids, too. Parco Askenasi (formerly known as Luna Park), which sits at Lungomare D'Annunzio, is the largest and most popular. It has a playground, lots of space to run around and play, and a tiny planetarium, which occasionally organizes activities for the public. The park is open daily, 8:30—20:30 (until 18:00 off season). There are two additional (and much smaller) parks on the island: One at Via Quattro Fontane, and one at Via Simone Occhi.

BURANO

Getting there: From the Fondamente Nove Vaporetto stop, take Line 12.

Charming Burano sits an hour (by public vaporetto) from Venice, at the north end of the lagoon, near Torcello. The island is tiny and can be toured in half an hour. The main draw here is that all the houses on the island are painted in vibrant, bright colors. There are no specific attractions here, but this little gem is a lovely place to wander around with no particular goal and take an unreasonable number of pictures. Given the considerable distance from Venice, we recommend making it part of a day where you visit other islands, such as Torcello. Alternatively, make a stop here on your way to Jesolo (the popular beach town that boasts a waterpark, aquarium and amusement park—see the separate itinerary for Jesolo under 'Day Trips from Venice).

Mission: Find a green house, a purple house, a pink house, a red house, a blue house and a yellow house, and take a photo making a silly face in front of each!

There are many theories regarding Burano's particular fashion sense. Some say that the wild colors made it easier for fishermen to see their homes when they were returning from sea. Or perhaps it is simply because creativity is woven into the fabric of life on Burano. The second traditional draw here is the delightful lace that has been made here for centuries. There's a small lace museum on the island's main piazza, and several shops sell delicate pieces that make beautiful souvenirs.

MURANO

Getting There: From the Fondamente Nove vaporetto stop in Venice, take Line 4.1 or 4.2 and get off at Murano Faro. From the train station (Ferrovia), take line 3. From San Marco, you can also take line 7.

This small island is famous for its traditional, hand-blown glass, and you can watch the artisans at work at this mesmerizing craft. Back in the Renaissance, the island had another bragging point—this was the birthplace of Fra Mauro, the famous 15th century cartographer whose maps were heralded by kings, armies and merchants. It is no coincidence that so many glass blowers can be found here, and not in the mainland. In 1291, an edict was issued moving Venice's many glass blower artisans to Murano, apparently for safety reasons—glass blowing involves heating glass until it is liquid, and the edict came after a cluster of serious fires. But as so often happens, there were secret political reasons, too. The Serenissima was extremely jealous of its glass blowing knowledge, and the mandatory move to Murano was also motivated by a desire to protect the artistic secrets of the local glass industry from spies who posed as merchants and tried to steal the tricks of the trade.

Glass was a very important part of the Venetian economy, and the artisans who created the beautiful pieces that adorned the homes of Venice's nobility were widely respected and given many privileges. In fact, glass blowers could marry their children into noble families and wear clothing and swords that were normally restricted to noble families. But glory came with a price—the artisans lived in a golden cage, and could never leave Venice.

Murano is only 10-15 minutes from Venice by vaporetto. If you don't have much time, stop for a pre-booked or last-minute glass blowing demonstration. The Murano Glass Museum at Palazzo Giustinian organizes weekly glass blowing demonstrations (check their website to find our more: www.museovetro.visitmuve.it). Alternatively, Fornace Gino Mazzuccato, just 100 meters from the Murano Farro vaporetto stop is a large shop that also does demonstrations every half hour. Vetreria Estevan is another popular shop, and they also offer guided tours and demonstrations (check their website in advance): www.rossettomuranoglass.com/en/guided-tours

TORCELLO

Getting there: From Burano, take vaporetto line 9. Do check the ACTV vaporetti timetable in advance, the number of water buses going to Torcello (and then back to Venice) is very limited.

Located about an hour away from Venice in the northern part of the lagoon, Torcello is home to about ten permanent, year-round residents. But it was once densely populated and bustling with importance. It's been inhabited since the fall of the western Roman Empire, and the population grew when people moved to Torcello to avoid the Barbarian invasions. The island's strong economy was fueled by the salt trade, but the black death and deadly episodes of malaria reduced the population by more than 70%. The area around Torcello became known as the *Laguna Morta* (the dead lagoon, in Italian), and when Constantinople fell in 1453, Torcello received its final blow.

Today nothing in this peaceful nature reserve of an island hints neither at its glorious past or its tragic demise. Rather, it's a fun destination for nature lovers who want to get a break from the hustle and bustle of the city. Famous writer Ernest Hemingway loved Torcello, and even a quick stroll around this unspoiled island will make it clear why. The natural beauty here is serene, and the island also has an ancient church, Santa Maria Assunta, which is 1,000 years old and features beautiful Byzantine mosaics. If you come here, bring a packed lunch; the restaurants on the island are fairly expensive. The main issue with Torcello, as we've mentioned earlier, is that reaching the island aboard the vaporetti can be very time consuming (and there are very few vaporetti coming here daily to begin with). If you haven't got a lot of time in Venice, it might be easier to focus your attention on other, more accessible islands, instead.

●•••●•••●•••●•••●•••●•••●•••●•••●•••●•••●•••●•••

Mission 1: Inside the church, how many men wearing completely white robes can you spot?

Mission 2: How many angels are there in this mosaic?

●•••●•••●•••●•••●•••●•••●•••●•••●•••●•••●•••●•••

To make the most of your visit to Torcello, you can also visit the delightful Andrich Art Gallery and Garden. This was once the private home of artists Lucio Andrich and Clementina De Luca, and today their work is on display throughout the property. There are some 1,300 pieces to enjoy, and the 50-minute guided tour includes a visit to the beautiful garden, too. Find out more here: www.museoandrich.com.

KIDS' CORNER

Cool and Weird Facts about Venice

1. Does the vaporetto feel soooo slllooowwww to you? That's because it is! The speed limit on the Grand Canal is 5 km per hour (that's actually slower than most tortoises). But some boat can go faster: Fire boats, police boats and ambulance boats are allowed to speed through in case of a serious emergency.

2. All over the world, streets are usually named after heroes and civic leaders. But did you know that in Venice there's a street named for a notorious criminal? Riva de Biasio is named after serial killer Biagio Carnagio, a 16th century butcher who went mad and bad...

3. You must have noticed that Venice has lots of narrow streets, but can you guess just how narrow is the narrowest one? The answer may shock you! The most narrow alley of them all is Calletta Varisco, and it's only 53 centimeters wide! Better not try to pass through after eating too much pizza...

4. Mainland Venice is made of lots of little islands that are connected by bridges. How many bridges do you think there are? 100? 200? Actually, there are more than 400 bridges!

5. Venetians love seafood, and they will happily eat anything that the fishermen catch in their nets. In fact, many Venetian restaurants serve seafood dishes that can scare non-Venetian guests... One of the most popular dishes is black pasta, made with the cuttlefish's black ink (nero di seppia, in Italian). Are you brave enough to try it? If you are, make sure to flash a big smile after you finish and take a picture; your teeth and tongue will be completely black!

KIDS' CORNER

6. Venice is famous for its gondolas, and the men rowing these boats are the stars of the city. Gondoliers have to be very athletic to do their job, and they take great pride in being strong and agile. In the past, the gondolieri would compete in rowing matches that were as popular as any major league sport today. Because the gondoliers were real show-offs, they enjoyed demonstrating their strength on every occasion, and sometimes they held boxing matches, too. Venice's famous *Ponte dei Pugni* bridge (near Campo San Barnaba) is named for the boxing matches held there. It was a perfect spot because the bridge didn't have rails, and the loser would fall straight into the water!

7. Venice is one of the most famous cities in the world. It is featured in many books and movies including two James Bond films, an Indiana Jones movie and the adventures of Alex Rider. It's even in the Assassins video game!

8. The city of Venice is often flooded, but luckily, today the floods aren't that bad. In the past, they were much worse. Once, in 1966, the city was so flooded that the water reached 196 centimeters; that's higher than football star Tom Brady!

KIDS' CORNER

More About... Marco Polo!

Do you know the game Marco Polo? Of course you do. But did you know that Marco Polo isn't just an invented name? He was a real person! Marco Polo was a world-famous explorer and adventurer, and one of Venice's most famous citizens. Marco Polo began his travels when he was just 17. The year was 1270, and Venice was where everybody came to do business. Rich merchants sailed in big wooden ships across the seas, and brought spices, salt, wool and gold from all around the world. Marco Polo's father and uncle were merchants, too, and they took young Marco on a dangerous journey to Mongolia. They traveled more than 8,000 kilometers from Venice, to the royal court of Kublai Khan. Kublai Khan was not only the ruthless leader of the Mongolian empire, he was also the grandson of Genghis Khan.

The journey from Venice to Mongolia was difficult and full of obstacles. Marco, his father and his uncle crossed the sea and rode for hundreds of kilometers across the Gobi Desert on camels and horses, until they reached the royal court. Eventually, Marco Polo stayed to work for the Khan for 17 years. He collected taxes, gathered information, and served as Khan's representative in the far-flung corners of the empire. Traveling in foreign lands was very dangerous—Marco Polo could be attacked, or taken prisoner by hostile tribes. That is why he always carried a golden tablet called a paiza. The paiza was like a secret identity card. When he showed it, people knew that he worked for Khan and that he was under Khan's protection. If they harmed him, there would be consequences.

KIDS' CORNER

During his travels, Marco Polo learned a lot about other cultures, and saw some amazing things. He saw new inventions in China and tasted many weird dishes (including donkey milk, which one tribe called a real delicacy). He even saw incredible battles, in which soldiers rode elephants instead of horses into the battlefield!

After many years, Marco Polo returned to Venice. He started a new life in his old city, and lived in a house in Corte di Million (near the Rialto Bridge; you can visit it from the outside if you want). The world might never have known about Marco Polo's amazing life and journeys, had he not been captured during the Battle of Curzola. Marco Polo was thrown into a jail cell, but luckily his cellmate was a successful writer, who was so impressed with Marco Polo's life story, that he decided to write a book about him. The book became a bestseller, and inspired many adventurous travelers to go on similar journeys to far away lands. You may have heard about one of those adventurous travelers... His name was Christopher Columbus!

KIDS' CORNER

How to be a mask expert - know your mask!

Have you noticed that nearly every shop in Venice sells masks? Do you know why that is? The Venetian masks are more than just fun souvenirs—they have a cool and mysterious history that not everyone knows about. But if you come closer and listen carefully, we will tell you all about it...

Hundreds of years ago, all the Venetians wore masks at carnival time. But some noble people wore them all year, because they wanted to move around the city discreetly, and masks were an excellent way to conceal their identity from nosy neighbors and even spies. If you think about it, it's a lot like having tinted car windows or wearing a hat and big sunglasses today. In the 15th century, mask making was a respected profession. But times changed, and eventually laws were made to limit how much people wore masks. Today the masks are still a symbol of Venice, but people don't wear them daily. Instead, the masks are used in celebrations and also in the theater, especially in a traditional Italian theater called 'Commedia dell'Arte'.

- Columbina: This is the popular and pretty half mask with a handle to hold it in place. You'll see them decorated lavishly with feathers, gilding, sequins and ribbons; the more lavish it is, the better the mask! Can you guess why it's called the Columbina? The reason is simple: It's named for the actress who wore this type of mask in the Commedia dell'Arte theater.
- Plague Doctor: Can you imagine your physician wearing one of these masks while giving you a check up? No thank you! But in the 14th century, doctors really wore these masks, because they were afraid of the black

KIDS' CORNER

plague. The beak-like part of the mask was filled with herbs, that they believed protected them from illness.

- Bauta: This was an official mask that people were required to wear when they gathered to make political decisions. That way, everyone could remain anonymous when they talked or voted. The chin is curved outward so the wearer could eat and drink without removing it, and it was illegal to carry weapons while wearing the bauta mask.
- Pulcinella: Ask your parents if this mask looks familiar to them—it's the model for Punch in Punch and Judy. Pulcinella has a long, hooked nose, and this mask is associated with the city of Naples.
- Harlequin: This is the mask with the distinctive diamond pattern in different colors.

KIDS' CORNER

More About... Gondolas and Gondoliers!

When you are in Venice, you will see many gondolas all around the city. These boats are a famous symbol of the city, and you will see them everywhere you look. But in the past, there were many many more! Thousands of gondolas traveled the waters of Venice 500 years ago, in the 16th century. Today there are fewer than 500, and most give tours.

Gondolas must be built according to very specific measurements: They are 10.85 meters long by 1.40 meters wide, and are made of exactly 280 wooden parts. Gondolas have a flat bottom, so they can travel in shallow water, and the oars are 4.20 meters long.

If you look at a gondola, you will see that the front and back ends have a special design: The front part is called the "ferro", and it looks like a comb with six "teeth" (each "tooth" represent one the six districts of the city of Venice). This part is not just pretty, it helps balance the gondola, too. The "risso", a curved metal piece that looks a bit like a seahorse, is at the back.

The gondoliers have a unique technique they use to row the gondola: They stand behind the passengers and use only one oar, which they move with their hands and legs. And if you are wondering why they only use one oar, the reason is simple—

KIDS' CORNER

the waterways in Venice are too crowded and narrow to fit an oar on both sides of the gondola. If you tried to row another boat like a gondola, it would tip and dump everyone in the water, but the gondola has a special design. Because the rowing makes it tilt to the left, it is built to tilt to the right. Aren't the Venetians smart?

The gondolas you see in Venice now are sleek and black, but long ago, gondolas were painted every color and even decorated with gold gilding. Noble families had their own gondolas and private gondoliers, like rich families today have a limo and private chauffeur. The rich families liked to show off and outdo each other by having the most beautiful gondola. But this made the Venetian government angry, and finally, they were so fed up that they decided that all the gondolas had to be black, except for the Doge's gondola. His gondola was called the "Bucintoro" and it was much larger and more luxurious than anyone else's.

KIDS' CORNER

More About... The Plague!

The Black Death (plague) was a terrible disease that spread terror across Europe when it struck 700 years ago, in the 14th century. It was a very gruesome disease, and symptoms included horrifying things such as gangrene, high fever, seizures, vomiting blood, and excruciating pain. The skin even began to decompose while the victims were still alive! Many people didn't survive. In fact, the plague killed almost a third of the population. And because Venice was such a busy port city, with traders coming from all over the world, it was at great risk.

Every time an episode of the black plague started, the rulers of Venice did everything they could to stop it. They outlawed public gatherings and closed down churches, and people who were suspected of being ill were taken away from their homes and put in isolation on a distant island, where they couldn't infect anyone. Doctors didn't have the scientific knowledge they do today, and they didn't understand much about how the illness spread. Many of them believed that the plague was a punishment from God. Some thought it was caused by bad air, and this is why in many paintings you see the doctor protecting his face by wearing a strange black mask shaped like a bird's beak.

The real reason for the plague, of course, was quite different. The plague is caused by a strong bacteria called Yersinia pestis (named after one of the biologists who discovered it). The agent that carried it around was the common rat. Italian merchants who arrived by ship from China unknowingly carried with them infected rats, bringing the plague to Europe.

People were scared of the black death and tried to protect themselves with all sorts of magic potions and tricks. Some used a stone from a church as an amulet; others used earth

KIDS' CORNER

that a holy person had walked on. But none of this helped much. People kept dying from the disease, and so many people died so quickly that it was impossible to bury them all. Instead, a man in a special boat would crisscross the city shouting "*Chi gà morti in casa li buta zoso in barca*" – which means "those with dead people at home should throw them (through the window) into the boat." Luckily, today modern medicine can cure the plague, and we have antibiotics.

KIDS' CORNER

What Was Venice Like 600 Years Ago?

One of the best things about traveling is that you get to see history with your own eyes. All you have to do is use your imagination and all those tourists vanish, and instead you can see Venice in the time that it was an empire, 600 years ago...

Back then, there were no vaporetti (water buses) in the Grand Canal. Instead there were small wooden boats and gondolas. The city was filled with fascinating people from all over the world, animals, lively markets, beggars, and dramatic religious gatherings. If you walked near the main town squares, you could often see public punishments of criminals in front of a crowd. (The little piazza near the Rialto Bridge was a popular spot for such exhibitions.)

The clothes that people wore back then were very, VERY different from the clothes we wear today. Men wore a sort of leggings with long, loose tops that hung below their hips and had wide, billowing sleeves. A pair of boots, a belt and a large hat completed the look. If they belonged to the elite, they also had a cape and a ruffled collar. Most women covered their heads with a veil in public and in church (black veils for married women, yellow veils for servants). Women wore high heels back then too, but not only to appear taller—they had to keep their clothing from touching the ground, which was absolutely filthy and smelly and filled with horse manure and garbage and fish heads from the market. And you couldn't just decide on your own what to wear. Only noble people were allowed to wear certain colors, like purple and red. If you broke the law and wore a color that belonged to a different social class, you were put in jail! So what would you prefer - living in Venice today, or living in Venice 600 years ago?

Eating in Venice

Eating out in Venice, unlike in other cities in Italy, can be complicated for many families. Venice is heaven for those who love seafood, but if you and your kids don't go crazy for clams, sardines and cuttlefish, finding the right restaurant for your family can become an issue. Additionally, the prices here are usually about 30% higher than in other Italian cities—a *primo* that would cost 12 euro in Florence will easily cost 15 euro in Venice, and a *Secondo* will be around 20 euro or more. For this reason, our list of recommended Venetian eateries includes both quick-fix restaurants that make pasta and pizza, as well as a number of traditional restaurants that offer a more authentic dining experience.

NEAR THE RIALTO BRIDGE

Old Wild West: If the kids get homesick for hamburgers, this is the place to take them. The fun wild west theme is a nice change of pace if you need a little break from all things Italian. The convenient location, right on the famous Calle Nuova shopping street, makes this an easy stop to make between sights. Strada Nuova, Cannaregio 3660A. Open daily, 12:00—midnight. www.oldwildwest.it/code/20100/Venezia-Strada-Nuova.

Hard Rock Café: For many teens, the Hard Rock Café still hits the spot, whether they are missing the food back home, or just want to take some selfies. There are two locations in Venice—by the Rialto Bridge, and behind Piazza San Marco. Hard Rock Cafe Piazza San Marco, Bacino Orseolo, San Marco 1192. Open daily 11:00—23:00 (later on Saturdays); Hard Rock Cafe Rialto Bridge, Salizzada Pio X. Open daily, 10:00—19:30 (until 21:00 on weekends). www.hardrock.com/cafes/venice.

Farini: It's easy to see why this place is so popular just from walking past it. This isn't a restaurant but a take-away diner, with a selection of delicious sandwiches and pizzas at budget-friendly prices. They have three locations, all close to tourist sites: San Polo 655 & 379 (both near the Rialto Market), and Castello 5602 (right off Campo Santo Maria Formosa). Open daily, 8:00—20:00 p.m. www.farini.com.

NEAR PIAZZA SAN MARCO

RossoPomodoro: With so much to see at Piazza San Marco, and with so many touristy and over-priced restaurants on every corner, it's great to find excellent pizza right off the square. Location, ample seating and quality make this the perfect pizza pitstop for families. Calle larga San Marco 404. Tel: 041.243.8949, www.rossopomodoro.it/ristoranti/VENEZIA/centro-storico. Open daily, 11.30—22:30.

Taverna Scalinetto: With its high ceiling and linen tablecloths, Taverna Scalinetto is sophisticated enough to feel fancy to children, but friendly enough that parents are comfortable bringing them. The food is delicious, and you can enjoy some very good traditional dishes, beyond the usual pizza, just a few minutes from Piazza San Marco. Castello 3803. Tel: 041.520.0776, www.tavernascalinetto.it. Open daily, 12:00—23:30.

NEAR FONDAMENTE NOVE

Ristorante Alvise: Care for a view with your pizza? This one is right on the waterfront near the vaporetto stop for Murano and Burano, and a short walk from Santa Maria dei Miracoli church. The menu is ample and caters to every taste, and both kids and adults will enjoy the relaxed atmosphere. Fondamente Nove, Cannaregio 5045. Tel: 041.520.1515, www.ristorantedaalvise.it. Open mid-March—early November, daily, 12:00—14:00 & 19:00—23:00 (the pizzeria is open 12:00—22:00). Closed off season.

Cicheti!

When you are on the go sight-seeing, it works well to stop for lots of snacks instead of a big meal. And in Venice, you'd be in sync with the locals doing just that. **Cicheti** are small snacks such as fried meatballs, polenta with creamed cod and finger sandwiches, and **bacari** are the tavern-cafes that serve them. Venetians often go hopping from bacaro to bacaro for some cicheti and a glass of spritz cocktail before dinner, and your teenagers will probably enjoy doing the same. Plus, you could easily fill up on these alone! You'll find several good bacari (the plural form of bacaro) around the Rialto Bridge and Campo San Giacometto and Erberia. We like **Bancogiro** (Campo San Giacometto, closed Monday), **Naranzaria** (next door to Bancogiro) and **Osteria Ciurma** (Calle Galeazza 406, closed Sunday) in this area. Near the Accademia, don't miss **Cantinone Già Schiavi** (Dorsoduro 992, closed Sunday), and in the Arsenale area, try the hugely popular **El Refolo** (Via Garibaldi, Castello 1580, closed Monday).

NEAR THE ACCADEMIA

Trattoria San Trovaso: This solid and very good choice is just meters from the Accademia, and on the route to the gondola garage. The menu here is both child-friendly and budget-friendly with a wide selection of pasta and meat dishes to keep everyone happy. Fondamenta Priuli, Dorsoduro 1016. Open daily, 12:00—14:45 & 19:00—21:45. Tel: 041.520.3703, www.tavernasantrovaso.it.

Bar la Toletta: This is a case of 'don't judge a book by its cover'. Behind the uninspiring façade, you'll find delicious sandwiches and pastries for great prices. Nothing fancy, but a good selection to satisfy everyone. Via Toletta, Dorsoduro 1191, Venezia. Tel: 041.520.0196. Open daily, 7:00—20:00.

Nico's Café: When in Venice, do like the Venetians and stop at Nico's for an ice cream or drink and some people watching. Come here before or after you visit the nearby Guggenheim collection, and enjoy a moment away from the crowds, a stroll along the waterfront, and some creamy gelato, of course. Fondamenta Zattere, Dorsoduro 922. Tel: 041.522.5293, www.gelaterianico.com. Open Friday—Wednesday, 7:00—21:00. Thursday closed.

NEAR THE FRARI CHURCH AND THE SCUOLA DI SAN ROCCO

La Bottiglia: Traveling with children should not condemn you to weeks of pizza and burgers. Even if you can't get the kids to enjoy a full meal at a serious restaurant, a light lunch of delicious panini made with the finest Italian products, from Mozzarella di Bufala to Parma prosciutto, will help them discover their inner foodie. La Bottiglia is a good starting point, and the location, just a couple of minutes from the Frari church, makes it a comfortable stop to make before or after your visit to the many sights in the area. San Polo 2537, Campo San Stin. Cell: 335.593.0910. Open daily in season, 10:00—22:00.

NEAR THE ARSENALE

Al Giardinetto: Escape the crowds for a delightful meal in their beautiful, shaded garden without breaking the bank. Then you can walk around the intriguing Castello neighborhood, off the beaten path. Salizada Zorzi (Ruga Giuffa), Castello 4928. Tel: 041.528.5332, www.algiardinetto.it. Open Friday–Wednesday, 12:00—15:00 & 19:00—22:00.

NEAR THE TRAIN STATION & JEWISH GHETTO

Ristorante Upupa: You will find this stylish choice in the historic Jewish ghetto, just five minutes from the train station. Their modern take on Venetian classics makes this a good spot for all members of the family. Campo di Ghetto Novo, Cannaregio 2888. Tel: 041.476.4288, www.upupaghettovenezia.com. Open Thursday—Tuesday, 12:00—15:00 & 19:00—22:30. Wednesday closed.

Ai Tre Archi: Delicious food, huge pizzas, and a fun, friendly ambiance. What more can you ask from one of our favorite neighborhood eateries? Cannaregio 552. Tel: 041.716.438, www.aitrearchivenezia.it. Open daily for lunch and dinner, reservations recommended.

VEGETARIANS

La Zucca: If your family is vegetarian, you could wind up as regulars here—it's Venice's only all vegetarian restaurant. The food is homey and very good, and made with fresh local ingredients. Via Santa Croce 1762. Tel: 041.524.1570, www.lazucca.it. Open Monday—Saturday, 12:30—14:30 & 19:00—22:30. Sunday closed.

SPECIAL RESTAURANTS

If you are celebrating a special occasion, or simply looking for a more sophisticated Venetian restaurant to try, there are a number of good options that still manage to remain family-friendly. **Bistrot de Venise** offers a fantastic menu of perfectly prepared Venetian dishes in an elegant setting (Calle dei Fabbri 4685, www.bistrotdevenise.com); **Ristorante Riviera** offers some excellent seafood and fresh fish dishes, right on the waterline (Fondamenta Zattere Al Ponte Lungo 1473, www.ristoranteriviera.it); **Al Gatto Nero** on Burano island is slightly more expensive but it is unique, intimate and known for its fish and seafood (Via Giudecca 88, Burano, Venezia, www.gattonero.com). Reservations are required for all three venues.

Gelato, Ice Cream and Waffles!

Suso take themselves seriously, and they even have branded wafers. But if we made such delicious gelato, we would probably proudly put our names on it, too... There are several gluten-free choices, and their chocolate, Gianduja and fruit gelati are some of the best we've tried. The convenient location, just minutes from the Rialto, is an added bonus. San Marco 5453, Calle della Bissa. Open daily in season, 10:00—midnight.

White: Paying by weight for your treats is a novel way to work a math lesson into your vacation, but the kids won't object when they see what's in it for them! Enjoy yogurt with loads of toppings at this super popular spot two minutes from the Rialto Bridge and in front of the popular Al Arco bacaro. San Polo 480, Ruga Vecchia San Giovanni. Tel: 041.528.5109. Open daily in season. 10:30—21:00.

Fontego delle Dolcezze hides in the Santa Croce ward, near Campo San Stae and La Zucca, Venice's (only) vegetarian restaurant. The gelato here is some of the best we've tried in the city—creamy, rich, and full of flavor. Santa Croce 1910, Salizada San Stae. Open daily, 11:30—21:00.

La Mela Verde: In the unlikely event of anyone in your family being sick of gelato, they can choose a crepe or waffle here, too. Or you can do as we do, and order it all together! Fondamenta de l'Osmarin, Castello 4977. Cell: 349.195.7924. Open daily in season, 11:00—23:00.

La Maison della Crepe: Yes, this is a crepe place, but they also have wonderful gelato. Can't decide which to try? Get both. You're on vacation, after all. Cannaregio 5781. Tel: 041.277.0565. Open daily in season, 10:30—21:00 (weekends until 22:00 or later).

Sleeping in Venice

Hotel rooms in Venice may seem foreign to many travelers, especially North American visitors. Rooms here are small, even by Italian standards, and you might feel crowded. Luckily, this is Venice, and you won't be spending much time in your room. There are hundreds of accommodation options in town, from B&B and hotels to Airbnb apartments for rent; choosing the right one for you depends on your budget and personal preferences. Our general recommendation is that you find a hotel that is easy walking distance from the vaporetto because it really is all about location here. Know that many of the city's most charming mansions have been converted into hotels, but that charm comes at a price: modern conveniences may be lacking. Many 3-star hotels and even 4-star hotels don't have elevators, and some don't have air conditioning. Almost all self-respecting hotels offers Wi-Fi, but in some of the older hotels, service can be a little tricky.

Travelling with a family is expensive, and it helps if you can find some discounts and deals. Try booking websites that offer savings such as www.budgetplaces.com/venice, and don't be afraid to politely ask hotels if they can match or beat the prices you've seen online before you book. Sometimes they prefer that people book directly through them and are happy to give you an incentive to do so.

Hotel Tivoli: This simple and clean budget hotel is in an excellent location. It's got two stars, so don't expect luxury, but it is very serviceable and convenient with a vaporetto stop and many good restaurants as well as Venice's best loved pastry shop – Il Tonolo – nearby. www.hoteltivoli.it.

Hotel Violin d'Oro: The location near Piazza San Marco can't be beat, and it offers good value for the money. But do be clear about what size room you need, as some are too tiny to accommodate a family. www.violinodoro.com.

Friendly Venice Suites: This is a good family-friendly option with free Wi-Fi in public areas, a baby-sitting service available (for a fee), and a breakfast buffet. And the décor is oozing Venetian charm without sacrificing comfort or convenience. www.friendly-venice.it.

Antico Doge: Offering exceptionally spacious rooms for Venice, this three-star hotel is close to the Rialto and Ca d'Oro. You'll definitely feel like a doge here! www.anticodoge.com.

Locanda La Corte: Simple, modern and stylish, this guest house features a courtyard that is a charming place to relax and plan the next chapter of your Italian adventure. The prices are very good for a location that is both quiet and close to San Marco. www.locandalacorte.it.

A Tribute to Music: If you stay here, you might be inspired to pen an aria about the helpful staff, the stunning views of the basin or the quirky charm of this family-owned hotel with rooms decorated in splendid Venetian style. It's surprisingly good value considering the location, and family rooms are available. www.atributetomusic.it.

Special Events in Venice

Carnival: Long ago, life in Venice was pretty severe. The government and church imposed strict laws year round, which covered not only commerce and social issues but set more guidelines too, including what people could wear, where they could work, and more. But before the 40 days of sacrifice and penance of Lent, people let loose at carnival. The tradition of Venice's carnival began so long ago, it is hard to say exactly how it started. The word 'carnival' comes from the words for meat and farewell, which makes sense because people gave up meat for Lent. The first known record of Venice's carnival was in the charter of Doge Faliero in the year 1092, but the event grew into something bigger in 1162, when Venetians celebrated their victory over the Patriarch of Aquileia. The carnival grew more and more raucous until in 1268 the council outlawed the custom of masked men throwing eggs at women; the Venetians continued their celebrations without the egg-throwing for centuries. Nobles and commoners partied together joyfully in elaborate masks and cloaks (called tabarro) and even allowed themselves to blur the lines between social groups. They played music in the streets and squares, feasted, enjoyed performances by acrobats and attended after-hours parties in the most chic salons. Venetians have always known how to party! But when the Republic of Venice fell in 1797, the carnival fell too and faded out.

In 1979, the city revived the traditional carnival as part of their efforts to celebrate Venetian culture and heritage. Today, locals and visitors party together at grand balls with different themes (and different price tags up to €2,000), cruises and parades. While some events are adults only, the **parades on the canals and costume competitions in Piazza San Marco** are a magical event for all ages. It can be crowded, but not in an overwhelming way, and even toddlers can enjoy the fun. The precise carnival program can be downloaded yearly from www.carnevale.venezia.it. We recommend reviewing it before you go to choose the events you want to attend. (Many are free and open to the public.)

Festa del Redentore: The Feast of the Most Holy Redeemer began in 1575 to give thanks for the end of the plague. Venice lost 50,000 people to the black death, so to show their gratitude for its end, they built the Andrea Palladio-designed Church of the Redentore on the island of Giudecca. Today the tradition continues each July with decorated boats and fireworks in St. Mark's Basin, a special mass and thousands of visitors who come to Venice to participate in the fun.

Festa della Sensa: Every May, Venice commemorates its triumphant victory in the year 999, when the city conquered Dalmazia and defeated pirates in the Adriatic Sea. In 1177, Venice saved Pope Alexander III from Federico

Barbarossa, and the pope thanked them with a golden ring and declared the city sovereign over the sea. This sparked the annual tradition of the doge throwing a gold ring into the sea to symbolize Venice's marriage to it. Today, boats parade from St. Mark's Basin (Bacino di San Marco) to St. Nicolò di Lido church, where the ring is ceremoniously thrown to the sea. There are rowing contests and other fun events across the city to celebrate.

Festa della Salute: In 1630, the city was in the grip of a round of the plague. Desperate, the doge summoned the population for a special prayer procession for St. Mary, which went on for 15 consecutive Saturdays, as a penance and plea for divine help. When the city was finally freed of the plague, the doge fulfilled his promise and built the iconic Basilica di Santa Maria della Salute (designed by the great Baldassare Longhena). Today, Venetians celebrate the Festa della Salute every November 21st with a procession to the church to light candles. Naturally, other cultural events are organized, too (the yearly program can vary, find out more at the tourist office).

Regatta Storica: On the first weekend of September, Venice commemorates the return of Caterina Correr, a Venetian who married King Giacomo II of Cyprus, who ceded control of his kingdom to the republic. A beautiful *regatta* of decorated gondolas with gondoliers in period costume makes its way down the Grand Canal, carrying a 'doge', his wife and city officials through the city. Come early to catch a spot and see the entire colorful event. You can also see gondola races on the day as the city celebrates.

Feast of San Marco (Il Bocolo): April 25th is the feast day of Venice's patron saint, Mark the Evangelist. It's also Il Bocolo/ Rosebud Day in this romantic city, when men give a single rosebud to the woman they love in memory of a peasant man who fell in love with a noblewoman, went to war to impress her family, and managed to pick a single rosebud for her after being mortally wounded. The 25th of April is also a national holiday commemorating Italy's liberation from fascists in 1945.

Vogalonga: This celebration of traditional Venetian boating began in 1974 as a protest against the growing trend of motorboats in the canals. Now, more than a thousand gondolas and other traditional, non-motorized boats gather for a procession around the city at a date in late May or early June, find out more here: www.vogalonga.com.

The Biennale: The Venice Biennale is one of the most famous art exhibitions in the world. It takes place every two years (hence the name) from late spring to early autumn, and consists of a number of separate but interconnected events, which include biennales for art, music, theater, and architecture, and the Venice Film Festival. The biennale was established in 1893, and in 1895 foreign artists were invited to participate. This prestigious art exhibition has drawn over the years some of the best-known artists in the world, from Pablo Picasso and Gustav Klimt to Anish Kapoor and Jeff Koons. Undoubtedly, the glamorous and exclusive parties, closed auctions and high-brow seminars that accompany the exhibition today have all added to the allure of this event. Visiting the biennale is a special experience for seasoned art lovers, but it can also be intriguing for curious passers-by. With such a wide array of events and exhibitions, spread all across the city, it is more than likely that you will find something that will pique your interest. The main venue for the biennale is the Biennale Gardens, where the pavilions for each country participating in the event are located, but several additional exhibitions are scattered around Venice in various private *palazzi*. Touring these annexed exhibitions is a unique opportunity not only to see innovative contemporary art, but also to get a peek inside some of Venice's most beautiful mansions, which are normally closed to the public. Find out more here: www.labiennale.org.

OUTSIDE OF VENICE (UP TO ONE HOUR AWAY)

Human Chess, Marostica: Do you like chess? Children might enjoy this version more than using pieces on board. This biennial event (held in **June, on odd years**) is part of a Renaissance Festival, and the pageantry alone is breathtaking. The precise dates and program change yearly, find out more here: www.damacastellana.it.

Palio dei 10 Comuni, Montagnana: More than a horse race, this festival in **early September** is one of the largest in northern Italy, and showcases ten villages in a daring competition with dazzling color and history. People race carrying banners, and they race riding horses bareback. Find out more about the precise yearly dates and program, here: www.palio10comuni.it.

Joust of the Fortress (La Giostra della Rocca), Monselice: Sure to fire up little imaginations, this event in late September features Middle Ages jousting and village streets filled with people in period costumes. It also commemorates Emperor Frederic's 1239 visit to the village of Monselice. The precise dates and program change yearly, call the Monselice tourist office (IAT Monselice) before driving here. Tel: 0429.783026. www.giostradellarocca.it.

Voices from the Middle Ages (Rievocazione Storica Cittadella), Cittadella: Experience the Middle Ages with a meal and a stroll through soldiers' camps and medieval markets where you'll encounter jesters, musicians and bowmen. Don't miss the falconry show or the torch-lit procession to set the castle on fire! The yearly program may change, it's recommended to verify all the details with the tourist office before driving here, call: 049.940.4385. Read more about the event here: www.padovamedievale.it/events

Renaissance Festival, Noale: A 35-minute drive from Venice, this town puts on a fun Renaissance festival with a race and a procession in June. The town has some nice sights including a fortress, and there's a nature reserve just a short walk outside the *centro storico*. Find out more here: www.palionoale.it.

Palio della Marciliana, Chioggia: The third weekend of June is the time to be in Chioggia, which is just 40 minutes from Venice, to see this impressive medieval festival. In addition to the music and procession, kids will love seeing the crossbow tournament and the boats. A marciliana is a type of local boat that symbolizes the town's history as a center of trade, and the festival commemorates the War of Chioggia fought between Venice and Genoa. Find out more about the precise yearly program and dates, here: www.marciliana.com.

Special Activities in Venice

Venice is full of amazing sights, but sometimes, children need to do, not just see. Happily, Venice offers kids many unforgettable activities to put the city's culture and heritage on their terms. By combining one or more of the hands-on activities in this itinerary, the kids will use up some of their boundless energy, and learn about the local art and culture while having a blast.

GET YOUR GONDOLIER ON!

Gondoliers and their gondolas are an iconic symbol of Venice. Touring the city by gondola is a classic, essential Venice adventure. You not only get to see the city, you get to experience it the way Venetians have for centuries.

Children will love the ride, and older children will be thrilled at the chance to take it further, and learn to row a gondola themselves. **Row Venice** offer rowing lessons and promote traditional Venetian boating. They organize 90-minute lessons for up to four people per boat, which are perfect for families. This activity is very popular, and we recommend you book your spot well in advance: www.rowvenice.com.

Alternatively, try **Venice on Board**. They offer a similar experience, and the classes are organized by professional rowers who also build and mend their gondolas and oars themselves. You can choose between their voga lesson (the classic Venetian style of rowing), a night tour, or even a sailing lesson in the lagoon. Book in advance: www.veniceonboard.it.

BOOK A BOATING OR KAYAK ADVENTURE

In another city, you might hop on a sightseeing bus tour or even a taxi tour. But in Venice, it's all about the boats. Travelling by vaporetto is fun, but if you want something more, consider booking a full tour of the city and the lagoon. Try **Laguna Escursioni** for a leisurely and novel tour, and don't forget to book in advance: www.lagunaescursioni.com.

If leisurely isn't your family's style, you can go for a more adventurous experience and explore by kayak, which most kids will find very exciting. **Venice Kayak** offers a variety of guided tours, including tours specially geared for families. This activity is popular, book your spot in advance: www.venicekayak.com.

MAKE A REAL VENETIAN MASK!

Has all this art inspired your little ones? Children tend to view art as something to do rather than something to look at, so why not encourage their creativity and book a workshop that will let them bring home some unique souvenirs along with fun memories?

Ca Macana offers workshops where your whole family can make beautiful and traditional Venetian masks of papier mache. Classes are offered in English, and should be booked in advance: www.camacana.com.

Carta Alta is a mask-making studio that also offers 90-minute classes on weekday mornings and welcomes families. They are located on the peaceful Venetian island of Giudecca. Book in advance: www.cartaalta.com.

The famous mask shop **Marega** also offers classes and workshops, but is aimed more at adults. This serious and hands-on experience will appeal to mature tweens and teens, while younger children will do better with one of the other workshops. All classes must be booked in advance: www.marega.it.

If your children are artistic, consider trying something different, such as a screen printing workshop. **Fallani Venezia** offers hour-long screen printing classes suitable for children who are old enough to learn about this art, and master the techniques involved in creating the designs. Book in advance: www.fallanivenezia.com.

MAKE YOUR OWN MURANO GLASS BEADS

Glass blowing is an amazing art, and mesmerizing to watch. If your family would like to try some glass art, you can take a workshop to make beads from Elena Rosso while you are visiting Murano. All lessons must be booked in advance: www.elenarosso.com.

VISIT A SPECIAL AVIATION MUSEUM

All museums should send your imagination soaring, but Venice has a museum that is the result of one man letting his passion take flight. Giancarlo Zanardo was a pilot who truly loved everything about aviation and the history of flight. He devoted himself to building replicas of famous early planes, and the result is this amazing museum of flight – the **Jonathan Collection** – just north of Venice. See a replica of Orville and Wilbur Wright's famous plane and intriguing inventions such as the Rotorway Scorpion, an experimental one-person helicopter. If flying to Italy has your little explorers fascinated by flight, this is a fun day trip and you can even book to see a flight demonstration for a fee. For details, see www.jonathanaereistorici.it.

ESCAPE THE CITY AND HEAD TO THE WATERPARK

The town of Jesolo, just 40 minutes outside of Venice, is a popular destination for active families because it has a great concentration of kid-friendly attractions including a waterpark, aquarium, beaches and more. See the our detailed itinerary for Jesolo in the 'Day Trips from Venice' chapter.

Day Trips from Venice

Chapter 2

Day Trips from Venice

While Venice is magical, the surrounding countryside offers some charms of its own. Beyond the city you'll find ancient castles, quaint hill-top villages, intriguing museums even children will love, and, of course, stunning natural beauty. Venice gets crowded in peak season, and crowded city streets and museums aren't the most child-friendly spaces. Away from the maze of historic palazzi and romantic canals, the kids will appreciate the chance to run around, experience things at their own pace, and recharge. A balance of city and countryside experiences makes for a vacation with something for everyone. Hopefully, the suggested itineraries in this chapter will help create the perfect mix for your family.

Itinerary N. 1: Lake Santa Croce, The Caves of Caglieron, and Castel Brando

This itinerary is packed full of natural beauty and adventure. If the weather is hot, you'll have plenty of opportunities to cool off by the water, and if the kids have hit their limit of sitting still and looking at pretty things they can't touch, then a day of exploring caves, swimming and visiting a real castle will be just what they need. Before you leave, dress for adventure—this trip requires comfortable clothes, good tread walking shoes, a sweatshirt or light jacket, and swimsuits. It's best to bring a change of clothes, too.

Caglieron Caves

Getting there & parking: From Venice, head north for about one hour on the A27 autostrada, and exit at Vittorio Veneto. The caves are five minutes from Vittorio Veneto, at Fraz. Fregona. The parking lot is 100 meters from the entrance to the caves. There is a charge to park here, but the caves themselves are free entry.

Tourist information office: Proloco Fregona, Via Marconi 6, Fregona. Tel: 0438.585487 / 337.517218, www.prolocofregona.it/grotte-del-caglieron.

Day Trips from Venice

A narrow road lined with farms and vineyards leads to the village of Fregona and the Caves of Caglieron. Once you step inside, you will discover a series of mini-gorges carved out over centuries by the Caglieron River and some human helpers. Following the kilometer-long path, you'll encounter little waterfalls, mysterious stalactites hanging from the cave's ceilings and towering stalagmites rising from the ground. You can explore smaller side caves, too, including one that was once used to conserve and mature cheese. During the Renaissance, workers quarried the sumptuous stone from these caves to build elegant mansions for the rich and powerful of Venice. (When you return to the city, play a little game—can you guess which buildings in Venice might have stone from these caves in them?) 🕒 Grotte del Caglieron, Via Ronzon, località Breda di Fregona, Fregona. The caves can be visited independently or with a guided tour. The tourist office leads guided tours of the Caves on Sunday mornings at 10:30 a.m (€3 per person, children under six are free), book in advance.

> **Tip:** Unless you specifically want to join the guided tour, it's best to avoid the caves on weekends. Not only are they crowded with locals, but the narrow roads leading up to Caglieron are full of cyclists and bikers.

Lake Santa Croce

Getting there & parking: Drive back down to Vittorio Veneto, get on the A27 and proceed north for about 15 minutes to reach the lake. Set your GPS to Viale al Lago 13, Farra d'Alpago, a parking lot which sits right on the shore. The local tourist office is located there, too.

After exploring the caves, it's time for some well-deserved splashing time by the lake. Lake Santa Croce is the second largest lake in the Veneto region, and the scenery is quite impressive, with the Bellunese Dolomites towering above the dazzling blue water, and vineyards clinging to the hillsides. Lake Santa Croce can be enjoyed at every speed: You can go on a hike; chill out with a cappuccino at **Bar Fortunato** and enjoy the jaw-dropping panoramic view from their terrace (they even have a Foosball table to keep the kids occupied); or you can dive right in and splash around at one of the beaches. ⊙ Bar Fortunato, Via Poiatte 16, Farra D'Alpago. Tel: 0437.4244. Open in season, 11:00—18:00.

The **two best beaches** for families are the Free Beach and Baia delle Sirene (Mermaids Bay), which are located just a couple of minutes apart by car. **The Free Beach** is next to the tourist office, and is a good option for kids because just down the road from it you will also find **Campeggio Sarathei,** a popular camping village with a playground and bouncy castles. Non-campers are welcome too, for a fee of €6 an hour (ask if discounts are available). ⊙ Via del Lago 13, Farra d'Alpago,Tel: 0437.454937, www.sarathei.it.

Baia delle Sirene Beach (marked on Google Maps) is located farther up the road, and is perfect for lazing by the water and soaking in the scenery. Because of the strong winds here, it's also a popular spot for kitesurfing and other water sports. If you are feeling adventurous, you can even try a lesson with **Ride with Us,** a local operator (book in advance): www.ridewithus.it.

Nature lovers will find much to do around the lake, too: There's a small bird-watching oasis just a short drive away (pick up a detailed map at the tourist office), and the famous **Foresta del Cansiglio** (Cansiglio Forest), a popular hiking destination, is only 20 minutes from here. If your children love horses, you can easily indulging them, too: **Agriturismo Rio Cavalli** is a charming farm experience where you can meet horses, donkeys, pigs, sheep and even deer. Book ahead for riding lessons, farm tours and fishing lessons, or simply stop by for lunch at their rustic restaurant (call first to make sure they are open, especially off-season). ⊙ Agriturismo Rio

Cavalli, Loc. Sagrogna 74, Belluno. Tel: 0437.927.380, www.riocavalli.it. All activities should be booked in advance.

Castelbrando

Getting there & parking: Take the A27 south, towards the village to Cison di Valmarino (30 minutes). Park at the entrance to the castle.

End your day with a visit to a real castle. CastelBrando is situated in **Cison di Valmarino,** which is listed as one of Italy's prettiest villages. With just 2,500 residents, its streets are full of charm but not much else—the castle really is the only thing to see. Built originally as a fortress in ancient Roman times, CastelBrando still stands tall, commanding a regal view over the forested valley. It has been expanded and altered over the centuries, notably in the middle ages and 15th century, and served as a military hospital in WWI and even as a monastery.

Now a sprawling complex including an elegant hotel, the castle still operates a small museum, filled with cool armor and interesting costumes that is open for tourists on **Sundays only (or by special appointment on other weekdays).** Once you've seen all that there is to be seen here, it's time to enjoy some ice cream! The castle's very own coffee and ice cream shop is located high up on the battlements. Check their website before you leave to verify which tours are available, and to learn more about the special events that happen here regularly. One of the best events is the Vivo Crafts Exhibition in August. This huge festival is when artists and craftsmen fill the streets of Cison di Valmarino with their gorgeous wares in a celebration of traditional crafts: www.artigianatovivo.it. ⊕ CastelBrando, Via Brandolini Brando 29, Cison di Valmarino. Open April—September, Sundays, 10:30—12:00 & 15:00—19:00. October—March, Sundays, 10:30—12:00 & 14:00—18:00. It is usually possible to book in advance a tour on other weekdays, too. Call: 0438.976.611 or email info@castelbrando.it.

Eating in the Area

CAGLIERON CAVES

After a visit to the caves, everyone will be hungry. Luckily, there are a few good restaurants nearby. The restaurant nearest to the caves, **Ristorante**

Bar Alle Grotte Da Nereo is very good but they specialize in seafood, which may be less suitable for most children. For something more-easy going and yet unique, visit **Casera le Rotte**. A Beautifully positioned farm, they offer homey and well-made local specialties, including pasta and fluffy gnocchi. Booking a table in the weekends is highly recommended, as they are almost always full. Casera Le Rotte, Via dei Cimbri, Loc. Pian Cansiglio (near the Cansiglio forest), Fregona. Cell: 338.142.5385. Open mid-June—mid-October, Tuesday—Sunday, 12:00-14:30 & 19:00-21:30. Monday closed. Off season usually open only in the weekends. Opening hours may vary, call before driving here.

CISON DI VALMARINO

Tenuta La Pila is a popular agriturismo that sits just outside of Cison di Valmarino. The antipasti platters and the homemade pasta dishes are especially good here, and booking in advance is recommended. This is also a B&B, and they offer family rooms and activities such as pony rides for children (which must be booked in advance). Agriturismo Tenuta La Pila, Via Pila 42, Località Spinimbecco, Villa Bartolomea. Tel: 0442.659.289, www.tenutalapila.com.

LAGO SANTA CROCE

There are a number of kiosks and small diners on the shores of Lake Santa Croce; the choice is really up to you. One of our personal favorites is **Snack Bar La Vela**. It's about 100 meters after the church of Santa Barbara, and offers outside seating with a beautiful vista of the lake. Via Poiatte 1, Farra d'Alpago. Open daily in season only.

If the children want pizza, then good pizza they shall get! **Pizzeria Dora Di Bona Mariella** offers a selection of pizzas as well as pasta dishes and tasty desserts. This isn't exactly haute cuisine, but it's reasonably priced and very tasty. The restaurant is in a little village called Spert, 10 minutes from the town of Farra D'Alpago and the lake. Via Spert 83. Tel: 0437.472.000. Open Monday—Saturday for lunch and dinner. Sunday closed. May close off season.

Day Trips from Venice

Itinerary N. 2: Cruise through the Ferrari, Lamborghini and Ducati Car and Motorcycle Museums

For kids and adults alike, Ferrari and Lamborghini cars, and Ducati motorcycles are a fantasy. So why not take your family to the source, to the Mecca of sports cars and motorcycles? This itinerary is perfect both for car-obsessed children who vrooom vrooom everywhere they go, and for parents who enjoy watching the Formula One races and follow the victories of international drivers. Depending on how much time you have, you can work just one of these museums into your itinerary, or plan a more ambitious day and visit two or even three sights one after the other for a motor-themed day of fun. **All three museums are quite close to Lake Garda and Verona, too,** and can easily be combined into a tour of that area as well.

Ferrari Museum

Getting there & parking: From Venice, take the E70 and the A22 (two hours). From Verona, take the A22 to Maranello (40 minutes). From Lake Garda, take the A22 (90 minutes). Park at the museum's lot.

For a hands-on Ferrari experience, visit the **Ferrari Museum in Maranello.** This museum is filled with dozens of stunning Ferrari cars, and that's only the beginning! Depending on your schedule and budget, you have a variety of choices for your Ferrari experience: You can add a turn with a semi-professional racing simulator to your museum tour (for an additional fee), or you can let the kids pretend to be one of the pit crew and change a tire while being timed and photographed. Another popular option is the factory tour, which will take you to where it all happens, though you should be aware that photographs are strictly forbidden there. You'll be entering an area steeped in secrecy, and Ferrari requires that visitors remain on the tour bus the entire time. Find out more on the Ferrari museum website.

If all that leaves you itching to get behind the wheel, you have a couple of ways to include a memorable driving experience in your day. You can

Day Trips from Venice

drive your rental car on a professional track by booking ahead with the Ferrari Museum, or, better yet, you can take a genuine Ferrari for a short spin courtesy of any of several car rental agencies near the museum (their representatives will jump on you as soon as you park in the museum's lot). This is a perfect indulgence for the adults who secretly dream of racing as they drive to work or to do errands every day. The only drawback is that once you've had the feeling of flying around a purring Ferrari, sitting in traffic in your minivan or sedan back home is going to be a little painful...
🕒 Ferrari Museum, Via Dino Ferrari 43, Maranello. Tel: 0536.949.713, www.musei.ferrari.com/it/maranello. Open April—October, daily, 9:30—19:00; November—March, daily, 9:30—18:00. Hours of operation for specific activities (guided factory tours and more) tend to vary and should be confirmed and booked in advance. 🕒 Pushstart Ferrari Tour and Rental, Via Dino Ferrari 41, Maranello. Cell: 346.370.5035, www.pushstart.it.

If you have some extra time, you can also visit the museum dedicated to the company's founder, Enzo Ferrari, in nearby **Modena**. This museum is a more sedate experience geared at the grown-ups as it focuses on his life rather than the excitement of car racing. 🕒 Museo Casa Enzo Ferrari, Via Paolo Ferrari 85, Modena. Tel: 059.439.7979, www.musei.ferrari.com/en/modena. Opening times are the same as the museum in Maranello.

> **Tip:** If motor racing is your passion, plan your trip for September, and book front row tickets to one of the most famous car races in the world—the Formula One race. Find out more here: www.monza.net

Lamborghini Museum and Factory

Getting there & parking: the museum is located east of Modena. From the Ferrari museum, take the SS274 to Sant'Agata Bolognese (40 minutes). From Venice, take the A13 (two hours). Park at the museum's lot.

The Lamborghini Museum is the perfect place to learn about these exquisitely designed cars and their dramatic history. Ferruccio Lamborghini founded the company in 1963, and through a rocky history with a series of financial crises, these luxury vehicles continue to accumulate admirers around the world. At the museum, you can see the evolution of Lamborghini cars and get a front-row view of the most famous models from the early creations including the 350 GT and the Miura. You can also **tour the production lines** (recommended, though pricey) in the original factory and see step by step how the powerful V12 Aventador is put together from the impressive engines to the luxurious interiors. ⊙ Lamborghini Museum, Via Modena 12, Sant'Agata Bolognese. Tel: 051.681.7611, www.lamborghini.com/it-en/experience/museo. Open April—October, daily, 9:30—19:00. November—March, 9:30—18:00. Guided factory tours must be booked in advance, consult the website.

Ducati Museum

Getting there & parking: From the Lamborghini Museum, head south on the SP568 (25 minutes). From Lake Garda, take the A22 (90 minutes). From Venice, take the A13 (90 minutes). Park at the museum's lot.

For avid motorcyclists, a visit to the **Ducati Museum** is a must. Antonio Cavalieri Ducati and his three sons set up a small factory in 1926 in the basement of the family villa to initially produce radio components. They continued production throughout World War II, despite being bombed repeatedly. One of their factories was destroyed in the war, but the company bounced back in the post-war years. For almost a century, Ducati has been a pillar of Bologna's industrial scene. They began producing motors in the 1950s and eventually developed their trademark bikes with the famous four-stroke, 90-degree V-twin motors. Now you can learn all about the motorcycles and the company's history in their newly revamped museum and see why they have racked up more than 300 race wins. ⊙ Ducati Museum, Via Antonio Cavalieri Ducati, Bologna. www.ducati.it/museo_ducati/il_museo.do. The museum is open April—early October, Thursday—Tuesday, 9:00—18:00. Wednesday closed; off season, hours of operation change, consult the website.

Eating in the Area

MARANELLO (FERRARI MUSEUM)

Vigna Sul Colle is just around the corner from the museum. The pasta and salads are especially good here, and you can also ask the owners to show you their *acetaia* (authentic Balsamic vinegar aging cellar). Via Dino Ferrari 49, Maranello. Tel: 0536.185.6177. Open for lunch only, Monday—Saturday. Sunday closed.

For something more serious try **Ristorante Montana,** a locals' favorite spot that is famous for its steaks and pasta. They sit right next to the Fiorano track, and proudly display photos of the various international race stars that have dined here over the years. They cater to a lot of foreign groups, racers and dealerships, so make sure you book a table in advance or they won't be able to accommodate you. Via 20 Settembre (XX Settembre, on some maps) 3, Fiorano Modenese. Tel: 0536.843.910, www.ristorantemontana.it. Open Monday—Friday, 12:00—13:30 & 19:30—22:00; Saturday open for dinner only, 20:00—22:00; Sunday closed.

SANT'AGATA BOLOGNESE (LAMBORGHINI MUSEUM)

Trattoria Piazzetta: If you don't mind driving an extra 15 minutes, this is our favorite of several more options in the next town over—San Giovanni in Persiceto. The fresh, homemade pasta here is especially good. Reservations are required. Via Betlemme 31, San Giovanni in Persiceto. Cell: 392.0462.046, www.trattoriapiazzetta.it. Open Thursday—Sunday, for dinner only, 19:30—21:30. Closed Monday through Wednesday.

BORGO PANICALE—BOLOGNA (DUCATI MUSEUM)

The Ducati museum is located in the industrial area outside Bologna, so you'll have to move 10 minutes away to find some good restaurants. There are a number of options: If you have the time, you can enter Bologna itself, visit the historical center and stop for lunch at one of the many restaurants here. (Bologna is a foodie's dream; the selection is endless!). Alternatively, in a 10-minute driving range from the museum you'll find two good options: **American Graffiti Diner** is an American diner style restaurant with a fun atmosphere. Via Antonio Cavalieri Ducati 74, Borgo Panigale Bologna. Open daily, 12:00—15:00 & 19:00—midnight.

Pizzeria Il Desiderio is very close to the museum, and you can treat yourself to some good pizza served at an easy-going spot. Via Marco Emilio Lepido 193, Bologna. Tel: 051.641.4207, www.ristoranteildesiderio.it. Open daily, 12:00—15:00 & 19:00—midnight.

Itinerary N. 3: Discover Jesolo, A Popular Seaside Town

Jesolo, a seaside resort town, is the complete opposite of Venice in many ways, and that is exactly why a visit there can be perfect for families. While Venice is elegant and magnificent, full of artistic riches and cultural treasures, Jesolo is family-fun central, with plenty of activities for children and teenagers to enjoy. Within a short distance of each other you will find a popular water park, an aquarium, go karts, well-equipped beaches, an amusement park, and more. Half a day here, away from the sights, is a great way to break things up and provide some balance that the kids will appreciate.

Getting There: You can reach Jesolo by car, bus, or by boat (battello, in Italian). **Bus:** Take bus number 10A from Piazzale Roma in Venice to Piazza Drago in Jesolo. **Car:** Take the SS14, exit at Jesolo, and continue along that road until you reach Jesolo Lido. **Boat:** There is a public ferry service connecting Punta Sabbioni (a large port in the Venetian lagoon, near the island of Burano) with Jesolo. Combo bus and boat tickets are available. Children under six don't pay. Please note that from Punta Sabbioni you will have to take a second boat (circa one hour) to reach Venice itself. You can save on travel time by taking the private boat service instead (operated by Azzurra Boats). They offer a direct line from Jesolo to Venice in just under an hour. Check the precise times and pickup location on their website: www.turisticaazzurra.it.

Day Trips from Venice

Parking: Jesolo has two sections—the town (Jesolo) and the beaches (Lido di Jesolo). Most of the town's attractions are at the beach (Lido), so it is much easier to park there. The most convenient parking lots are: Parcheggio Piazza Brescia (in Piazza Brescia), Parcheggio Volta (at the corner of Via Aquileia and Via Nausica), Parcheggio di Piazza Internazionale (enter from Via Aleardi.) Expect to pay about 20-25 euro for an entire day.

Moving Around: You can walk from one attraction to the next, or if that is too much for the little legs in your family, you can avail of one of the bike rental or bike sharing options in Jesolo (pick up a map of the bike sharing spots at the tourist office). There is also a bus and shuttle system that is very convenient.

Tourist information office: The large and well-equipped tourist office is in Piazza Brescia 13, Lido di Jesolo. Tel: 0421.922.88 / 0421.370.601, www.jesolo.it. Open daily in season.

> **Tip:** If you are going to stay in a hotel in Jesolo, consider choosing one of the better ones with its own private beach and parking. What you save on beach fees and parking fees will help offset the extra expense.

Start your day in Jesolo in Piazza Brescia, at the tourist office. Pick up a free map of the town, and use it to decide the order in which you want to visit the sights. In other itineraries in this book, we've suggested visiting attractions in a certain order, but Jesolo is different, and offers a very wide range of attractions, both large and small. We've listed them all, in no specific order. That way, you can create your own custom mix-and-match itinerary based on the interests of your family.

Aqualandia

Aqualandia is the main reason families come to Jesolo. It is one of the largest and most popular water parks in Italy, and children taller than 1.40 meters love it. (Children below that height won't be able to go on many of the rides, and are likely to find it very disappointing, as will parents who pay their entrance fee.) Aqualandia boasts a good range of activities for children, tweens and teens. Join an epic water battle, plunge down towering water slides, or watch a show and be catapulted from the top of Jungle Falls. This is a great day for adrenaline junkies, and parents should not expect to stay dry on the sidelines. 🕒 Parco Aqualandia, Via Michelangelo Buonarroti 15, Lido di Jesolo. Tel: 0421.371.648, www.aqualandia.it. Open daily, late May—early September, 10:00—18:00 (last entry at 16:00). The park may closer later in peak season, consult the website.

> **Tip:** Aqualandia is extremely crowded on weekends and holidays, so it is best to avoid those times. Note that the entry fee isn't cheap, but some hotels offer discounted tickets to guests. And you can bring your own food and drinks to keep costs down.

Sea Life Jesolo

Sea Life Jesolo is a well-presented indoor option for rainy days or when your family needs a break from the sun. It's one of those fun attractions where your children will learn lots without realizing it: They can see seahorses, turtles, rays, octopus and more up close, and learn about local and exotic sea life as well as Aqualandia's 'Breed, Rescue, Protect' conservation efforts. And they won't soon forget the shark feeding time! ⊙ Sea Life Jesolo, Piazza Venezia 28, Lido di Jesolo, within the Laguna Shopping Center, www.visitsealife.com/jesolo-en. Open late May, June & September, daily, 10:00—18:00; July—August, Monday—Sunday, 10.00—23:00, Weekends 10:00—18:00. Booking your ticket in advance is highly recommended (especially on weekends) as the park has a limited daily capacity.

> **Tip:** Morning is the best time for the aquarium because it is busiest between 11:00 a.m and 15:00 p.m. Feeding times are twice a day, and the first sessions are between 10:30 and 12:30 p.m, so it is possible to do it all, finish with the 12:30 ray feeding and then go feed yourselves before heading to another local attraction for the afternoon.

Tropicana

Tropicana will be a hit with children who love animals and nature. You can tour the three sections of the park—predators (sharks, crocodiles), aquarium and of course tropical animals (iguanas, turtles). The park also features a butterfly house so you can see these flying beauties up close, which will delight many children. ⊙ Tropicana, Pala Arrex, Piazza Brescia, Lido di Jesolo. www.tropicarium.it. Open daily, 10:00—22:00. Children under 3 enter for free, children 4-14 pay a reduced entry, discounted family tickets available.

New Jesolandia Luna Park

The New Jesolandia Park is a classic seaside amusement park with 35 rides for thrill seekers of (almost) all ages. This is no Gardaland, obviously, but it is a fun amusement park with options ranging from the classic Ferris wheel and (small) roller coasters to canoes and quads. For teenagers craving a more extreme ride, there's the scary Slingshot, and the littler members of the family can jump into the playground ball pit or enjoy the easy-going Flintstones ride. The park opens every evening, so you can cap off your day at the beach with the amusements, an ice cream, and a stroll along the promenade. 🕒 New Jesolandia Luna Park, www.newjesolandia.com. Open June—August, daily in the evenings, 20:00—01:00.

Jesolo Military Museum

The small Military Museum, one of the few attractions in the town of Jesolo itself (and not the Lido), offers history buffs a chance to get a detailed view of tanks and helicopters, like those used during WWII. Families who find guns upsetting should know there are a lot of them on display here. 🕒 Military Museum, Via Roma Destra 131, Jesolo. Tel: 0421.350.898. Open June—August, daily, 10:00—12:30 & 16:00—19:30; September—May, open by appointment.

Smaller Parks & Attractions

Those who prefer a low-key attraction can spend an hour or so playing mini-golf at **Adventure Golf,** navigating the ball through some crazy waterfalls in a tropical forest. Show your entry ticket from Aqualandia to get €2 off the (hefty!) admission fee, or buy the combo ticket in advance. 🕒 Adventure Mini Golf, Via Buonarroti 15, Jesolo (near Piazza Marina). Tel: 0421.371648, www.minigolfjesolo.it. Open daily in high season, 10:00—19:00. Opening times may vary.

Teens and adults can imagine themselves behind the wheel of a sleek Italian race car zooming around the track at the **Pista Azzurra Go-Kart Park.** Various motor sizes from 50cc for children (at least 7 years old) to 270cc (for adults over 18) can be rented, and these are serious engines! 🕒 Pista Azzurra Go Kart, Via Roma Destra 90, Lido di Jesolo. Tel: 0421.972.471, www.pista-azzurra.com. Open daily in season, 10:00—13:00 & 16:00—midnight. Sunday open 16:00—midnight. Closed in case of rain. Check their website before you go to learn about any variations.

Day Trips from Venice

Younger children can let loose at **Gommapiuma**, a large bouncy park with trampolines and similar activities. ◎ Gommapiuma, Via Firenze 16, Lido di Jesolo. Cell: 333.884.4889, www.gommapiuma.net. Open in the evening only, 20:00—midnight. Access is limited to children who are 12 years old or younger. Adults enter for free when accompanying children. Bring a pair of socks, you'll have to take off your shoes here.

If your kids and teenagers love horses, head to **Equitrek**. Located 30 minutes from Jesolo (in Eraclea), they offer one- and two-hour horseback riding expeditions. Explore the beach, the pine forest, the lagoon and the countryside on horseback. It's an unforgettable experience for everyone age four and up. Equitrek Horse Tours ,Via Dancalia 136, Eraclea Mare. Cell: 338.1842.511, www.equitrekmaneggio.it. Tours must be booked in advance.

Jesolo's Best Beaches for Families

Jesolo sits right on the Adriatic Sea, and its proximity to the water draws in the crowds. Many hotels have their own private beaches for guests, but there are also other fun beaches where you can rent lounge chairs for the day. Note that many of the popular beaches for families offer more than sea and sand, and in the summer months organize activities for children—find out more at the tourist office in Piazza Brescia. The beaches on Via Andrea Balfie (Lido centro) and Piazza Trieste have activities as well as shows and live music concerts. You can rent a paddle boat at Oro Beach (see www.jesolospiagge.it). Relax Beach (www.relaxbeachjesolo.com) and Riva Levante Beach (www.rivieradilevantejesolo.it) are also popular because of their activities for families.

Eating in Jesolo

Oasi del Panino makes exceptionally tasty sandwiches. Piazza Aurora 27/b, Lido di Jesolo. Tel: 0421.972076. Open Tuesday—Sunday, 7:00—20:30. Monday closed.

Semiramide has a location on the river you'll savor as much as their delicious food. It's worth leaving the beach for a sunset dinner here. Via Ca Nani 42, Jesolo. Tel: 0421.359614, www.semiramidejesolo.com. Open Thursday—Tuesday 12:00—15:00 & 19:00—midnight. Wednesday closed. Closed in January.

La Marachella offers a friendly, relaxed atmosphere with wonderful pizza, pasta and seafood at reasonable prices. Via Andrea Bafile 566, Jesolo. Tel: 0421.972.746, www.lamarachella.it. Open March—October, daily, 11:30—14:30 & 17:30—23:30. Off season, open on the weekends only.

Pizzeria Capri at the beach is pizza for foodies. They take the humble pizza to new levels, using quality ingredients and inspiration. Piazzetta de Santis 9, Lido di Jesolo. Tel: 0421.382.055, www.pizzeriacaprijesolo.com. Open Wednesday—Monday, 19:00—21:30. Tuesday closed.

Picnics!

Picnics are a great way to save money and try new flavors. In Jesolo you'll be happy to find three **big supermarkets** where you can get everything you need for a fabulous family picnic, from prosciutto, pecorino and mozzarella cheese to fresh bread, olives, fruit, juice and more. (Just make sure picnics are permitted at the spot you choose or you might be fined.) The best supermarkets to try are: **Famila Superstore,** Via Equilio 19, Lido di Jesolo. Open daily, 8:30—20:00.; **Coop,** Via Reghena 1, Lido di Jesolo. Open Monday—Saturday, 8:30—19:30 & Sunday, 8:30—13:00; **Supermarket Iper Tosano,** on the first floor of the Giardini di Jesolo shopping center, Via Piave Vecchio 47, Jesolo. Open daily, 8:30—20:30 (Sunday until 20:00).

Sleeping in Jesolo

Domino Suite Hotel boasts a kids' club, baby pool and free beach access a short walk from the hotel. The family rooms are equipped with kitchen basics. www.dominosuitehotel.com.

Hotel Bolivar has a great location by the water and competitive prices. It's simple but modern. www.hotelbolivarjesolo.it.

Hotel delle Mimose is a gorgeous, modern hotel with a private beach, pool and children's pool. They offer family rooms and superior family rooms. www.dellemimosejesolo.it.

Jesolo Palace suits families who want a quiet retreat with all of the benefits of a big hotel. Located in the Cavallino district, it has family suites, a private beach and a pool. www.jesolopalace.it.

Malibu Beach Camping Village offers something different for outdoorsy families. Choose between camping, glamping, cottages and mobile homes, and enjoy a good range of facilities and activities including children's dance, theater, kayaking and much more. www.campingmalibubeach.com.

VERONA

Chapter 3

Verona

Welcome to Verona, one of northern Italy's best loved cities. Though often overshadowed by Venice, its famous neighbor to the east, Verona is a UNESCO World Heritage site that will conquer your heart. Stunning art and architecture can be found on every corner, the historic center's quaint streets are a pleasure to wander along, and the enticing local dishes and wines will tempt any foodie. In short, it is no wonder that Shakespeare set not one, not two, but three of his plays in this fair city…

Top 5 Family Activities in Verona

1. Visit Juliet's house and take a picture on the famous terrace.
2. Tour the ancient Roman Arena that is the heart of Verona.
3. Enjoy the spectacular view of the city from Castel San Pietro.
4. Climb up the popular Torre di Lamberti.
5. Discover the stunning art work at Verona's Santa Anastasia church.

Even if you are on a tight schedule, you won't have to skip Verona; the town is quite small, and its main attractions can be visited in a few hours of sightseeing on a day trip from Lake Garda. You can also combine a tour of Verona with a visit to the popular Sigurta park, or the Nicolis Car Museum (see full details under: 'Day Trips from Lake Garda"). In Verona itself, focus your attention on Piazza Bra, the Arena, Piazza della Erbe, Juliet's house, and the Duomo or the church of Sant'Anastasia, all of which are described in detail in the itinerary below. Then cross the Ponte Pietra (Pietra bridge) and go to the Roman theater or Castel San Pietro to end your day with a panoramic view of the city. If you have more time on your hands, your visit will be even more satisfying—follow the full walking itinerary suggested in this chapter, and consider booking a special activity in the area to complete your day.

Verona: A Brief History

Verona has been inhabited since the Neolithic Period. Once the land of the Veneto and Gaul tribes, Verona's strategic position made it a potential target for any conquering force that passed through the area. During the first century BC, Verona became a Roman colony and quickly grew and developed. In the 5th century it was conquered by the Goths; then by the Langobards, who remained until the 8th century; and then by Charlemagne. The city flourished under French rule, and soon the local noble families decided Verona should declare itself an independent city-state, governed by a *Signoria*. After a bloody power struggle between the Ghibellin and Guelph noble families, the mighty della Scala family (also known as the Scaligero family) took control, and remained the city's leading force and dynasty for nearly 200 years. Of the many Scaligero family members, the most famous was Cangrande I della Scala, who was also Dante Alighieri's chief patron, and is mentioned in both the *Decameron* and the *Divina Commedia*. Cangrande I expanded Verona's rule and power over the entire Veneto territory, reaching as far as Padova, dramatically altering the political map. In 1387 Gian Galeazzo Visconti, of the famous Milanese family, conquered Verona, putting an end to Scaligero rule. In 1405 the city was once again conquered, this time by the mighty Republic of Venice. Verona thrived under the rule of the Serenissima, as is evidenced by the many winged lion statues and symbols that can be seen throughout the city even today.

When the Venetian republic fell, defeated by the armed forces of Napoleon in 1797, Verona was hit hard. A brief French and Austrian occupation followed (the city was literally divided between the two armies), until finally it was conquered in 1866 by the Italian royal family – the Savoias—and became a part of Italy.

Tip: Try not to schedule your visit to Verona to Monday mornings, since most of the museums in town are closed on that day. If you plan on visiting the Arena and at least one more museum, consider purchasing the Verona Card combo ticket: www.veronacard.it.

Our walking tour of Verona begins at Castelvecchio. If you came to Verona by car, Castelvecchio is just a short walk from the Cittadella and Arena parking lots. If you came to Verona by train, simply hop on Bus No. 21, 22, 23, 24, 93, 94, 95 or 30 from the Verona Porta Nuova train station (note that buses making their way to the city center leave from platform D2, in the parking lot in front of the train station).

Literally meaning "the old palace / fortress," **Castelvecchio** is Verona's most imposing public building, and was built by the mighty della Scala dynasty. Its relatively peripheral location was common practice for the della Scala rulers, who preferred to position their forts away from the city center, to keep a watchful eye while still having the possibility of fleeing in case of an uprising against their tyrannical rule. When the Visconti counts conquered Verona and built a new castle—Castel San Pietro (see later in the itinerary)—the palace's name was changed to "the old castle" and it was turned into a military warehouse and academy.

Castelvecchio is a real treasure trove for history and art lovers, but families can have a great time here, too. The medieval halls were elegantly renovated by Carlo Scarpa, one of the greatest Italian architects of the 20th century, and the result, while highly controversial at the time, is admired today. The artwork on display is beautiful, though children will probably find the space itself more interesting, especially the dramatic medieval architecture, the statues of knights and the battlements on the second floor. Sadly, several of the original pieces of art are long gone. When

Napoleon invaded northern Italy, Verona suffered the same fate as many other cities: Several of its churches and public palazzi were looted, and the art was taken to France (mostly the Louvre museum).

End your visit with a walk along the stunning **fortified Castelvecchio Bridge** (commonly referred to as the **Ponte Scaligero**), a true symbol of Verona. At the time of its construction, it had the longest span in the world (48.7 meters). The original bridge was blown up by German troops in April 1945 as they were fleeing—the one you stand on today was rebuilt in the same style after the war. 🕒 Corso Castelvecchio 2, Verona. Tel: 045.806.2611, www.museodicastelvecchio.comune.verona.it. Open Tuesday—Sunday, 8:30—19:30; Monday 13:30—19:30 (last entry at 18:45).

●•••●•••●•••●•••●•••●•••●•••●•••●•••●•••●•••●•••

Mission 1: How many turrets can you count on the bridge?

Mission 2: Imagine that you are one of the knights protecting the castle. Take out your binoculars and write down: what is the farthest point you can see, looking west? North? East? West? Describe what you saw in your detective journal.

●•••●•••●•••●•••●•••●•••●•••●•••●•••●•••●•••●•••

> **Tip:** On the other side of the bridge you will find a small park and playground that is perfect for relaxation or a picnic. The park is called **Giardini Pubblici Piazza Arsenale,** and is located at Piazza Sacco e Vanzzetti. For more parks in the area, consult the list at the end of this itinerary.

From Castelvecchio, cross the street and walk along Via Roma, towards Verona's main piazza, Piazza Bra, where you will also find the world-famous **Roman Arena.** This impressive theater dates back to the first century AD, and is a testament to Verona's importance during Roman times. In fact, the Arena was large enough to accommodate up to 30,000 people—three times the local population back then. The interior part of the Arena has remained intact. The exterior rings, however, have been damaged by earthquakes and sneaky local builders, who turned the Roman monument into a illegal quarry, using its stones as building materials for new public buildings, churches or even private homes.

For nearly 2000 years, the Arena has served its purpose as the city's main theater: In Roman times, gladiators fought here; in medieval times, the Arena was used for public spectacles, bull fighting, jousting matches and noble banquets—when Antonio della Scala (of the famous Scaligero family) married Samaritana da Polenta, their marriage was celebrated with a wild feast at the Arena that went on for 25 days! Sadly, the Arena was also the preferred venue for public executions. On February 13, 1278, 166 people who were accused of heresy were burned here at the stake.

The last jousting match in the Arena took place in 1716, but it remained a stylish venue for concerts throughout the 18th and 19th century—Buffalo Bill Cody preformed here in 1890 and in 1906, and in 1913 this was where Giuseppe Verdi chose to hold the world premiere of his new opera—Aida. Today, the Arena regularly hosts opera shows as well as rock concerts by international stars, from Sting to Adele. The Arena can be admired from the outside, or you can purchase a (rather pricey) ticket to get a better look. Entrance is free with the Verona Card. 🕒 The Arena, Piazza Bra, Verona. Open Tuesday—Sunday, 8:30—19:30; Monday 13:30—19:30. Opening hours may vary if there's a concert taking place. The ticket office closes at 18:30.

Mission 1: back in those days, size was measured with hands and feet, and the Arena measured 250 x 150 standard roman feet (that would be 75,68 m x 44,43 m in modern terms). Pretend you are a Roman architect—can you measure the distance between the entrance to the first row of seats in YOUR feet?

Mission 1: Outside the Arena, near Via Mazzini, there's a statue of a heart. Can you find it? Take a picture inside it!

Mission 2: (hard!): can you count how many entrances (including doors and windows) does the Arena have?

Once you've visited the Arena, stay for a while in Pizza Bra itself. This vibrant town square is the perfect place to enjoy a cappuccino or a creamy gelato while doing some people watching. Simply sit down and relax on one of the benches scattered among the cedar and pine trees or at one of the many cafés that line the square, and enjoy the view.

Before moving on, don't forget to stop by the **tourist office,** which is located at Piazza Bra number 9 (open daily, 9:00—19:00). The friendly staff will provide you with a free map of the *centro storico*, and you can even book a hotel for the night, or purchase the Verona Card (the all-inclusive card that grants you entry to Verona's various sights and museums).

> **Tip:** Toddlers will love the small tourist train leaving from Piazza Bra on fun tours of the city. The train leaves in season, daily, 10:00–19:00, every 25 minutes. www.visitareverona.it.

Next, exit Piazza Bra onto **Via Mazzini**—Verona's main shopping street. This marble-lined via is a shopper's dream, featuring just about every favorite brand in Italy. The street running parallel to Via Mazzini (Via Cavour) is also filled with fantastic shops. Continue walking along Via Mazzini all the way to the end of the street, until you come to a T intersection; to your left you will see the famous Piazza Erbe, and to your right, Via Capello, which will lead you directly to Juliet's house (at number 23).

La Casa di Giulietta (Juliet's house) is without a doubt one of Verona's best-known sights. Shakespeare set Romeo and Juliet's story in a historic time in which Verona was indeed fair, and much more; back in the 14th century, the city was one of Italy's brightest shining jewels—a strong and rich city, blooming and growing under the rule of the Scaligero dynasty.

Romeo and Juliet's tragic love story has crowned Verona as one of the most romantic cities in Italy, but, as often happens in such cases, fact and fiction have become intertwined. Both the Montague and Capulet (Montecchi and Capplletti) families really did exist, and are even mentioned in the writings of Dante Alighieri, though in a different context. Furthermore, the Capulets really did have a house on Via Capello, where today hundreds of thousands of tourists stop for a quick peek. Sadly, that is where the historical certainties end. There is no proof that other sites in the city, such as Juliet's grave and Romeo's house, are real. To be honest, though, historical accuracy is hardly the only reason to visit them.

Once you reach Juliet's house, you will be overwhelmed by both the sheer number of people who stop for a visit and the amount of graffiti

Verona

on the wall, written by couples proclaiming their undying love. Until a number of years ago it was common practice to stick love notes to the wall with a piece of used chewing gum, but the 500 euro fines the city started issuing to violators put an end to that questionable practice.

Step inside to see the inner court, where Juliet's statue stands, and take the obligatory photo caressing Juliet's left breast—according to local tradition, touching the statue will bring love into the lives of those who are unlucky in romance. You might notice that the statue looks practically new, and that is because it is. What stands before you is a replica from 2014; the previous statue had to be replaced after years of being caressed and hugged by hundreds of thousands of romantic tourists.

Then, look up and you will see the famous balcony where Juliet stood when her star-cross'd lover came to visit her at night. For a fee, you can enter the house and visit the medieval-style rooms, which are decorated with costumes and artifacts from MGM's classic 1936 production of Romeo and Juliet, starring Leslie Howard as Romeo and Norma Shearer as Juliet. Naturally, there is a popular gift shop in the courtyard, filled to the brim with romantic souvenirs that your teenagers will love. 🕐 Casa di Giulietta, Via Cappello 23, Verona. Open Tuesday—Sunday, 8:30—18:45; Monday 13:30—18:45.

●•••●•••●•••●•••●•••●•••●•••●•••●•••●•••●•••●•••

Mission 1: Take a picture with Juliet's statue.

Mission 2: Juliet's famous balcony has a unique decoration on it—how many decorative arches can you count?

●•••●•••●•••●•••●•••●•••●•••●•••●•••●•••●•••●•••

Some tourists hope to visit Romeo's house, too, but sadly, this is impossible as the house is located on private property. You can, however, visit Juliet's supposed tomb, which is located in the charming garden of the San Francesco al Corso convent (marked on all the tourist maps). While there is no historical proof that Juliet is actually buried here, the setting is picturesque, and you wouldn't be the only ones drawn to this very spot.

Lord Byron visited it, too, and by his own admission, even stole a few pieces of the granite to take back home with him and give to his nephew.

> ## Discover Verona from Like a True Explorer—Rolling on a Segway, or Floating in a Dinghy!
>
> A leisurely walk is the most popular way to enjoy Verona, but it certainly isn't the only way. **Segway Verona** offers guided tours that will take you to the main tourist sights aboard one of the coolest means of transportation. A 90-minute tour will cost about 50 euro, and advance reservations are required: Segway Verona, Tel: 045.594.949, www.segwayverona.com. Alternatively, leave the dry land to others, board a rubber dinghy, and float down the Adige River on a **Boat Tour of Verona.** While you won't be able to see the sights themselves, obviously, since they are not accessible from the river, this fun adventure is great for families who want to get away from the crowds and insert some kid-friendly activities into their itineraries. In high season, booking usually isn't necessary—you can simply arrive 15 minutes before departure time and join the tour (though we do recommend calling, just to be on the safe side). If you are traveling off-season, between September and May, always call in advance: Verona Boat, tours leave June—September daily at 10:00, 12:00, 14:00, 16:00 and 18:00. Cell: 393.300.3030, www.veronaboat.com / www.tryverona.com.

Next, backtrack and make your way to **Piazza delle Erbe** (literal meaning, "the herb market"). This is Verona's market square, and the second most famous piazza in the city (after Piazza Bra). Small and rectangular, Piazza Erbe is always buzzing with life. People wander

Verona

among the stalls or enjoy an *aperitivo* or a meal in one of the many cafés that line the piazza. It is incredible to think that this square has been serving the same purpose for over a thousand years—in Roman times, this was the forum, and a bubbling market and commercial center like today.

As you stand in the entry to the Piazza, you will see on your right the famous Torre dei Lamberti, the highest tower in Verona (see next stop on this itinerary). On your left you'll find the ancient market *loggia*, the **Domus Mercatorum.** Built in 1210, this unique *palazzo* with striped walls is where Verona's powerful merchant guild held its meetings. In front of you is the magnificent **Palazzo Maffei,** built in typical Baroque style and decorated with statues of six divinities: Hercules, Apollo, Jupiter, Minerva, Venus, and Mercury. As you look up, you'll notice that one of the palazzi, Case Mazzanti, is still decorated on the outside with colorful frescoes. Sadly, many have been damaged over the years, but back in the early 16th century, several of the palazzi here were similarly colorful.

The tall marble column in front of Palazzo Maffei, featuring a large winged lion, is one of the many reminders across the city of when Verona was under the rule of the Serenissima—the Republic of Venice (the winged lion is Venice's symbol). Venetian rule was a golden age for Verona, and when the Serenissima was defeated by Napoleon's army, Verona was hit badly, too.

In the middle of the piazza stands an impressive fountain, built in 1368, during the Scaligero family's time on the throne. The delicate sculpture at the center of the fountain, know as Madonna Verona, is even more ancient, and dates back to Roman times (circa the 4th century).

Next, exit Piazza delle Erbe on the right, towards Torre dei Lamberti. As you exit, look up. Can you see that strange curved bone hanging from the arch? According to the local tradition, this 300-year-old "rib," after which the street is named (Via della Costa means Rib Road in Italian), is presumably the rib of a whale, and is said to predict the weather—if the rib is perpendicular to the arch, make sure you bring your umbrella with you!

Almost as soon as you exit Piazza Erbe, the entrance to **Torre dei Lamberti** will be on your right. This 84 meter tower dates back to 1172, and was renovated in the 15th century, after it was hit by lightning.

> **Tip:** You can reach the top of the tower on foot, or with the help of the elevator. If you are travelling with toddlers and carrying a stroller, please note that because of the tower's narrow medieval structure, the elevator **doesn't** go all the way up—you will still have to climb the last flight of stairs to reach the tower's terrace.

Once you reach the top, a beautiful view will compensate your efforts. Don't forget to look up, too—the two large bronze bells hanging directly above you are a reminder of a time when the tower served an important role in Verona's civic life. The smaller bell is called the *Marangona* bell, and it was used to signal the beginning and end of every work day, and to alert people in case of emergencies. The second bell is called the *Rengo* bell, and it was used to summon the citizens to special council meetings. Ringing the bell was a serious job—the city appointed official bell ringers, and while their annual salary wasn't exactly that of a CEO, they did enjoy some perks, such as living for free in the tower. 🕐 Torre dei Lamberti, Via della Costa 1, Verona. Tel: 045.927.3027. Open daily, 11:00—19:00. Last entry 45 minutes before closing. Free for children under 7 years old. The price of the elevator is not included in the Verona Card.

Exit Torre dei Lamberti, and turn right and step into **Piazza dei Signori** (often referred to as Piazza Dante). This delightful square is lined with elaborately decorated medieval buildings, most of which were built by the della Scala family. The impressive 12th century terracotta and white striped palazzo is Palazzo della Ragione (enter through the arch to see it properly), which today houses the municipal offices and a modern art gallery (entry to the gallery is free with the Torre dei Lamberti ticket).

The beautiful palazzo with the large open arches is the Loggia del Consiglio, which dates back to 1476. Right next to it stands the dramatic Palazzo del Podesta, built in typical Scaligero style. This was once the official residence of the Scaligero (della Scala) family, and it is where the most important guests were invited to stay when visiting Verona—everyone from Dante to Giorgio Vasari slept here. The palazzo was once decorated with beautiful frescos by Giotto, but sadly none of them survived.

Verona

In 1865, right in the middle of the Austrian occupation of the city, an important (and very Italian) monument was added to this piazza by the defiant citizens—a large statue of Dante Alighieri, who had played an important role in Verona's civic and political life after he was exiled from Florence. The statue of a man on the arch between the loggia and the terracotta-colored Casa della Pieta is the Renaissance doctor Girolamo Fracastoro, one of the leading physicians of his time. Fracastoro was one of the first to believe in the theory that illness is caused by living things. Curiously, he is also the man who gave syphilis its name, in a long poem he wrote, dedicated to the mysterious "French disease."

The most interesting monument in the piazza, however, hides on the wall next to the pizzeria restaurant—a real **denunciation box,** similar to the ones found in Venice. Back in medieval and Renaissance times, these boxes served an important function in city life, and people could anonymously tattle on their neighbors if they suspected any wrongdoing.

●•••●•••●•••●•••●•••●•••●•••●•••●•••●•••●•••●•••

Mission 1: Find the denunciation box. What animal is it shaped like?

Mission 2: How many statues decorate this piazza? Don't forget to look up, some of the statues here are located in surprising places…

●•••●•••●•••●•••●•••●•••●•••●•••●•••●•••●•••●•••

Exit Piazza Dante and walk along via Santa Maria in Chiavica and you will immediately reach the **Arche Scaligere**—the Scala family Gothic funerary monument. The first tomb in the complex is that of the father of the dynasty, Cangrande I, and is easy to spot, thanks to the large tabernacle surrounded by dog statues ("cane grande" in Italian means "large dog"). Richly decorated reliefs and arches also mark the tombs of the other four members of the family who are buried beside him.

From here, continue along the same street for a few more meters, turn left onto Via Cavaletto and then immediately right onto Corso Sant'Anastasia. After a short walk along this charming shop-filled street, you will reach one of the most beautiful churches in Verona—the **Church of Sant'Anastasia.** Built in 1280 in classic Gothic style by monks of the powerful Dominican order, the church of Sant'Anastasia is a treasure for art lovers. The church was constructed over the ruins of a Roman temple, and its impressive bell tower is almost as tall as Torre dei Lamberti, standing at 72 meters. Sant'Anastasia is built in the shape of a Latin cross and the red, white and black colors that dominate it are symbolic: The red represents Verona, the black and white represent the Dominican order.

Mission 2: As soon as you enter, you will see that this church has two very unique holly water fonts. Can you find them? That are they shaped like? Take a picture standing next to them, hunching like them.

The ceiling is decorated with light, elegant frescos, and the main chapels, on either side of the altar, hold some incredible art work. On the right, in the Pellegrini Chapel, you will find the famous St. George and the Princess fresco by Pisanello. He was one of the most important and talented painters in the early Italian Renaissance, and was employed by several noble families and even by the Vatican. St. George and the Princess is considered one of his finest works thanks to the vivid storytelling and beautiful details. Sadly, over the years the fresco has been seriously damaged due to neglect. Other noteworthy works in the church are the Centrego altar, featuring the famous *Our Lady Enthroned* painting by Girolamo dai Libri; the *Giudizio Universale* by Turone Mazio; the beautiful Capella Salerni; and, of course, Capella Cavali, featuring the impressive *L'Adorazione della Vergine*. 🕑 Piazza Santa Anastasia, Verona. Tel: 045.592.813, www.chieseverona.it. Open Monday—Saturday, 9:00—18:00; Sunday and holidays, 13:00—18:00. Off season, open until 17:00.

From Sant'Anastasia walk along Via Massalongo, which turns into Via Ponte, towards **Ponte Pietra,** one of the prettiest bridges in Verona. The original bridge was built 2000 years ago of wood, but it collapsed several times, and was finally built of stone (pietra—thus giving it its name) in the 13th century. The bridge you see before you, however, isn't the original—in 1945 the retreating German army blew the bridge up, and the one before you is a well-designed reconstruction from 1959.

Verona

To really appreciate the beauty of the bridge and its scenic surroundings, you must cross it and admire it from the other side of the river (walking towards the Roman theater). As you stand on the banks of the Adige river, it will be easy to see why Verona inspired so many love tales.

Stay on this bank, and continue walking for about two minutes towards the **Roman theater.** Dating back to the first century AD, this monument is even older than the famous Arena in Piazza Bra. The theater recently opened after a long renovation, and today serves a dual function—the theater itself regularly hosts concerts and shows, while the former Jesuit convent that looms above the theater hosts a very small archeological museum. To be honest, the collection here is so tiny that it may not justify the price of the ticket. But the view from the open terrace on the museum's top floor most certainly is worth your time and money (and if you've bought the Verona Card, entry to the museum is free). ◉ Rigaste Redentore 2, Verona. Tel: 045.800.0360, www.museoarcheologico.comune.verona.it. Open Tuesday—Sunday, 8:30—19:30; Monday 13:30—19:30. Last entry at 18:30. Opening hours may change when concerts are held here.

Enjoy the Best Views in Verona!

The vista from the Roman theater is lovely, but to enjoy the best views in the city, you'll have to climb up to Castel San Pietro, which stands directly above the theater. To reach it, you can either walk up the (many, many) stairs, drive up with your car, or take the recently opened funicular, which will take you right to the panoramic viewpoint! The Funiculare di Castel San Pietro starts from Piazzetta Santo Stefano (by the Roman theater), and is open daily, 11:00-21:00. If you'd like to extend your stay, know that there is a small cafe at Castel San Pietro, called TedoricoRe (www.reteodorico.com). Sitting here for a cold drink at sunset is one of the best ways to end your day in the city.

Verona

One you have completed the tour of the Roman theater and museum, retrace your steps and go back across the Ponte Pietra, turn right onto Piazza Broilo and then continue straight until you reach the back entrance to the Duomo.

Verona's main cathedral, the **Duomo,** is actually a complex of three adjoining buildings—the Cathedral itself; the church of San Giovanni in Fonte (where the famous baptistery is located); and the ancient church of St. Elena (where the archeological excavations can be found). All three are quite beautiful, and merit a visit.

The Duomo was built on the orders of Verona's famous bishop, San Zeno, though the current building that stands in front of you is somewhat "newer," and was built in 111 A.D., after the previous basilica was destroyed in an earthquake. The location in which San Zeno chose to build the Duomo was hardly accidental—right on top of the ruins of a temple dedicated to Minerva, among the large villas and thermal baths of one of the richer quarters in Roman Verona. The elegant Romanesque structure holds a majestic interior. Frescoes of the Veronese school cover the walls, as do works such as Titian's Assunta; the dramatic Cartolari chapel; the poetic Adoration of the Magi by Liberale da Verona; and Francesco Torbido's frescoes in the presbytery.

Don't forget to enter the small church of San Giovanni in Fonte where the famous baptistery is located (included in the price of the ticket). Dating back to the 10th century, this octagonal christening font is carved with scenes from the New Testament. The choice of form is symbolic, and refers to the eighth day, on which the Messiah will return and judgment will begin. The archeological section and mosaics next door, which are what remains from the earliest Christian basilica in Verona, are interesting, too. ☻ The Duomo, Piazza Duomo. Tel: 045.592.813, www. chieseverona.it. Open Monday—Saturday, 10:00—17:30; Sunday 13:00—17:30. Off season, closes at 17:00.

●•••●•••●•••●•••●•••●•••●•••●•••●•••●•••●•••●•••●•••

Mission 1: One of the benches in the baptistery holds a secret... it used to be a door! Can you find it?

Mission 2: Which of the scenes carved to the font is your favorite? Why?

Mission 3: stand in front of the main entry to the Duomo, and look at its facade. How many animals can you find here?

●•••●•••●•••●•••●•••●•••●•••●•••●•••●•••●•••●•••●•••

The final part of the walking tour will take you to the most famous church in Verona—San Zeno. Located a at some distance from the city center, this church is not only a treasure for art lovers, it is also where Romeo and Juliet were secretly wed. San Zeno is a pleasant 2.2 km (1.5 miles) walk from the Duomo. If that's too far, you can take bus number 31, 32 or 33 from Via Diaz, right next to Porta Borsari–the next stop in the itinerary.

> **Tip:** If you are not interested in visiting San Zeno, you can cut your tour short, and instead head to the beautiful Giusti gardens, instead (described in detail below).

From the Duomo walk to Via Garibaldi, and continue walking straight ahead, until Via Garibaldi becomes Via Rosa. Turn right at Corso Porta Borsari and continue along this shop-filled street until you reach Porta Borsari (the Borsari gate). This ancient Roman white limestone gate dates back to the first century BC and was once the main entrance to Verona. Today, it is a testament to the vibrant city that Roman Verona was. From this point, continue by foot along Corso Cavour until you reach Castelvecchio (the starting point of this tour) and from there walk along the river, and turn at Via Barbani Berto—the **church of San Zeno** will be in front of you.

Of the many churches in Verona, this 1100-year-old basilica is probably the dearest to the Veronese heart, and was the model for the rest of the churches. The location, though slightly remote, is also symbolic—back in Roman times, this area was the city's cemetery; the church and adjacent Benedictine monastery were built to surround the grave of San Zeno himself. As you stand in front of the impressive cream-colored marble Romanesque church, the first thing you will notice is the large bronze doors, which are decorated with 48 panels depicting scenes from the lives of various saints and allegorical scenes showing some Christian virtues. The panels were made in collaboration by a number of artists between the 13th and 14th centuries. Look up, and you will see the large rose window, known as the "wheel of fortune."

Enter, and walk down the main nave, lined with beautifully decorated and carved pilasters, until you reach the jewel of this church—Andrea Mantegna's triptych, known simply as the San Zeno Altarpiece. This is considered the first real Renaissance work of art to be displayed in Verona. Sadly, only parts of this beautiful work have survived; a number of pieces were looted by the French army during the Napoleonic invasion. Naturally, your visit here won't be complete without stopping by the crypt, where, according to tradition, the body of San Zeno is kept, his face covered by a mysterious silver mask. ⊙ Piazza San Zeno 2. Opening hours vary, and depend on the religious events celebrated here.

To end your day the right way, spend an hour or two in Verona's magical **Giusti Garden.** This is a splendid classic Italian and English garden is just a short walk from Piazza Erbe and the Roman theater, and offers kids some space to run around, while adults will admire its beauty. The garden is suffused with history, and was built in 1570 by Agostino Giusti, a cavaliere of the Venetian Republic. His Tuscan origins explain the choice of style and décor, especially the deeply symbolic statues in the garden, which are reminiscent of the art work that can be found in the famous Boboli gardens in Florence. There's a fee to enter the garden; for other parks in the city, see the box below. ⊙ Via Giardino Giusti 2, Verona. Open daily, 9:00—19:00.

Eating in Verona

Ristorante La Vecia Mescola is a good choice—welcoming, traditional, and reasonably priced given the quality of the food. Book a table in advance as they are always full. Vicolo Chiodo 4, Verona. Tel: 045.803.6608, www.trattorieverona.it. Open Sunday—Thursday, 12:00.—15:00 & 19:00—22:30.; Friday—Saturday, 12:00—15:00 & 19:00—23:30.

For Pasta lovers, **Parma a Tavola** is a very good option. Comfortably located on Corso Anastasia, just minutes from Piazza Bra, this venue specializes in the most Italian dish of them all. The pasta is fresh, hand-made (of course!), and served with selection of traditional and seasonal sauces. Corso Sant'Anastasia 20, Verona, Tel: 045. 8012001, www.parmatavola.com. Open Wednesday—Saturday, 12:30—16:00 & 19:30—22:20; Sunday—Tuesday, open for lunch only.

Ristorante Pizzeria Nastro Azzurro is a popular quick fix for many families—centrally located and reasonably priced, they specialize in tasty pizza and pasta to please all. And, since their hours of operation are extended, you can come here for a late lunch or an early dinner, too. Vicolo Listone 4 (near Piazza Bra), Tel: 045.800.4457, www.ristorantenastroazzurroverona.it. Open daily, 12:00—23:00.

If you are curious about trying some of the most typical Veronese dishes, head to **Osteria Macafame**. The menu changes daily, and includes some well-loved classics (try the gnocchi!) as well as a few dishes for the brave only (such as horse tartare, a Verona specialty). Via delle Fogge 6. Cell: 347.873.0150. Open Tuesday—Saturday, for lunch and dinner; Sunday open for lunch only; Monday closed.

Parks & Where to Picnic in Verona

There are a number of parks in Verona, but not all of them are suitable for for picnics. If you prefer an outdoor family meal, try one of these options:

Giardini Pradaval, on Piazza Pradaval (near Parcheggio Arena) offer families a playground, picnic benches, and lots of free space.

Parco Giardino Valdonega, on Via Ippolito Nievo (marked on Google Maps as 'Parco Giocchi Nievo') has a play area, picnic benches, and more.

Giardino Arsenale, off the Castelvecchio Bridge (mentioned in the itinerary, too) offers a picnic area and a large playground.

Outside the centro storico, on the way to the Castel San Pietro Panoramic Viewpoint, there's the very large public park called **Parco delle Colombare** where kids can play, picnic, and run around freely.

Sleeping in Verona

B&B Villa Beatrice is located right outside Verona and offers guests modern, comfortable family rooms (make sure you book the ones with a private bathroom), a garden with BBQ facilities and a pool, and a delicious buffet breakfast. B&B Villa Beatrice, Via Bonuzzo S. Anna 18, Verona. GPS: N 45° 29' 13.536" - E 10° 59' 57.948". Cell: 349.730.0751, www.bbvillabeatrice.com.

Hotel Accademia is located right in the historical center, just two minutes from Piazza Erbe. The rooms are a good size, the breakfast buffet is generous, and the staff is friendly. Via Scala 12, Verona. Tel: 045.596.222, www.hotelaccademiaverona.it.

Special Events in Verona

Many of Verona's best events take place in the winter, which makes them irrelevant for most families. But if you happen to be visiting in February, don't miss the town's wildly colorful **carnival** (www.carnevaleverona.it) as well as the Verona in Love Festival, which take place on Valentine's day, and celebrates Verona's reputation as the city of love.

In the summer, Verona comes to life with endless shows. Kids may be too young, but teenagers will enjoy either the **dramatic operas** or the **rock concerts** that are organized at the Arena. Note that many events sell out very early on, so check the Arena's website well in advance, and if you find a show that interest you, book it: www.arena.it. The Roman theater hosts many shows of its own, and is worth checking out, too: www.estateteatraleveronese.it.

Special Activities in Verona

ADVENTURE PARKS

Two excellent adventure parks await families visiting the Verona area. The first, **Boscopark Adventure Park,** sits in Bosco Chiesanova, 45 km north of

Verona, and offers visitors 6,000 square miles of fun with 70 activities kids can climb up or hop on. For younger children (over 80 cm tall), there's even the baby trail. Boscopark Parco Avventura, Via Aleardi, Bosco Chiesanuova. The park is usually open from Easter to September. Cell: 348.8984.881, www.boscopark.it.

The Jungle Adventure Park is highly popular with action-loving families. It is located 45 minutes west of Verona (just 10 minutes from Lake Garda), and offers parkour trails within the forest. Both kids and teenagers will enjoy the various routes, that range from the easy green route to the adventurous and thrilling black route. Even toddlers can join the fun, at the baby section (designed for 3—6 year old). The park is open May—mid-September, daily. Off season (April & mid-September—mid-October), open on weekends only. Opening times depend on the weather conditions—call first. Strada per Lumini, Pineta Sperane, San Zeno di Montagna. Infoline: 045.628.9306, cell: 348.244.3543, www.jungleadventurepark.com.

FARM VISITS & PONY RIDES

Animal-loving toddlers and children will enjoy a visit to **Agriturismo Spigollo,** a farm that offers educational workshops, activities and tours, too. They are located just 10 minutes from Verona's city center, and you can either stop here for lunch and say hello to the goats, pigs and horses, or book in advance a full visit, including a riding lesson. Find out more, and book your tour on the agriturismo's website: www.agriturismospigolo.com/eng.

LAKE GARDA

Chapter 4

Lake Garda

Welcome to Lake Garda, one of the best-loved tourist destinations in all of Italy. Stunning landscapes of sparkling blue water surrounded by dramatic mountains set the scene, and the mild climate makes it comfortable to explore the dozens of engaging attractions for families. Both quiet nature-lovers and energetic thrill-seekers will find much to do. Being close to Verona and the Dolomites, and just a 90-minute drive from Venice, Lake Garda is easy to reach and even easier to love.

Lake Garda is not just one single destination—the area includes many towns, each offering something different. The towns of Sirmione, Malcesine, Gardone and Salò all offer easy access to the beach, lovely promenades, and family friendly shops and restaurants. They are some of the best villages to stroll around with a *gelato* in hand—the architecture will transport you to another time, and the picturesque streets, quirky boutiques and medieval fortresses will make you want to stay there. The southern shores of the lake are best for swimming, while the northern shores are known for water-sports, hiking trails, and even rock climbing.

The sheer number of attractions Lake Garda is known for is almost overwhelming, which is why we've focused our attention on the best and most interesting suggestions specifically for families. This will enable you to make an informed decision, and focus on what your family hopes to experience in Italy. We've also added dozens of practical tips and ideas; knowing what awaits you—both the best attractions and the potential pitfalls—means you can build a personalized itinerary to make the maximum of memories to treasure. Check the section at the end of this chapter titled "Special Activities in the Area" for details about family-friendly beaches, adventure parks and even a chance to go hiking with alpacas. The "Special Events in the Area" section also includes some outings and medieval festival sure to delight children.

189
Lake Garda

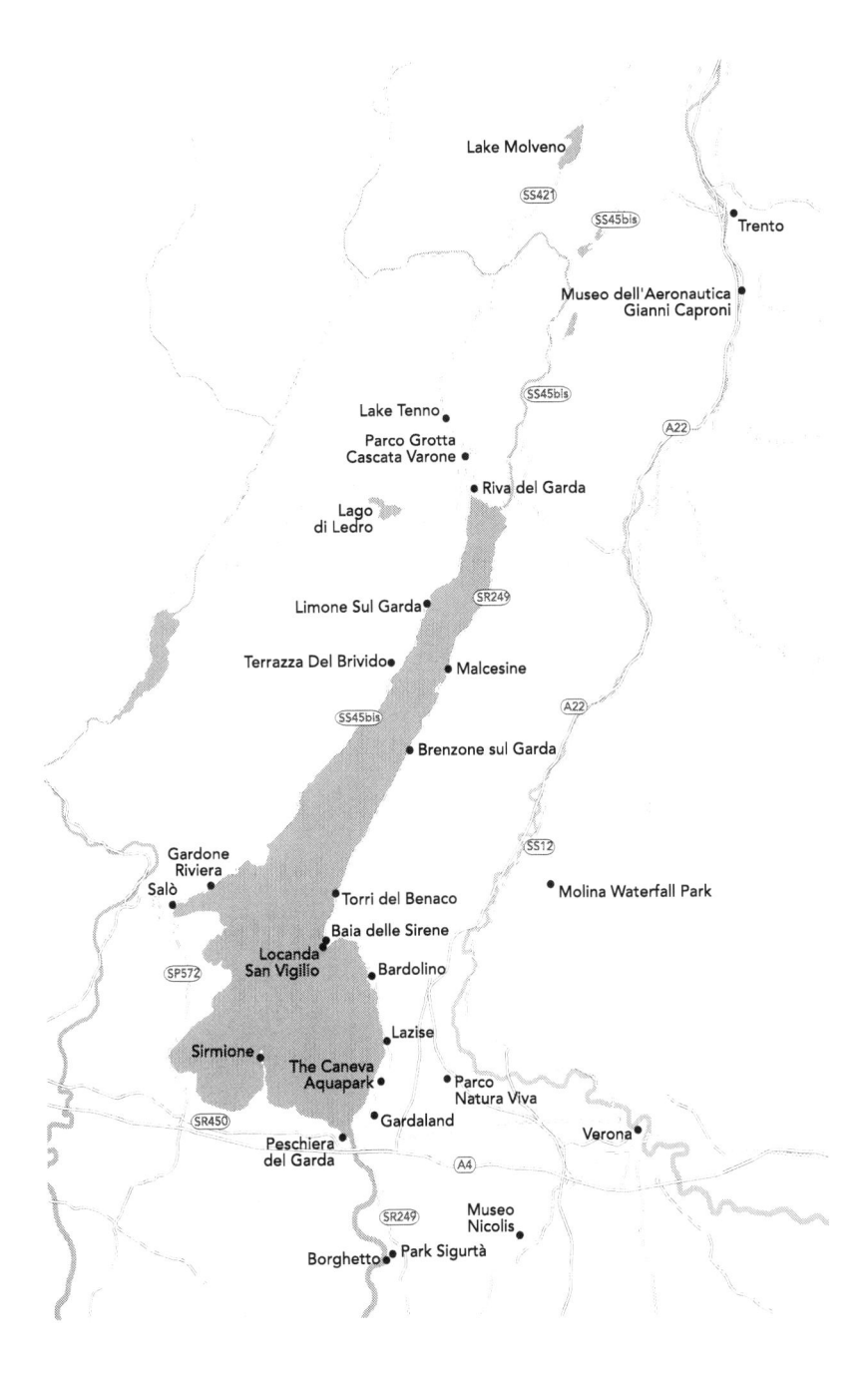

Top Ten Family Attractions

1. Enjoy a wild day of fun at the popular Gardaland park.
2. Dine like lords at the knights' dinner at Canevaworld.
3. Relax at one of Lake Garda's beaches.
4. Take the cable car from Malcesine up to the top of Monte Baldo for glorious views.
5. Visit the beautiful and poetic town of Sirmione.
6. Marvel at the stunning Varone waterfalls.
7. Explore one of the Scaliger fortresses on the shores of the lake.
8. Splash around at one of Garda's popular water parks.
9. Jump, roll and climb at one of the many adventure parks surrounding the lake.
10. Rent a small family boat and explore the lake like real captains!

Planning Your Visit to Lake Garda

GETTING AROUND LAKE GARDA

With so much to see and do, you'll need to travel around the lake a bit. What's the best option for your group? That depends on where you plan to base yourselves and where you want to go.

BUS

The main towns around the shores of Lake Garda are well-connected by bus routes, and you can even cross the lake by ferry. If you plan to stay here for no more than a couple of nights, spending most of your time at the beach, you could rely on public transportation. You won't have to worry about parking, and you can enjoy the scenery instead of focusing on traffic. The main disadvantage of this is that the local buses can be very crowded, especially in high season, and their schedule is sometimes erratic. Reaching the more remote attractions in the area may turn out to be complicated and time consuming; if you plan on visiting adventure parks and nature reserves and not just the lake itself, you might find you'd rather spend money to save time.

CAR

Renting a car gives you the freedom to venture off the main roads and explore ancient hamlets and castles, tiny farms and hidden lakes, and, more importantly, the local amusement parks (such as Gardaland). Driving in this area is easy: Lake Garda is framed by two main roads—the SR249 on the eastern side of the lake (this road is quite scenic), and the SS45bis on the west (which features many tunnels through the mountains; honking in tunnels is frowned upon in Italy.) Malcesine, Gardaland, Canevaworld, Parco Natura Viva Zoo, Torbole and the waterfalls are spread along the eastern bank of the lake, while Limone, Salò and Gardone are on the west. Riva del Garda is at the northern tip, and Sirmione is nestled at the southern edge. The disadvantages of going by car are the heavy traffic on the narrow roads, especially on weekends and holidays, and the difficulty of finding parking in peak season.

> **Tip:** make sure you carry plenty of change for the parking meters as they don't accept banknotes or cards.

FERRIES & BOATS

The roads are not your only option! Using the public ferry system—**Navigazione Lago di Garda**—can give you a welcome break from the wheel.

Traveling by boat is more time consuming than by car, but it's also a novelty that kids will love, and a ferry trip can substitute for a (more expensive) boat tour of the lake. Ferries connect all the major towns along the shores of Lake Garda, including Sirmione, Malcesine, Riva del Garda, Torri del Benaco, Lazise, Salò, and Gardone. If you plan to use the ferries more than a couple of times, you can save some time and money by buying a family pass, valid for one or three days. Up to two children who are under 12 years old are included and kids 4 to 12 pay a reduced fee. Please note that such offers may change, so you should confirm all details at the ticket office. In addition to the public service, there are also private companies who offer similar tours. **GardaExpress** (www.Gardaexpress.com) is a local operator that offers a basic tour from Malcesine to Limone del Garda that costs nine euro per person.

Even if you've rented a car, you can combine car and ferry travel with the **Traghetto Autoveicoli** (ferries for cars). From June through October, there's a ferry from Maderno to Torri every 35 minutes between 8:00—20:25 and a ferry from Limone to Malcesine every hour between 8:45—18:20 (except at lunch time). Ticket prices are around 13 to 16 euro, depending on the type of car. Find out more about the regular ferries and the ferries for cars here: www.navlaghi.it.

Avoiding the Crowds

Italy's most famous lake is crowded with attractions, natural beauty, history ... and of course visitors. For this reason, we've included many suggestions to take you off the beaten path and away from the flocks of other tourists. The chapter on 'Day Trips from Lake Garda' provides especially valuable information on such hidden attractions. The roads less taken will lead you to a more authentically Italian experience at a more relaxed pace, offering a nice break from the must-see spots that everyone else is also seeing.

To avoid the crowds while touring Lake Garda itself, try to schedule your visit to mid-June—late July, and avoid the weekends. Remember that August is the busiest time in Lake Garda, since Italians are on vacation, too, and the beaches and amusement parks can get very crowded.

# How to Build a Family-Friendly Itinerary in Lake Garda

All of the main attractions around the lake are listed in this chapter in geographical order, starting from the southernmost point in the lake (Sirmione). The sample itineraries bellow can be followed to the letter, or they can simply provide you with inspiration for your own custom itinerary.

Itinerary N. 1: Family with Two Children, 3 and 5 Years Old

Day 1: Start in Sirmione with a visit to the Scaliger Fortress, then chill with some ice cream before taking a boat ride on the lake, or relaxing at one of the beautiful beaches. (Check the recommendations for the best family beaches later in this chapter.) If the kids are still full of energy, visit the Jungle Park adventure park before dinner. All the details can be found in the itinerary itself.

Day 2: Head to Malcesine, and take the cable car up to Mount Baldo to enjoy some panoramic views. If everyone wants to keep their feet on the ground, hike up to the Scaliger Castle or visit the Parco Natura Zoo and Safari.

Day 3: Gardaland. Yes, it will keep everyone entertained for a full day! Do check the height and age restrictions for the rides before you go (consult the Gardaland website), to avoid disappointments. If your children won't be able to get on most of the rides, consider a different park (see 'Special Activities' at the end of this chapter), or perhaps focus your visit on Gardaland's aquarium, instead of the amusement park.

Day 4: Visit the toddler-friendly Lake Molveno for a day exploring the beaches, playing at adventure parks, and paddling across the lake. If you don't have time for a drive to the Dolomites, this is a great alternative that lets you get close to the mountains and enjoy the outdoors without the long trip. See the 'Day Trips from Lake Garda' chapter for more details.

Itinerary N. 2: Family with Two Children, 6 and 8 Years Old

Day 1: Sirmione offers great adventures for children this age including boat rides, the beach, and dinner at the exciting knight feast and show at Canevaworld. (As well as all the fun listed above for younger kids.)

Day 2: Malcesine is a great day, as described in the previous itinerary, and older kids will probably enjoy the cable car ride up Mount Baldo even more and can go exploring along one of the family trails up the mountain.

Day 3: Gardaland is a perfect day for this age range.

Day 4: The kids probably won't appreciate that Franz Kafka and Thomas Mann visited Riva del Garda and drew inspiration from the wild landscape, but they will love Busatte Adventure Park, just 10 minutes (by car) from Riva itself. While you are here, try some of the watersports on offer, see some snakes the local reptile museum, or a visit to Varone Waterfall. Alternatively, if you leave early in the morning, you will be able to enjoy an exciting day at Merano (90 minutes from Riva del Garda, see Dolomites chapter).

Day 5: Leave Lake Garda and visit a popular attraction in the vicinity such as Lake Ledro or Lake Molveno, both of which are perfect for children 3 to 12 years old. You could even spend the day hiking with alpacas! (See the 'Special Activities in the Area' section at the end of this chapter.)

Itinerary N. 3: Family with Two Children, 10 and 12 Years Old

Day 1: In Sirmione, older kids will enjoy visiting the Catullo Roman Villa and the adjacent beach, going on a boat ride, and having dinner at the knight festival or at the Rock'n'Roll restaurant.

Day 2: This age group will love a whole day at Gardaland and/or Canevaworld because they are big enough to get on all the rides.

Day 3: A day combining the beauty of Lake Tenno with visits to the Trento science museum, the aviation museum, and the enormous Beseno Castle is a nice balance after the amusement parks.

Day 4: Malcesine and a ride up to Monte Baldo in a cable car make a great day for all ages. For dinner, either try one of the town's many waterfront restaurants, or consider a picnic by the beach, which can be more intimate and fun.

Day 5: If your kids have the patience for a longer journey—head straight to the Dolomites. You need at least one full day to visit this region, but two is much better. The Dolomites are full of exciting cable car rides and hiking opportunities, and the views are far superior to what you might find in Lake Garda. If you enjoy the outdoors, and have only five days, you might wish to skip the Mount Baldo cable car in Malcesine in favor of one of the more dramatic rides in the Dolomite Alps, such as Pass Pordoi, the Seceda near Ortisei, or the Marmolada. See the Dolomites chapter for full details.

Itinerary N. 4: Family with Two Children, 14 and 16 years old

Day 1: With teens, you can do a more grown up visit to Sirmione. After the speed boat ride and visit to Catullo Villa and beach, you can all relax at the Sirmione thermal spa, or the cool Baia delle Sirene pools and spa complex (see detailed description in the itinerary itself) and they'll feel very worldly.

Day 2: Teens are old enough to enjoy the guided tour of Malcesine's stunning Isola del Garda Villa, which is great for lovers of art and history. An alternative historic spot to explore is Il Vittoriale, in Gardone Riviera. Combine this with a visit to Limone sul Garda, and a sunset *aperitivo* by the water, complete with non-alcoholic cocktails.

Day 3: Gardaland is a fantastic day for teens. They'll be able to get on the best and scariest rides, and they will love enjoying all the fun of an amusement park but with an Italian twist.

Day 4-5: Two days in the Dolomites are a wonderful experience for teens who love the outdoors. Your hiking and cable car rides will be rewarded with jaw-dropping views, and you can even go on an easy hike / horse ride in Alpe di Siusi. If your kids don't enjoy the outdoors, consider visiting one the attractions listed in the 'Day Trips from Lake Garda' and 'Day Trips from Venice' chapters, such as: A visit to the Ferrari Museum, a visit to Sigurta park, and more.

More About Lake Garda

Lake Garda is not just Italy's most famous and popular lake; it's also the largest and deepest lake in the country. Its perimeter is 155 kilometers, and its deepest point measures 346 meters, which is nearly as deep as the Empire State Building is tall! The lake was formed in the Pliocene age, when a large section of Mount Baldo sank, creating a huge hole. As the glaciers from the Alps continued to erode the land, the lake grew larger and developed its particular fjord-like shape. The lake is fed by several underwater springs.

The lush landscape surrounding Lake Garda includes vineyards and olive groves. The town of Bardolino is especially famous for olives, and the olive oil from this region is known for its excellent flavor. The wines produced here, particularly the Bardolino and Lugana wines, are well respected.

With such fertile land, it is no surprise that humans have lived around Lake Garda since prehistoric times, leaving their mark here quite literally—some prehistoric graffiti is still visible today near Mount Baldo. Waves of different peoples lived here—Etruscans, Eugenians, Celts and of course Romans.

The region suffered greatly during the Barbarian invasions, and revived in the Middle Ages. It may be hard to imagine these serene waters turbulent, but during Italy's fight for independence from the Austrian occupation, brutal naval battles took place in the middle of the lake. In fact, the full drama of Italian politics through the centuries played out in this region, with prominent players such as the La Scala of Verona and the Visconti from Milan, the Republic of Venice and Napoleon claiming the land at various times in history before the current borders of Italy solidified. During WWII, the lakeside town of Salò became the capital of Benito Mussolini's Nazi-controlled puppet state known as the Italian Social Republic.

Sirmione

Getting there & parking: The easiest way to reach Sirmione is by car. From Verona, it's about 40 minutes on the A4 autostrada. The historic center of Sirmione sits at the very tip of the peninsula; avoid the parking lots near the main road and instead set your GPS for the huge parking lot at Piazzale Porto or Piazza Montebaldo (depending on the map).

Tourist information office: Viale Marconi 2. Tel: 030.374.8721, www.sirmionebs.it. Stop here to pick up a free map and to learn about events and special activities. Open Easter—the last Sunday of October, daily, 10:00—19:00.

Sirmione, the famous town which enchanted so many visitors from Maria Callas to Alfred Tennyson to James Joyce to D.H. Lawrence, lies at the peninsula jutting into the southern part of Lake Garda. Sirmione has been populated since prehistoric times, and it's been a tourist hot spot since Roman times. Today's population of less than 10,000 hosts an endless stream of tourists every summer in the fortified village of 33 square kilometers.

When you cross the drawbridge and walk into the village to start your tour, you'll feel like the stars of your own fairy tale. That small, perfect fortress ahead is the **Scaligero Castle,** and it was built in the 13th century by Mastino I of the della Scala family from Verona. You can explore the empty inside and climb up for a fantastic view of the surrounding area.

(Malcesine has its own larger Scaliger Castle, complete with two mini-museums and even better views due to its elevated location, but it is less suitable for young children, who might find the walk up tiring.) ◉ Scaligero Fortress, Piazza Castello 34, Sirmione. Tel: 030.916.468. Open Tuesday—Saturday, 8:30—19:00; Sunday, 8:30—13:00. Monday closed. May close down off season.

Follow the main street, **Via Vittorio Emanuele,** to explore the plethora of little boutiques and souvenir shops. We subscribe to the belief that the calories in ice cream eaten on vacation don't count, which is nice because it is impossible to resist the allure of all the *gelaterie* you'll pass. Our favorites are Gelateria Scaligeri (Via Colombare 113) and Cremeria Bulian (Via Vittorio Emanuele 30). And the ice cream should give the children the energy to continue on to the very tip of the peninsula, where you'll find Sirmione's most renowned sight—The Roman Villa known as **Le Grotte di Catullo.** Dating back to the first century BC, its exact origins are a mystery, but its current name is in honor of the Roman poet Gaius Catulus, who wrote several verses celebrating the beauty of Sirmione, the pearl of Lake Garda. The small adjacent museum displays a collection of artifacts from the site. ◉ Grotte di Catullo, Piazza Orti Manara 4, Sirmione. Tel: 030.916.157, www.polomuseale.lombardia.beniculturali.it/index.php/grotte-di-catullo. Summer: Tuesday—Saturday, 8:30—19:30; Sunday, 9:30—18:30; Monday closed. Winter: Tuesday—Saturday, 8.30—17:00; Sunday, 8:30—14:00; Monday closed.

Lake Garda

> ## Rent a Speedboat!
>
> A speed boat tour of Sirmione and the lake is an exciting and wildly fun way to see the peninsula. Many companies offer tours, and you can learn about them online and book in advance, or walk around the pier and choose on the spot the one that suits your family best. (In high season, consider reserving a tour in advance, as many operators are fully booked.) The speed boats are known in Italian as *motoscafi*, and they leave from Via Marconi near the bus parking area, from Hotel Sirmione, and from the Lungolago (lake promenade). Try www.cosorziomotoscafisti.it or www.Sirmioneboats.it/en/boat-rental-service. Naturally, you can rent or join tours in other towns around the lake including Desenzano, Brenzone and Bardolino.

Gardaland and Canevaworld Amusement Parks

Getting there & parking: Driving is the easiest way to reach these neighboring parks, although it is possible to get there on public transportation: Both parks operate their own free shuttle bus (*navetta*, in Italian) from the Peschiera del Garda train station. Be advised the shuttles can be very crowded, and their hours of operation are limited. Parking is free at Gardaland, but Canevaworld charges 5 euro per car.

Top Tips for Visiting Gardaland and Canevaworld:

1. Gardaland is a dream come true for children. Children taller than 110 cm, that is. Children shorter than 110 cm are likely to be frustrated and disappointed because they won't be allowed on many of the rides. Children under 1 meter don't have to pay an entry fee, but they can't go on most rides, either, which means they will probably have more fun at other parks, suitable for toddlers.

2. Spare yourself and your children the hassle of standing in line by buying your tickets in advance, either online (both parks), at your hotel (Gardaland), by phone (Canevaworld) or from the tourist office (Gardaland). Canevaworld has two sections (Movieland and the Waterpark), and you can get a discount if you buy in advance a ticket for both sections.

3. Gardaland offers express tickets that let you skip the line for most rides. If you are going in peak season (July and August) it might be worth the hefty price to enjoy the VIP treatment and avoid long waits, standing in the heat.

4. With so many rides and so little time, a visit here can be overwhelming. To avoid wasting your morning on the "wrong" rides, preview everything on each park's website, ask your kids which rides they want to try, and map a route to follow through the park. This way you can hit the best rides first (such as the jungle rapids ride, or the blue tornado) and keep the excitement coming without any time lost debating what to do next.

Lake Garda

> 5. A change of clothes comes in handy because you can get fairly soaked on some of the rides in both parks. Ironically, you can also get dehydrated spending the day exposed to the sun, so bring drinks. Water is important, but you will also want juice or energy drinks to keep everyone's electrolyte levels up.
>
> 6. Plan to visit the parks mid-week, and arrive early in the day. Holidays and weekends see massive crowds, and it can add real stress to the day. An early start means you can enjoy some of the rides before the crowds arrive and the temperatures soar.

Gardaland is one of the most popular amusement and activity parks in Italy, and you can easily spend an entire day here. It consists of two main sections: the **amusement park**, which features themed rides grouped into 'fantasy', 'adventure' and 'adrenaline', and the **Sea Life Aquarium**, which is home to 5,000 aquatic creatures including fish, jellyfish, sharks, ray fish and more.

Before you visit the park, consult the website to find the best rides for your children's age group. For teenagers, the Raptor wing style roller coaster gets high marks for thrills, and as a perk it also offers fantastic views of the area. Warning: you will get wet on this ride! If just sitting on an amusement ride isn't enough, try Ramses: Il Risveglio where you can partake in a dramatic battle as you zoom along. Gardaland does themed areas exceptionally well, and in 2018, they will open a new section where the littlest ones can join Peppa, George and their friends on three new rides in Peppa Pig land. Be sure to catch a show while you are here; you'll have a good variety to choose from so you're sure to find something to suit your children's ages and tastes. 🕐 Gardaland Park, Via Derna 4, Castelnuovo del Garda, www.Gardaland.it. Open early April—mid-June, daily, 10:00—17:00; mid-June—mid-September, daily, 10:00—23:00; Opening times vary yearly, consult the website first. Gardaland Sea Life, open mid-April—late September, daily, 10:00-18:00.

Canevaworld is sometimes overshadowed by Gardaland, but it is a great park that offers enough of its own attractions to merit a visit. It too has two sections: the **Aquapark (waterpark)**, which is a great way for families to cool down without slowing down, and **Movieland** which has stars actors and stunt men and a variety of rides with Hollywood blockbuster themes from Route 66 to dinosaurs. Fittingly enough, you can also watch a show here, and they offer something for all tastes from vintage musicals to wild west to action. Canevaworld is also home to the famous Medieval Times Dinner (see box), which is an unforgettable delight for the family. 🕐 Canevaworld AcquaPark & Movieland, Via Fossalta 58, Lazise. www.canevaworld.it. Open June–mid-September, 19:00–18:00. July & August, open until 19:00.

Medieval Times Dinner!

This is one dinner time battle parents and children will actually enjoy. Eat medieval style without cutlery in a fantastic castle while you watch knights in armor joust and sword fight. And cheer on your table's knight as he battles to win the hand of the princess. The show is in Italian, but even without speaking the language, the kids will get the gist of what is going on. The menu itself is very child-friendly, and advance booking is essential for this massively popular event: www.medievaltimes.it. Little ones less than a meter tall are admitted for free, and there are two seating times–19:30 and 21:30. If you a prefer some Rock'n'Roll over medieval knights, try the **Rock Star Café** (think a family-friendly version of the Hard Rock Café). They are open from June to September, and the buffet with live music will appeal to tweens and teens. Advance booking required: www.rockstarcafe.it.

Parco Natura Viva Safari

Getting there & parking: From Peschiera del Garda, take the SR450 (20 minutes). Watch out for the small brown signs leading to the zoo and safari. There's a parking lot for guests.

Italy is not the most obvious destination for a safari, but if you are willing to settle for a small one, you can see 250 species of animals from around the world at this 49-hectare park. Located in the southern lake area near the town of Bussolengo, it is a short drive from Gardaland and Canevaworld. Like both of those attractions, this popular park is divided into two parts: First drive (in your own rental car) through the **Safari Park** and then walk through the **Fauna Park (zoo)** to see animals from the various continents in their reconstructed habitats. In addition to the lions, tigers and bears, your little monkeys can swing around the playground and enjoy feeding time at the restaurant. You can download a map from the park's website at www.parconaturaviva.it to preview the layout and plan to see everyone's favorite animals. 🕐 Parco Natura Viva, Località Quercia, Bussolengo (marked on some maps as: Strada provinciale 27, Pastrengo). Safari: Open daily, 9:30—16:30 (Sunday until 17:00). Zoo: Monday—Thursday, 9:30—18:30; Friday—Saturday 9:00—21:00; Sunday, 9:00—19:30. In high season (weekends only), the staff organize cool nocturnal visits of the zoo, which must be booked in advance.

Lazise

Getting there & parking: Drive along the SR249 to Lazise's centro storico. Set your GPS to the large parking lot on Via Gardesana, near the supermarket, and from there proceed by foot (two minutes) along Via Cansignorio to the lakefront promenade.

Travelers who are looking for a picturesque lake shore village with fewer tourists will enjoy Lazise. Because it is so close to Sirmione, it is often overlooked by visitors. And while it does not offer quite as much as Sirmione or Malcesine, it has a pretty promenade by the lake and Piazza Vittorio Emanuele is delightful. Plus, one of our favorite ice cream shops on the lake is here—**La Cremeria di Lazise** (Via Fontana 8, two minutes from the Scaliger fortress).

Lazise is ideal for a few hours of tranquility—teenagers will appreciate the shops and fun vibe, and the younger children will have fun at **Play Village** on the outskirts of town, which has bouncy castles, a playground, mini-golf and go karts. This town is also a good spot for dinner, especially in one of the lakefront restaurants. ◎ Lazise Play Village, via Pra del Principe 3. Open in season. Cell: 347.610.6062 , www.playvillagelazise.it.

Bardolino

Getting there & parking: From Lazise, continue north along the SR249. The closest lot to the town center is on Piazzale Gramsci. If that is full, there's a very large lot on Via Peschiera (immediately after Hotel Vela d'Oro), which is attached to a small park, with a play area for kids. Further down that same road you will also find the popular Palafitte beach (see below).

Bardolino will sound familiar to wine enthusiasts because of the ruby-red Bardolino DOC wine made here from Corvina and Rondinella grapes. This is a wonderful spot to stop in the afternoon. When it is very hot, you can escape the sun in the small wine museum or the olive oil museum; older children might be intrigued by the machinery and processes of making wine and olive oil, even if the products don't interest them. ◎ **Wine Museum,** Via Costabella 9, Bardolino. www.zeni.it / www.museodelvino.it. Open year round, late March—late September, 9:00—13:00 & 14:30—19:00. Off season the museum opens & closes half an hour earlier. **Olive Oil Museum,** Via Peschiera 54 Cisano, Bardolino (down the street from the wine museum). Tel: 045.6229.047. Open Monday—Friday, 14:30—19:00; Weekends open 9:00—12:30.

Bardolino's position on the lake and its harbor full of white boats make it an exquisite place to relax, enjoy a good meal with a view, and then stretch your legs with a walk along the port's promenade as the sun slides down the horizon. For the best views and delicious alcoholic and non-alcoholic cocktails, visit the vibrant **Palafitte Lounge Bar** (Lungolago Palafitte, www.palafittebeach.com); they often organize live music shows and parties in the summer, check their website for the monthly program and to see which events are suitable for teenagers, too.

> **Tip:** Even in glorious sunny Italy, summer showers can dampen the fun. If you are looking for shelter from the rain, visit the small **Sisan Ornithology Museum** (Via Federico Marzan 24, Cisano di Bardolino. Tel: 045.2377.935, www.sisan.it/museolagodigarda). This wouldn't be on our list of top recommendations, but as a pitstop, it can be fun for younger children.

Parco delle Cascate di Molina

Getting there & parking: From Bardolino, take the winding SP31 road up the mountain, pass the vineyards of Fumane (where Italy's famous Valpolicella and Amarone wines are made) and continue all the way to the town of Molina (50 minutes from the lake). Marked on Google Maps as: 'Waterfall Park'.

This region isn't all manicured lakeside towns and ancient Scaliger fortresses. Lake Garda also includes plenty of chances to get out in nature. If that appeals to your family, you'll love hiking through Parco delle Cascate di Molina to see the waterfalls. You can get a map there, and take the short hike down the path to discover small waterfalls and pools, ziplines and even a swing that swings right into the waterfall.

Come prepared for slippery trails and lots of water! Parco delle Cascate di Molina offers a few hours of fantastic fun for active families with older children, but it is a non-runner for babies in strollers and toddlers. Families with younger children might prefer the smaller and more accessible *Grotte di Varone* Park near Riva del Garda, which is described later in this chapter and requires almost no hiking to reach its (much smaller) waterfall. ☻ Parco delle Cascate di Molina—Waterfall Park, Località Vaccarole, Molina, Fumane. Tel: 045.772.0185, www.parcodellecascate.it. Open April—September, 9:00—19:30 (last entry at 17:30). May close down even in high season in case of bad weather; October open daily 10:00—18:00; November—March, open on Sundays and holidays only. Children under 6 enter for free.

Punta San Vigilio

Getting there & parking: Set your GPS to San Vigilio Lat. Nord 45°34'25.77" Long. Est 10°40'22.38".

This exceptionally scenic bay is where you will find one of the loveliest beaches in Lake Garda—the **Parco Baia delle Sirene** (www.parcobaiadellesirene.it; See the list of best beaches in Lake Garda at the end of this itinerary for the others.) Leave your car at the parking lot, and continue along the cypress-lined road to the beautiful 16th century Renaissance villa surrounded by olive and lemon trees. Winston Churchill found solace and refuge here after WWII. Walking along this secluded path, you will find your own peace, too. Bring a picnic, uncork a bottle of wine and let the gentle breezes blow your cares away.

Torri del Benaco

Getting there & parking: Continue along the SR249. Set your GPS to the large parking lot at the entry to town, on Via Gabriele d'Annunzio.

This cute little town features a small Scaliger fortress, a pleasant central street filled with shops, and a low-key ambiance. The della Scala family built the Scaliger fortress in 1383 on the ruins of an even earlier medieval castle, which dated back to the 10th century. The small museum inside it can be skipped, or you can stop by for a quick visit to see the antique fishing equipment, tools and olive press. Climbing up to the battlements to take in the views is the literal and figurative high point of Torri del Benaco. ⊕ Museo del Castello Scaligero, Viale Fratelli Lavanda 2, Torri del Benaco. www.museodelcastellodiTorridelbenaco.it. Open daily in season, 9:30—13:00 & 16:30—19:30 (hours may vary off season). Children under 14 pay just 1 euro, family tickets are available.

> **Tip:** Halfway between Torri del Benaco and Malcesine, in the town of Assenza, there's a fun beach restaurant and bar called Bar Lido di Assenza. The food is tasty, the view is beautiful, the ambiance is laid-back, and in the summertime they often organize live music shows in the evening. In short—this is a place your teenagers might like. Call in advance to learn more about their monthly program: 045.7402 0050. Via Gardesana 24, Assenza.

Malcesine

Getting there & parking: From Torri del Benaco, continue driving up north along the SR249 (45 minutes). Finding parking in Malcesine can be challenging. One option is to park at the Funivia (cable car) parking lot, at Via Navene Vecchia 12, Malcesine. If you can't find a free space (which often happens), try the centrally located lot in Piazza Statuto (right off Corso Garibaldi). It's often full, too, but the turnover is quick, so don't despair. Note that there's a small **playground** attached to the end of the Satuto parking lot.

Tourist Office: Via Gardesana 238. Open daily mid-March—November. Tel: 045.740.0044.

Romantic and picturesque with charming cobblestone streets, Malcesine is a must-see for any visitor to Lake Garda. The historical center is tiny, and you can take in the sights and tour the boutiques and souvenir shops in a couple of hours. Malcesine has long had a focus on commerce—the **Palazzo dei Capitani** on Via Portici Umberto once housed the offices of Malcesine's medieval customs officer known as the 'captain of the lake' who collected duties from arriving boats. This structure, like many in the area, was built by the Scaliger family between the 13th and 14th centuries as a residence for their governors. Today it is the City Hall, and the interior is decorated with pretty frescos. It also features an enchanting terrace garden bursting with fragrant flowers and tall trees that dance in the wind, which makes it a popular stop for tourists, too.

Next, visit the famous **Malcesine Scaliger Castle** perched at a strategic point high up above the lake. The Scaliger family built this one (on the ruins of an earlier 5th century fort built by the Logonards) during their expansion mission across the Verona territory, before they were defeated by the Viscontis of Milan. If you could only visit one Scaliger castle on Lake Garda, this would probably be the best one to pick. The views of the lake and whole region from the top of the ramparts and the tower are worth every step of the climb up. You can also tour the frescoed halls, and enjoy the beauty that inspired the German poet Goethe to sketch pictures during his visit to this castle in the late 18th century. If you feel inspired to do the same, you can relax knowing that unlike Goethe, you will not be arrested for spying ... Today you can even visit the old guard rooms and see the castle's collection of arms. The fortress includes two minuscule museums—one featuring historical artifacts, and another dedicated to the local flora and fauna. ☺ Scaliger Castle, Piazza Castello 1, Malcesine. Open daily in season, 9:30—18:00.

> **Tip:** If you want to visit both the fortress and the Monte Baldo Funivia (Malcesine's famous cable car), you can buy a combined ticket to both at the castle. The financial savings are not significant, but avoiding having to stand in line to buy a ticket at the funivia is priceless.

End your tour of Malcesine on a high note, specifically—on the top of Monte Baldo. The **Malcesine Monte Baldo Funivia** (cable car) will take you 1,800 meters up the mountain, and from there you can enjoy dazzling views. Many visitors think that is enough, but if you want more of Monte Baldo you can take a short hike to the Prá Alpesina Chair Lift and ride it over glorious green meadows to a higher point on the mountain ridge. The chair lift (unlike the funivia) only operates from early May until mid-September, depending on weather conditions. You can find more details on their website. ✆ Funivia Monte Baldo, Via Navene Vecchia 12, Malcesine. Tel: 045.740.0206, www.funiviedelbaldo.it. Open late March—early November, daily, 8:00—18:15 (until 16:00 September through November). A ride leaves every 30 minutes, circa.

Riva del Garda

Getting there & parking: From Malcesine, continue north along the SR249 (45 minutes). Set your GPS to Piazzale Lido and park at the large lot there, near Palazzo dei Congressi. Continue by foot along the promenade.

Riva del Garda can't boast of a major tourist attraction, but it has a lovely promenade and is one of the main towns in the region for watersport activities (the best operators are listed at the end of this itinerary). The landscape is wilder and more dramatic here than in many of the villages in the southern parts of the lake, with mighty grey cliffs that frame the sapphire blue water and tiny villages that cling to the rocks at impossible angles. The dramatic views attracted and inspired tortured writers Frantz Kafka and Thomas Mann, and it is easy to see why. Mann was so enthralled with Riva that he visited no fewer than 20 times!

The main square, Piazza III Novembre, and the streets leading off it feature too many delightful pizzerias and cafes to list them all, and if you are in good shape and have the extra time, hike to the Bastione, a 15th century guard tower high above Riva del Garda. The path, which is off Via Monte Oro, is shady and well-marked, but might be hard for younger children. The Bastione was a strategic watchtower, so it is up high enough to provide a good view of the neighboring town just in case any trouble was brewing there.

Lake Garda

You can also enjoy some of attractions outside Riva itself: **Reptiland** is a small museum dedicated to reptiles where you can see a Burmese python and other scary snakes, a giant tarantula, arachnids and insects. If the creatures don't appeal to you, the fact that children under 8 enter for free might. ◯ Reptiland, Piazza Garibaldi 2, Riva del Garda. Open year round, 11:00—20:00 (hours vary off season, call in advance). Tel: 348-7948389. www.reptiland.it.

The popular **Parco Grotta Cascata Varone,** a more toddler-friendly alternative to the Cascate di Molina (reviewed earlier in this itinerary), is immediately outside of Riva del Garda (10 minutes by car). Follow the 150 meter path into this 20,000-year-old canyon's upper and lower caves passing many small waterfalls fed by Lake Tenno. Make sure to wear shoes with good traction as it can be slippery, and you will definitely get wet. It's a great choice for a hot day because part of it is inside the caves, it's wet and even outside you will get some shade from the lush forest around the caves. While you are there, you can also relax in the park and botanic gardens with a picnic. This is an easy but exciting visit for toddlers, but older kids will probably crave more. ◯ Parco Grotta Cascate del Varone, Tel: 0464.521421, www.cascata-varone.com. Open May—August, 09:00—19:00. Off season (March, April, September-November, closes one hour/two hours earlier).

Additionally, the **Busatte Adventure Park** in nearby Torbole (see our full recommendation under 'Special Activities in the Area' at the end of this itinerary) and the beautiful **Lake Tenno** are both just a short drive away.

Limone sul Garda

Getting there & parking: From Riva del Garda start driving down south, towards Limone, along the SS45BIS. Sadly, this road isn't as scenic as the SR249, because entire sections of it are covered by tunnels. Try to find parking near the Limonaia (this village's main attraction, at Via Orti 17) and if you can't, park at the Parcheggio Multipiano, Via Lungolago Guglielmo Marconi 50, Limone sul Garda.

Whoever thought life giving you lemons was a bad thing has never been to **Limone Sul Garda**. Yes, 'limone' is Italian for lemon, and this town is famous for them. Lemon groves were introduced to Lake Garda more than 800 years ago, and were initially regarded as ornamental plants. Large terraced greenhouses were built to protect the trees from the harsh weather conditions in the winter, and a successful export business was born, bringing lemons to the homes of the rich and noble across Europe. Today what remains is mostly the stories. Limone sul Garda is also famous for longevity—residents here have such a long lifespan that scientists have studied them and discovered a specific protein in their blood which might explain this phenomenon. Today, despite the lack of any specific attractions, tourism drives the town's economy; it's simply a beautiful spot to enjoy.

Terrazza del Brivido—the Panoramic Terrace

Getting there & parking: To reach the famous terrace (at the Hotel Paradiso), drive From Limone sul Garda south along the SS45BIS in the direction of Tremosine. Note that there's a series of tunnels along the road and then suddenly a turn right to Tremosine. Use your GPS and slow down as you get near the turn or you'll miss it. Park at the hotel's lot, meant for guests.

The **Terrazza del Brivido,** aka Shivers Terrace, is a fun little detour. The terrace hangs over the lake, making it both chilly and a bit scary, hence the name. Even the drive up the narrow road is a bit of a white-knuckle experience! It's not suitable for anyone with vertigo, but for everyone else—it's a great stop for a coffee break and snack. The terrace is in the

Hotel Paradiso, which hasn't seen much change in the last 50 years, so we probably wouldn't recommend it for a full meal; the lake views are the main draw here. 🕐 Terrazza del Brivido, Viale Europa 1, Tremosine. Tel: 335.5448156 / 0365.953.012, www.terrazzadelbrivido.it. The hotel & terrace are open from early March—end of November. Closed off-season.

Gardone Riviera

Getting there & parking: From Limone sul Garda, head south along the SS45bis (35 minutes). Parking is problematic in Gardone Riviera. There are seven small public lots around town, but even there space is limited, and some apply time restrictions, too. Your best option is Parcheggio Agli Ulivi, on Via Vittoriale, which is located near the main entrance to the Vittoriale (Gardone's main tourist attraction). It's very large, and you can leave your car there for a few hours if you want to visit the town center, too.

Tourist Office: Corso della Repubblica 1, Gardone Riviera. Tel: 030.3748.736. Open in season.

Gardone Riviera was founded in 1879 as a lakefront resort town for the rich and weary, who came by the hundreds to this popular and chic vacation site. Two big attractions make Gardone a beautiful stop on the western shore of lake Garda: The extravagant **Il Vittoriale** estate, which was the residence of writer and poet Gabriele d'Annunzio, and the privately-owned postcard-pretty **Heller Botanical Garden**, featuring plants from around the world.

Il Vittoriale

Il Vittoriale is a unique spot, to say the least. Roughly translated into English as the 'Shrine of Italian Victories', this intriguing and eccentric estate was where the influential, controversial and possibly insane fascist poet Gabriele D'Annunzio resided until his death.

One of the best-known writers in Italy, D'Annunzio fostered intense relations with some of the leading artists and actors of his time, not least countess, fashionista and actress Eleonora Duse. At the height of his power he devoted himself mainly to his image, residing in dramatic mansions, holding grand parties, and employing a large number of servants. When his finances couldn't keep pace with his lifestyle, he hid from his creditors in France, where he dived into the bohemian art world and collaborated with Debussy. He eventually returned to Italy where he collaborated with Puccini, and wrote for the newspaper Corriere della Sera. He also visited the battlefields of World War I, which inspired him to join the army. But instead of the usual approach to enlisting, he wrote a letter to the prime minister threatening to kill himself if his application was denied. Unhappy with the post-war peace agreement, D'Annunzio decided to conquer the Croatian town of Fiume himself. He then declared himself governor, but he was eventually forced to return to Italy and settled in Garda, where he remained until his death in 1938, angry at the state that had sidelined him.

The original villa in the complex was built by German art historian Ernst Thode. When D'Annunzio acquired the property in 1921, he launched an elaborate reconstruction, and today you can visit and see D'Annunzio's antique cars, the mausoleum, the boat he used to sail to Croatia, and numerous artistic artifacts. The Villa's gardens are beautiful, as is the impressive amphitheater overlooking the lake. (Concerts are held here regularly in the summer; check the Vittoriale website for details.) 🕐 Fondazione Il Vittoriale degli Italiani, Via del Vittoriale 12, Gardone Riviera. Tel: 0365.296.511, www.vittoriale.it. Open from the last Sunday in March to the last Saturday in October, Tuesday—Sunday, 9:00—19:00; From the last Sunday in October to the last Saturday in March, Tuesday—Sunday, 9:00—16:00. Closed on Mondays throughout the year. The priory can only be visited with a guided tour (included in the price of the ticket).

After that intriguing madness, you can rebalance in the delightfully poetic botanical garden **Giardino Heller**. It boasts plants from around the world, selected by a passionately devoted owner, Austrian artist Andre Heller. The entire garden is a work of art featuring nature's best flora mingling

Lake Garda

with fountains, statues and other human creations. 🕒 Heller Garden, Fondazione Andrè Heller Via Roma 2, Gardone Riviera. Cell: 336.410.877, www.hellergarden.com. Open March—October, daily, 9:00—19:00.

Salò

Getting there & parking: Continue south from Gardone along the SS45bis. There are a number of parking lots in town. The largest one is on Piazzale Martiri della Libertà, right next to the Italmark supermarket, 300 meters from the town center. Alternatively, try the lot on Via Landi, which is just located on the other side of town (a few minutes by foot from the Duomo).

Tourist Office: Piazza Sant'Antonio, Salò. Tel: 030.3748.745. Open in season.

When the Romans built this town, they called it Salodium. It became an important trade center, and in medieval times Beatrice della Scala, wife of Count Bernardo Visconti, moved her court here. During the 15th- 18th centuries, the town was part of the Venetian Republic, and a column with Venice's symbol, a winged lion, still stands on Salò's main square. The town was the seat of government of Benito Mussolini's Nazi-backed puppet state, the Italian Social Republic (also known as the Republic of Salò) from 1943 to 1945. Many of the official state buildings from that period still stand today.

Salò's 15th century Duomo (dedicated to Santa Maria Annunziata and built in Gothic style) is worth a quick visit before you head to the town's three-kilometer long promenade and take in the gorgeous views. The fun is never quite complete without some *gelato*—try **Gelateria Blu Garda** on Lungolago Zanardelli 26; the kids will love the Smurf blue ice cream there.

Best Family-Friendly Beaches in Garda

Adventure parks and beautiful villages aside, some downtime lounging on the beach is part of what will make your vacation here memorable. You need to know two key things to really enjoy the shores of Lake Garda. First, most of the beaches are gravel, not sand. Second, some sections are not safe for swimming. If you want to swim, chose a regulated beach. If you'd like to organize a picnic, too, consult the special box at the end of this itinerary listing the best lakeside spots for a picnic.

So where are the best beaches on Lake Garda? Here are our top picks:

1. **Lido delle Bionde** next to the famous Grotte di Catullo in **Sirmione** offers wild charm in easy walking distance. (Just follow the signs to the Grotte and the lido.) This is a great evening stop because you can enjoy a pleasant dinner at the Ristorante Pizzeria Lido delle Bionde. (Nearby **Jamaica Beach** is also quite beautiful and famous, but less suitable for families.)

2. **Lido Galeazzi** (Via Lucchino 6, Sirmione) is quite good for sports lovers. You can rent canoes, paddle boats and windsurfing gear, and there's a volleyball court. Find out more at www.spiaggiagaleazziSirmione.com.

3. **Spiaggia Brema** (Via Buozzi, Sirmione) is a quieter option that's also near Sirmione. It offers a big lawn, nice water, and reasonable prices, making it an ideal choice for families with small kids who need to run and splash on a budget.

4. **Baia delle Sirene** is a wonderful spot that's easy to find (set your GPS to Locanda San Vigilio, or Via Vigilio 17, Garda). Because it has so much to do, including a playground and a little wading pool for toddlers, you'll find it is very popular.

5. **Lido di Manerba sul Garda** is a quieter beach where you can soak up the natural beauty in tranquility away from the crowds. The nearby **Baia del Vento** offers a similar serenity.

6. **Baia Bianca**, near Lido di Manerba, is better suited for teenagers because of its organized events and chic restaurant: www.baiabianca.it. An evening and meal here will give the teens serious bragging rights when they get home; just check the program first to make sure it's suitable for your family.

7. **Mokai Beach** (Via Tavine, Salò) also has a young, laid-back vibe that teenagers will enjoy.

8. **Spiaggia Sabbioni** (Via Filzi 2, Riva del Garda) is an easy-to-reach, quintessential Lake Garda beach with dazzling views and some grassy lawns.

9. **Spiaggia Tifù** (Via 4 Novembre 2, Limone Sul Garda) is a great spot for either a quick stop or an afternoon of lounging. Views, some greenery and a space to play make it nice for families.

10. **Spiaggia Feltrinelli** (Lungolago Cesare Battisti, near Hotel Riviera, Desenzano del Garda) offers all the necessary amenities for kids. Plus, once you've dried off, you can make a stop at the small but entertaining amusement park, which is open in season every evening after 20:00. (Luna Park Desenzano, Località Monte Mario, Desenzano del Garda.)

Eating in Lake Garda

LIMONE SUL GARDA

Ristorante AL Tamas: You have to book in advance and drive up the mountain, but you'll be rewarded with amazing views and delicious pasta and fish dishes. Make sure you book a table on the terrace that overlooks the lake, and not outside, in the front section by the road. Via Alessandro Volta 86, Limone Sul Garda. Tel: 0365.954.298. Open March—late September, Tuesday—Sunday, 12:00—14:00 & 18:00—22:00. Closed Mondays. Closed off-season.

Al Vecchio Fontec: Enjoy an excellent selection of fish and pasta in a lovely courtyard with a fun atmosphere. Via della Corda 21, Limone sul Garda. Tel: 0365. 954.185. Open Friday—Wednesday, open for lunch and dinner.

Il Chiosco: A great place for a drink and a snack, with stunning views and a relaxing setting. Via Campaldo 7, Limone sul Garda. Open daily in season, 10:00—23:00.

GARDONE RIVIERA

Ristorante Emiliano's: This cozy pizza and pasta place offers tasty dishes and generous portions for reasonable prices near the lakeshore. Corso della Repubblica 57, Gardone Riviera. Tel: 0365.21517. Open Wednesday—Monday, 12:00—14:30 & 18:30—22:00. Closed Tuesday.

SIRMIONE

Il Girasole: This is a solid choice for families right in the historic town center. The selection of dishes caters to younger palates, too, and it's great for a between-sights meal. Via Vittorio Emanuele 72, Sirmione. Tel: 030.9191.82, www.ilgirasole.info. Open: March—late-October, open daily, 12:00—15:00 & 18:30—22:30.

Trattoria Clementina: Named for the family matriarch, this is like dining at your Italian grandmother's—generous platters of antipasti, braised beef with polenta and gorgonzola gnocchi made with local ingredients are worth the trip out of Sirmione itself. Piazza Rovizzi 13, Rovizza (between Sirmione and Lugana). Tel: 030.919.6663. Open Wednesday—Monday for dinner only, 19:00—22:00. Closed Tuesdays. In high season may open for lunch too on some days—call in advance.

BUSSOLENGO

Il Giardino dei Sapori: You won't regret stopping here after you visit the Parco Natura Viva (see itinerary) for some tasty basics, and the kids can run around the nearby playground if they have any energy left. Localita' Crocioni di Bussolengo 43, 37012, Bussolengo. Tel: 045.670.4615, www.giardinodeisapori.com. Open daily (in season) 12:00—14.00 & 19:00—22:00.

PESCHIERA DEL GARDA

Sapori in Cantina: Serious chefs at a family-run agriturismo with wine tastings make for a culinary symphony with everything perfectly tuned. If you love good food, this is the place for you. Via Strada Berra 4, Peschiera del Garda. Tel: 045.755.0949 / 349.420.4727, www.saporiincantina.com. The restaurant is open daily (in season), 12:00—14:30. The wine cellar is open daily, 9:00—18:00.

BARDOLINO

Relax: Perfectly named, this chilled out, waterfront restaurant offers tasty, hearty fare and welcomes children. They also serve exceptionally good mojitos. Via Passeggiata Rivalunga, Bardolino. Cell: 340 069 9280, www.facebook.com/pg/relaxbardolino

MALCESINE

Treccani Ristorante Pizzeria: This family restaurant offers a good balance of price, quality and location. Via Domenico Turazza 8, Malcesine. Tel: 045.657.0431, www.ristorantetreccani.it. Open daily in season, 10:30—midnight.

Hotel Ristorante Alpino: If you find yourselves hungry outside regular lunch hours, this is the place to go for a vast selection of sandwiches and pizzas. Piazza Statuto 23, Malcesine. www.hotelalpinomalcesine.com.

Ristorante Al Gondoliere: This is a fine dining experience that will appeal more to foodies than to young children, but their homemade pasta is outstanding. Piazza V. Emanuele 6, Malcesine. Open April—late October, Wednesday—Monday, 12:00—14:00 & 18:00—22:00. Tuesday open for dinner only. Reservations are highly recommended. Tel: 045.740.0046, www.algondoliere.com.

Ristorante Paradiso Perduto: At the foot of the stunning Scaliger Castle sits this upscale restaurant offering wonderfully regal meals. For a special night out in Malcesine—this is the place to go. Booking a table in advance is highly recommended. Via Castello 17, Malcesine. Tel: 045.657.0902. Open March—November, daily, 12:00—15:00 & 18:30—22:00.

SALÒ

Pizzeria LungoLago64: Salò's three-kilometer-long promenade is a favorite with families, and this tasty pizza place right on promenade is hard to resist. Via Lungolago Zanardelli 64. Tel: 0365 290030 www.pizzerialungolago64.it. Open Thursday—Tuesday, 12:00—14:30 & 18:30—23:30. Wednesday closed.

RIVA DEL GARDA

Pizzeria Leon d'Oro: The whole family will enjoy the homey atmosphere and generous portions of classic local dishes. Via Fiume 28, Riva del Garda. Tel: 0464 552341, www.leondororiva.it/ristorante. Open late March—November, daily, 12:00—15:00 & 18:00—23:00.

> ## Where to Picnic
>
> With all this scenic beauty, you might prefer a picnic even to the best, most child and budget friendly restaurant on occasion. Here are our favorite places to unpack our picnic basket:
>
> **Parco del Laghetto in Via Giotto, Desenzano del Garda,** at the southern part of the lake, has lots of grass, a picnic area and a playground for kids.
>
> **Parco Grotta Cascata Varone** offers an section near the entrance with benches and wooden tables for your picnicking pleasure.
>
> **Busatte Adventure Park in Torbole** at the northern part of the lake, near Riva del Garda, also has a nice picnic spot.
>
> **Passeggio della Pua** is a little picnic area with benches in Cisano di Bardolino, along the promenade.
>
> **Lido Campanello in Castelnuovo del Garda** (Località' Campanello) offers a picnic area and a small playground.
>
> **Spiaggia Cola on Via Lungolago Marconi, Limone del Garda** (next to Spiaggia Tiffu') has picnic tables and you can also rent a paddle boat.

Sleeping in Lake Garda

For families, Lake Garda offers endless options for accommodation to suit every style, budget and family size. You really are spoiled for choice with an assortment of camping sites, apartments, villas, B&Bs and hotels. **Before you choose, here are a few general tips to keep in mind:**

1. If you plan on doing some sightseeing, it's best to choose a location within a short drive from the main roads, and not an *agriturismo* deep in the countryside, so you don't spend precious time travelling the same stretch of road daily.

2. Just because you want to visit Sirmione, Malcesine and Gardaland doesn't necessarily mean you have to sleep there, too. You can save a substantial sum by staying in one of the lesser known towns by the lake. Check Google Maps to get a sense of the location first, and whether it's on the beach or in one of the villages in the hills.

3. Many families with younger children or with special dietary needs prefer to rent an apartment, either through Airbnb or in a residence, because this gives them a kitchen and more room. If you choose an apartment, make sure it has everything you need for daily living. Other families prefer the exact opposite, and book a hotel with full board, so they never have to worry about dinner after a day of sightseeing. On some nights, knowing that all you have to do for dinner is take the elevator down to the bottom floor, will be a huge relief.

4. If you have younger children and prefer a hotel, go for one with amenities such as a playground, kid pool, etc. so you can stay at the hotel if you want, instead of making separate trips to swimming pools, playgrounds, restaurants and the like with cranky toddlers.

5. With teenagers, on the other hand, we would suggest avoiding the family hotels and choosing something chic they'll think much cooler. Find a hotel that organizes special activities, sports or hikes, or one with an impressive pool and spa.

6. If you want to be able to walk from your hotel to the beach (without having to drive there), make sure you choose a hotel in a town that is right on the lake shores (such as Gardone, Toscolano Maderno,

Sirmione and Desenzano) and not in the mountains above the lake (such as Limone, Torbole, and Tremosine). Check the 3D images on Google Earth to get a real sense of where the hotel is located. And remember—while the views from the hill top villages are spectacular, booking a room up in the mountains also means you'll have to drive up there possibly twice a day, and again after dinner, in the dark.

7. We've focused our recommendations in this chapter on the most family-friendly lodging options, but naturally, a web search will yield several more results for every price range. Booking your room through websites such as booking.com and expedia.com can help you save money, but know that in recent years many hotels have started offering special discounts to those who book directly through them. Check each site individually to maximize your savings.

MANERBA DEL GARDA

Agriturismo La Filanda is a great choice for budget-conscious families. These simple but comfortable apartments offer friendly owners, well maintained grounds and a large pool. It's on the western shore of the lake (opposite of Gardaland–a 30-minute drive), and an easy 15-minute walk to the water. Via del Melograno 35, Manerba del Garda. www.agriturismolafilanda.com.

MALCESINE

Hotel Baitone, a bit north of Malcesine, is a family-run hotel with lake or mountain views and air conditioning. If you are renting a car, they have on-site parking. The restaurant has nice views, and the patio is stunning. Via Gardesana 516, Malcesine. www.hotelbaitone.com.

PESCHIERA DEL GARDA

Camping Bella Italia is a classic resort for families. Just a short walk from the lake, it has everything kids want—five pools, water slides, a playground, organized activities for children including a kids' club and evening activities. Parents will appreciate the grocery store, three restaurants on-site (including a pizzeria), free parking and being just 15 minutes by car from Sirmione. This is more like a small town than a resort. You get a map to find your way around the streets with their little houses. The family rooms and bungalows are simple but comfortable. Via Bell'Italia 2, Peschiera del Garda. www.camping-bellaitalia.it.

Camping Village San Francesco is a huge, beachfront resort near Sirmione with amenities such as wifi, an outdoor pool with a bar, tennis court, table tennis and a children's playground. Each of the air-conditioned mobile homes includes its own patio with tables and chairs, kitchenette, and private bathroom. You can also barbeque or eat at the restaurant. Bikes and water sports equipment can be rented on site, and there is a game hall and organized children's activities. Desenzano del Garda, GPS coordinates LAT 45.46565 LONG 10.59443. www.campingsanfrancesco.com.

Albatross Mobile Homes on Camping Bella Italia is a hugely popular resort 250 meters from the lake with lots of children's activities. The clean, modern mobile homes have kitchenettes, bathrooms and patios, and they are set on manicured grounds with swimming pools, a water park, a tennis court, and a restaurant with fantastic views. There's also a mini mart if you'd rather cook by yourself or use the BBQ facilities, and last but not least—it's close to Gardaland and Caneva World. Peschiera del Garda, www.albatrosscamping-bellaitalia.com.

SIRMIONE

Tenuta La Borghetta is an apartment residence on a working vineyard. This is a fantastic choice for those who want peace and quiet. It's not right on the lakefront, and without a playground or children's activities, it draws fewer families with little kids. The gracious hosts offer clean, spacious apartments, a good swimming pool and a delicious breakfast. Just a ten-minute drive from Sirmione, it makes a handy base for exploring the area. Via Borghetta, Sirmione. www.tenutalaborghetta.com.

Residence Nuove Terme offers 16 apartments in a perfect location just a 15-minute stroll from the beach. Run by the extremely knowledgeable and friendly Flavio, it offers good value for the money and an outdoor swimming pool. Via Alfieri 9, Sirmione. www.nuoveterme.com.

Villaggio Turistico Lugana Marina puts you right on the lake without breaking your budget or your heart. All units in this solid choice include kitchenettes, bathrooms, flat screen televisions, and a balcony or patio overlooking the pool or the gardens. Large families might prefer one of their modern bungalows. One of the two swimming pools has a hot tub. It also offers bike rental and a restaurant. Via Verona 127, Sirmione. www.luganamarina.it.

LAZISE

Residence Hotel Palazzo Della Scala is one of our favorites because it manages to be both family-friendly and a bit glamourous with gorgeous views of the lake. It is more high-end, but it's hard to resist the pool surrounded by dazzling white sand or the salt water hot tub. Perfectly positioned in Lazise, it is just a short drive from Gardaland, Canevaworld and Sirmione and a two-minute walk from the beach. You can rent bicycles. Via Gardesana 54, Lazise. www.palazzodellascala.com.

RIVA DEL GARDA

Hotel la Gioiosa is budget-friendly option with family suites less than 20 minutes from the lake. You don't get lake views, but you do get a pool, sauna, mini-golf, easy access to public transportation and excellent rooms. It is very convenient for northern parts of the lake, and even parts of the Dolomites. Via delle Cartiere 70, Riva Del Garda. www.gioiosa.it.

Hotel Campagnola is only 2.5 kilometers from the lake with a huge play area for kids, friendly staff, comfortable family rooms, a large pool, a very good restaurant with an ample selection of gluten-free dishes, and more. Via San Tomaso 11, Riva del Garda. www.hotelcampagnola.com.

Ambassador Suite Hotel is a three-star hotel with rooms, suites and apartments only 200 meters from the beach. It's very family-friendly, and you can get rooms with changing tables and cots. High chairs are available in the dining room, and there's a playground, bouncy castles, a swimming pool and bike rental. Via Longa 16, Riva del Garda. www.ambassadorsuite.it.

Special Events in Lake Garda

Lake Garda offers your family events of all sizes where you can really engage and experience the local culture. From small markets and concerts to lively medieval fairs, you can find opportunities to have fun, learn, and make memories together. The list below includes some of the biggest and best events, and the local tourist offices are a great place to find out what else is happening while you are in the area. The locals are very fond of fireworks shows and live music, and it is quite likely that you will find something happening during your visit. Whenever possible, we've added the specific dates for events. When such dates are unavailable, contact the tourist office in advance to learn more and schedule your visit accordingly.

MAY

Lazise became the first township in Italy in 983 when Emperor Otto II granted it administrative authority. Locals proudly celebrate this every May 7 with a medieval festival and reenactment featuring hundreds of actors.

JUNE

Wine lovers will want to schedule their visit to **Bardolino** for early June to celebrate Palio del Chiaretto, a festival dedicated to this popular local wine. The festival includes plenty for everyone to enjoy even if they don't like wine—live music, rowing competitions, food stands and fireworks.

The town of **Affi** celebrates Anno Domini, one of the largest medieval festivals in the area, in mid-June. Jousters, knights and parades fill the streets, along with live music, shows and flag throwers, as well as a medieval market. Find out more here: www.festamedioevalediaffi.it

In late June, **Desenzano Castle** hosts a small jazz festival. Contact the tourism office for details. www.facebook.com/desenzanojazzfestival

JULY

Malcesine honors its patron saints every July with lively processions, music and a firework show at the Festival of the Patron Saints Benigno and Caro, the two hermit saints who lived in the caves of Mount Baldo in the 8th and 9th centuries.

In mid-July, **Brenzone sul Garda** celebrates the Festa de l'Ondes de Luj. It began as a festival of thanks to the Virgin Mary for saving the population from an outbreak of plague, but has evolved into more. After a religious procession in the morning, locals and visitors enjoy music, dancing and food in the evening.

The town of **Garda** celebrates the **La Sardellata al Pal del Vò**, a culinary festival focused on local fish, in late July with live music at the lakeshore.

AUGUST

The night of August 10th is magical throughout Italy as communities celebrate 'the night of the falling stars', AKA—the *Festa di San Lorenzo*. **Peschiera del Garda** organizes one of the best celebrations, with a real show involving most of the town's people.

August 15th is a national holiday in Italy, and the neighborhoods in **Garda** face off at the *Palio delle Contrade*, a rowing competition. Don't leave too early because the fun begins after dark, when the entire lake celebrates the *Notte d'Incanto* with thousands of lights around the lake and fireworks.

La Notte di Fiaba, on the last weekend of August in **Riva del Garda**, is one of the most popular festivals in the area featuring artists, vendors, show and music, and a magical firework show over the lake. Find out more here: www.nottedifiaba.it

On the last week of August, **Peschiera** hosts the *Palio delle Mura*, a big rowing competition followed by a night of live music and fireworks. www.remierapeschiera.it.

In the town of **Gardone Riviera**, the Vittoriale hosts concerts by Italian and international artists all summer long: www.anfiteatrodelvittoriale.it.

SEPTEMBER

The most exciting boat race held on Lake Garda, the *Centomiglia* (which means 100 miles) starts in **Gargnano** in early September. World class sailors compete in yachts, sailboats and all sorts of pleasure boats. www.centomiglia.it.

Autumn is time for harvest festivals, and one of the best is the **Festa dell'Uva e del Vino Bardolino**, which has been going on for nearly 90 years. What better way to celebrate the grape harvest than to raise a glass of wine on the shores of Lake Garda?

Torri del Benaco has its *Carnevale Settembrino* to celebrate local heritage with folk dancing, medieval costumes, live music, food, fireworks and more.

WEEKLY MARKETS

All around the lake, towns and villages hold regular weekly markets for the locals, not tourists, which means they are more practical than quaint. Monday: Torri del Benaco and Peschiera; Tuesday: Castelletto di Brenzone; Wednesday: Lazise; Thursday: Bardolino; Friday: Garda; Saturday: Malcesine. This is a good place to find tablecloths, homeware, etc.

Special Activities in Lake Garda

A big part of Lake Garda's appeal to families is the great variety of activities. You can find fun things to do outdoors for every age, taste, and fitness level. From sailing and pedal boats to go karts and adventure parks, here are some of the best.

BOAT RENTAL

The lake is the center of everything here, and exploring it by boat can be relaxing or adrenaline-charged, depending on how you do it. **Renting a speed boat** is easy as you do not need a license, and it is more affordable than you might think. You are usually charged separately for fuel, and you must leave your ID with the operator for safety reasons. If you prefer not to drive you can go on a **guided boat tour**; there are several options available throughout the lake, many of which have immediate openings (especially in Sirmione and Malcesine). Touring with a guide will give you the chance to relax, and learn more about the lake. Companies offering both options are usually near the dock or the promenade of Sirmione, Malcesine, Brenzone sul Garda and Riva del Garda. You can take your chances and see what's available when you arrive, or you can book in advance to be safe. In **Sirmione**, try the popular **Sirmione Boats** (www.sirmioneboats.it); **La Barca di Salvo**, is another good option, and Salvo offers both private rentals and mini cruises (www.labarcadisalvo.com). **Bertoldi boats** is another good choice, and they offer private rentals and tours (www.bertoldiboats.com).

In **Lazise**, **Olimpia Boats** offer both speed boats and guided tours (www.reshot-olimpia.it); **Garda Charter** offers an identical service (www.gardacharter.it). In **Brenzone**, try **Nauticuore** (www.nauticuore.com) and **GoSail** (www.go-sail.it). In **Peschiera del Garda**, where all the family hotels are located, you will find the popular **Peschiera Boat Rent**: www.peschieraboatrent.com. In **Desenzano del Garda**, near Peschiera, you will find **Garda Boat Rent**, and they also offer jet ski experiences: www.gardaboatrent.com.

RENT A KAYAK

Another great option for families is renting a kayak—this experience is both easy and fun! Try the activities organized by Canoa Club in **Riva del Garda**: www.canoaclubriva.it

WATER PARKS

There's a lot of fun to be had on the water, but if the children want a serious waterpark, then a waterpark they shall get! **Canevaworld** (see the detailed recommendation in the itinerary) is the biggest and best, so it is a must for families with children age eight and up. For younger children, on the other hand, especially toddlers, such a venue might be too much of a good thing. They can't go on many of the rides, and the crowds and noise can be overwhelming. Smaller parks may be a better choice for younger children, exactly for the reasons that make them less appealing to older kids.

Ninfee Park is a small park on the right scale for toddlers and preschoolers to enjoy. They have a couple of pools, some little waterslides, a play area with bouncy castles and plenty of grassy areas to just sit and chill out. Via del Pilandro, Desenzano del Garda. www.leninfeedelgarda.it

Riovalli Parco Acquatico has a children's lagoon, pools, slides and a picnic area. It is in the town of Affi, near the Grande Mela shopping mall. Località Fosse, Cavaion Veronese. www.riovalli.it

Cavour Water Park is a great place to stop for a fun break if you are driving from the lake to Verona and Valeggio del Mincio. Loc. Ariano, Valeggio sul Mincio. For more details, see the Verona chapter. www.parcoacquaticocavour.it.

ADVENTURE PARKS

Waterparks and beaches aside, there is plenty of adventure to be had on dry land, too! Lake Garda has some excellent adventure parks for active kids who like a challenge, particularly kids who are eight or over, because they can enjoy most of the activities. Younger children are not allowed to do as much, and while some parks offer a special section for the youngest thrill seekers, others do not. Before arriving with small children, check the website to make sure the park in question is a good fit for your family.

Lake Garda

Rimbalzello Adventure Park near the town of **Salò** boasts five different action-packed routes where you will negotiate Tibetan bridges, nets and ziplines. You can also choose some action on the lake such as scuba diving, canoeing or pedaling a boat. Between adventures, you can catch your breath at the picnic area or beach. The park is open daily in June, July and August; weekends only in April, May, September and October. Via Trento, Barbarano. Cell: 331.843.8869, www.rimbalzelloadventure.com.

Le Busatte Adventure Park near **Torbole** will delight your family's daredevils because in addition to the rope bridges and playground, they have a BMX park where kids age five and up can learn bike tricks. The park is open mid-June to late-September, daily, 11:00—19:00; April, May and October, open on most weekends, 11:00—18:00 (always call first). Tel: 347.3880570, www.busatteadventure.it.

Park Jungle Adventure, which sits just 30 minutes from **Torri del Benaco**, has plenty to keep active kids busy. Four routes feature rope nets, jungle paths, monkey bridge, hanging rails, ziplines, cable cars and more. They even have a route specifically for children three to eight years old. Bonus: the drive to the park is stunning. San Zeno in Montagna, Lago di Garda. Tel: 045.6289306, www.jungleadventure.it. Open May—mid September, daily, 10:00—19:00; Off season (late March—late April & mid-September—mid-October), weekends only, 10:00—18:00.

Parco Avventura Polsa is a smaller park aimed at younger children, specifically those under eight years old. The disadvantage here, however, is that it is located up the mountain, about 40 minutes from the lake (check Google Maps first, to see if you are comfortable with the drive). Explore the adventure trails, play a round of mini-golf, enjoy the playground, and have a picnic. Via del Bosco 61, Polsa. Open June-August, daily, 10:00-18:00. www.familyadventurepolsa.it.

BoscoPark, which sits about one hour north of Verona, has some great activities for teenagers to challenge themselves high in the treetops of this forest setting. Open in high season only, may close down in bad weather, call before driving here—cell: 348.8984881, www.boscopark.it.

Lake Garda

QUAD TOURS

Want to try an exciting adventure on four wheels? **Crazy Wheels** leads tours that take you to hidden corners of beauty in the countryside. Drivers must be at least 18 years old. You can also rent one without a guided tour. Via Gardesana 45, Castelletto di Brenzone. Cell: 327.117.9168. crazywheels.hd@gmail.com.

GO KART

Has driving on Italy's narrow roads in the congested tourist season given you an urge to put your foot down and fly around the race track? Go karting in a mini F1 might be the answer. Children age six and up can join the fun at Affi-Kart on their two-level track. Advance reservations are recommended, as well as showing up 30 minutes before your time lot or your reservation may be cancelled. Via Archimede, Affi. Cell: 348.521.7227, www.gokartverona.it.

HORSE RIDES AND ALPACA HIKES

Four legged friends tend to make everything more fun, especially for kids. While the Dolomites offer more horse riding options, Lake Garda does have **Barlot Ranch** where you can go trekking with a guide to explore Mount Baldo. Tours must be booked in advance. The farm is located in Porcino, Caprino Veronese. www.ranchbarlot.com.

And if you're looking for something completely different, what about trekking with an alpaca? The treks explore Mount Baldo and are suitable for children, who will immediately fall in love with these sassy animals. You can choose between an hour and 40-minute route or a 45-minute route, and all excursions must be booked in advance. Warm clothes and trekking shoes are highly recommended. Via Navene Vecchia 79, Malcesine. www.elalpaca.it.

WATER SPORTS

The **Lake Garda Water Ski Center,** in Camping Serenella outside **Bardolino,** offers waterskiing for the whole family, including children from five years old. They also have banana boats and dinghy boats. www.waterskigardalake.com.

If you prefer to go out with an instructor, you could take **sailing lessons.** **Circolo Nautico Brenzone** offers lessons to children 6-16 (and adults, too, of course) from first timers to more advanced sailors as well as special activities for teens. www.cnbvela.it.

For **surfing**, the best spots are in the windiest part of the lake, near the town of **Torbole sul Lago.** Try **Conca Beach** or **Torbole Beach** (near Hotel Lido Blu). **Colonia Pavese** has a windsurfing school, or you can check out **Circolo Surf Torbole** for lessons in windsurfing, kite surfing and stand-up paddling. www.circolosurftorbole.com

Can't decide which watersport to try? Try them all! **Garda Surf & Sail,** in the town of **Brenzone sul Garda,** has almost everything—windsurfing, dinghy boats, paddles, kite surfing and even panoramic tours where you can simply relax and watch the lake go by. www.gardasurf.com.

Another one-stop shop is **Sailing Dulac-Pier Windsurf,** in the town of **Riva del Garda,** where you can rent windsurfing boards, sailing boats, bikes and kayaks for reasonable prices. www.sailingdulac.com or www.pierwindsurf.it

Also in **Riva del Garda,** you can try windsurfing, kitesurfing or sailing with **Surf Segnana,** which has been operating since 1980. www.surfsegnana.it.

PARAGLIDING

If none of that packs enough thrill for your family, what about **paragliding**? **Fly 2 Fun** are a team of adrenaline junkies and experts who operate in the town of **Malcesine,** and will take you flying, quite literally, from Mount Baldo over to the lake. Fly 2 Fun can take people with disabilities paragliding, and anyone weighing below 35 kg/ 77 pounds or over 95 kg/ 210 pounds should talk to them in advance. www.tandemparagliding.eu

Lake Garda

DIVING

If you are looking for a really different perspective on Lake Garda, how about exploring it beneath the surface? Lake Garda isn't a famous diving destination, but it does boast some impressive rock formations, colorful fish, and more. **Ambiente Acqua**, in **Torbole Sul Garda,** is one of the best-known diving centers at the lake. www.arcosub.com.

GUIDED HIKES

Hiking is a beautiful, healthy way to experience the area, but touring an area you don't know very well can be intimidating for beginners. Plus, going with a professional guide gives you insight and allows you to truly understand what you are seeing. The **Brenzone tourist office** (**IAT Brenzone**) organizes regular hikes in season, which are very reasonably priced and for all levels of fitness and experience. You can book through the tourist office: info@brenzone.it, Tel: 045.742.0076. Via Zanardelli 38, Porto di Brenzone.

Another option is the **Garda Touring Association**, which offers guided hikes, historical tours and more. Open 9:00—13:00 & 15:00—18:00. Cell: 347.749.1452, www.guidelagodigarda.it.

ROCK CLIMBING AND CANYONING

If you like your outdoor activities with a dash of adrenaline, you'll find plenty to do here. From climbing up the cliffs to plunging down through canyons, all kinds of adventure awaits you on shore.

Mountime offers rock climbing lessons high above the lake in the town of **Arco**, but if that sounds a bit intense, you can climb their indoor wall instead. www.mountime.com

MMove, also in Arco, organizes kid-friendly hikes along the splendid trails north of Garda, and even offer kid-friendly rock-climbing, river hiking and canyoning activities. Book in advance. Tours leave from Parcheggio Camping Arco, Via Legionari Cecoslovacchi 14, Loc. Prabi Arco. Cell: 334.219.3862, www.mmove.net.

Lake Garda

Canyon Adventure live up to their name, offering canyoning, kayaking, caving and rock climbing activities. They are based in **Torbole**, and no special equipment or experience is necessary as long as you are reasonably fit and don't mind getting wet. Book in advance. Activities take place April—early October. Via Matteotti 122, Torbole. www.canyonadv.com.

Garda Outdoor is the project of the very passionate alpine guide Demi Centi, and he'll guide you to all sorts of adventures at Lake Garda or in The Dolomites including canyoning, climbing and trekking. www.gardaoutdoor.it.

Day Trips from Lake Garda

Chapter 5

Day Trips from Lake Garda

ITINERARY N. 1: A Day in Lake Molveno and Its Surroundings

Getting there & parking: From Riva del Garda take the SS241 north (about one hour). Set your GPS to Viale Lungolago 9, Molveno. There's a large parking lot right by the lake.

This itinerary can take a full day or a half day, depending on the activities you choose to pursue. Lake Molveno is no poor relation of Lake Garda—it's a smaller gem, with sparkling turquoise water sunk deep in a wooded valley and forest-covered mountains rising around it. It could be described as "Dolomite lite"—much of the mountain majesty, but a lot easier to reach and tour. Lake Molveno's combination of stunning scenery and fun activities have made it increasingly popular with families.

After the drive here, nothing is nicer than getting right in the water. Lounge on a beach or grassy area and soak in the gorgeous views—you can bring the little ones wading or take bigger kids for a swim. Renting a paddle boat or canoe is fun for all ages, and there's a boat rental place on Via Lungolago 19. If your children want something more active, you can take them to the play area (complete with bouncy castles) and mini-golf that sits right on the lake, near the parking lot. There are trails for those who'd like to walk around the lake and discover hidden points, and for toddlers, there's even a small and colorful train that tours the streets. (It departs every 40 minutes, 9:30—12:00 & 15:00—18:30, from the Tourist Infopoint by the parking lot.)

For older children who'd like something more action-packed, take the **Molveno Cable Car (funivia)** up to the mountain top. The funivia sits 10 minutes from the lake and has its own little parking lot, but it fills up very quickly, so it's probably easier to come here by foot. This is a two-step ride: A cable car goes halfway up the mountain, and then you change to a chairlift that brings you the mountain top. Make sure you have your camera set for action—the view of the wooded slopes plunging down to the blue lake and the dazzling azure sky hanging over Molveno's red roofs is spectacular.

The cable car station is an excellent starting point for more outdoor activities. The popular **Forest Park Adventure Park** is 50 meters from the cable car station, and is suitable for children eight or older who love to jump, climb and explore. There's also a pizzeria here called **Ristorante del Brenta**, where you can enjoy a tasty slice with beautiful views. Then you can take the chairlift all the way to the top, and enjoy some coffee and cake at **Rifugio La Montanara Cafe'**, which has a play area featuring swings and a panoramic view point. ☺ Funivia Molveno, Via Lungolago 27, open daily in season, 8:00-18:45. ☺ Molveno Forest Adventure Park, cell: 334.162.4948, www.molveno.it/forestpark. Open mid-June—mid-September, daily, 10:00—17:30.

On your way up the mountain, you'll pass **Malga Tovre**, a farm and petting zoo halfway between the cable car station (first stop up the mountain) and the chairlift station (second and final stop). If you don't want to walk up, do what many families do—take the chair lift all the way to the top of the mountain, then hike down, following the marked path for about 15 minutes to reach the farm. There you can meet the donkeys and pigs, and sample some hearty farm fare, such as yogurt, cheeses and cold cuts. The view from here is just as delicious as the food.

For a good lunch after all this hiking and jumping and swimming, head back to Molveno, to our favorite restaurant in town: **Osteria del Maso** sits just minutes from the lake and is known for its delicious homey food and friendly atmosphere. Their pasta is simply fantastic, as are the polenta and meat. And the seasonal menu will tempt even tough to please foodies. Make sure you book a table in advance, they are always full in season. Via Lungolago 7, Molveno. Tel: 0461.586.345. Open June—September, daily, 12:00—14:30 & 19:00—21:30. Off season opening hours vary, call in advance.

ITINERARY N. 2: A Day Trip to Castel Beseno

Getting there & parking: From Trento, drive south along the SS12 (20 minutes). From Riva del Garda drive north-east along the SS240. The castle has a parking lot below it, and from there it's a 10-minute walk along a marked path up to the main entrance. Most of the walk is easy, but parts of it are somewhat steep. Parents pushing strollers might prefer a different destination, as there are several stairs everywhere in the castle.

Just an hour-long drive from Lake Garda sits one of the best-preserved castles in northern Italy. At 16,000 square meters, it is the biggest castle in Trentino and one of the largest in Italy. It's also one of the most fun for families, as it boasts a medieval theme play area where children can climb, explore, and dream of princesses and knights, kings and queens, and even dragons. Active kids can try the catapult, explore the old kitchen were feasts were once prepared, and put on the knight's gear. Once you've all had your fun in the various mysterious rooms, don't forget to climb the ramparts for an amazing 360-degree view. Plan on two-three hours to explore the castle's museum of armor and medieval weapons. And since Castel Beseno is so close to Trento and to Lake Garda, you can combine it with half a day of watersports in Riva del Garda, or with a visit to Trento.

With such a strategic position and brilliant view of the whole area, this peak has always appealed to humans—and has always been the site of battles. The castle is named after the noble Beseno family, vassals of the counts of Appiano, who lived here in the 12th century. At the highest point, you can still see traces of the two original fortifications built here by two branches of the family. A dispute within the Beseno tribe cost them this much-coveted asset, and in the following decades the castle changed hands many times. In 1487 this was one site of the particularly gruesome *Battle of Calliano* between the Republic of Venice and the Austrian forces of Sigismund de Habsburg. The Austrians triumphed, killing or taking prisoner more than 6,000 Venetians. Castel Beseno was restored in the 1600s, but over time, the political scene changed, and its position became less important. It was neglected and all but forgotten until finally, in the 1970s, it became a public monument and tourists and locals alike realized what a treasure it actually was.

The castle hosts many events and fairs on weekends in the summer, particularly from mid—July to early September. It's even more fun to visit here with a guide in period costume during one of the medieval fairs! **Il Mestiere delle Armi** on the first weekend in August is the most exciting event, with two days of medieval battle reenactments—find out more on their website, or at the Trento tourist office. 🕒 Beseno Castle, Via al Castello 4, Besenello. Tel: 0464.834.600, www.visittrentino.info/it/guida/da-vedere/castelli/castel. Open year round, Tuesday—Sunday, 9:30—17:00. In high season, the castle is open until 18:00.

ITINERARY N. 3: A Day at Lake Ledro, the Prehistoric Pile Dwelling Museum, and the Donkey Sanctuary

Getting There & Parking: From Riva del Garda, take the SS240 west to Lake Ledro (25 minutes). There's a parking lot by the Pile Dwelling Museum—set your GPS to Via Lungolago 1, Molina di Ledro.

Tourist information office: Via Nuova 7, Ledro, Tel: 0464.591222, www.vallediledro.com. Open year round, daily, 9:30—12:30 & 14:30—18:00. (Hours vary off season.) In June—late September they open a second, smaller info point in Molina, near the Pile Dwelling Museum. Open daily, 10:00—13:00 & 15:00—18:00.

Day Trips from Lake Garda

The sites in this itinerary are all within a 25-minute drive from Riva del Garda, and will appeal to families who want to enjoy a more tranquil day of lakeside fun. Nestled 650 meters above sea level, between Lake Garda and the Dolomites in the Ledro Valley, the often-overlooked Lake Ledro offers plenty to do for everyone in the family. In addition to the fun activities you expect at a lake, you'll find the Pile Dwelling Museum (which is a UNESCO World Heritage Site), a donkey sanctuary, an outdoor art experience and some serene hikes. The only thing "missing" is the crowds of other visitors!

Start your day at Lake Ledro with the most obvious activity—jump in for a swim. There are a number of beaches here, including a few that offer various watersports, from canoes to paddle boats to windsurfing lessons and more. There are free sections and private beaches, and the privately-owned beaches are where you will find operators renting equipment for watersports and offering lessons.

Four beaches are especially popular with families: **Pieve di Ledro's** free beach has a large parking lot, a playground, mini golf and even a pizzeria. **Molina di Ledro Beach** (marked on some maps as Besta Beach) is a private and spacious beach with lots of grassy areas for children to play; you can rent boats and kayaks, and if you fancy a game of tennis, there are courts here, too (entrance fees apply). **Mezzolago Beach** (in Mezzolago) boasts postcard-pretty good looks and a convenient location with all the basics including a playground for kids and picnic tables. The **Pur beach** is a very serene spot, but dogs are allowed on a section of this beach, so children who fear them might not feel very serene here. The usual playground, kiosks and other basics are also here.

Lake Ledro is also popular for **short hikes** that are manageable for most children. A trail runs all the way around the lake, and it's a nice 10 km/ 6 mile walk. You can do it all or just take in a section of it between sites you'd like to visit—the lovely stretch along Via Lungolago that leads to the Palafitte Museum, for example, is only 2.5 km/ 1.5 miles.

For an even more exciting experience, choose a different sort of hike, complete with donkeys. Just don't be surprised if your kids fall in love with these friendly animals and refuse to leave. **Le Vie Degli Asini Farm** is a serene oasis where donkeys and children both come to learn from each other. The donkeys have been rescued, and the children come for animal therapy. This is a joyful place, where you play with the animals and go on organized hikes with them. You'll soon realize these creatures are much smarter and gentler than you expect! Consult the farm's website for details.

All activities must be booked in advance. 🕐 Azienda Agricola Gianni Fruner, Loc. Ballino - Fiavè; GPS coordinates 45°57'51.1"N 10°48'40.2"E, Cell: 348.370.8251, www.leviedegliasini.jimdo.com.

Hikes aside, Lake Ledro also boasts two museums, and both are outdoors. **The Museo delle Palafitte (Pile Dwelling Museum)** is a UNESCO World Heritage Site that dates back to the Bronze Age. It sat undiscovered for centuries until the water level in the lake decreased in 1929, revealing the remains of the settlement. Pile dwellings—structures that are built on stilts to sit at the surface of a lake, similar to the way Venice was built—were actually quite common in the past, and this was one of about a hundred such villages in the Alps. In the Bronze Age, the huts were built in clusters—mini-villages with various structures dedicated to specific purposes. The water provided the men and women with a natural barrier and protection from animals and enemies alike.

Today, visitors to this site can examine three reconstructed huts showcasing what we know about the lives of those who inhabited the original dwellings 4,000 years ago. One hut features the tools and materials used by craftsmen of the time—tools for bronze and wood work, linen weaving, stone carving, net weaving, and ceramics making. Another shows how people actually lived in these huts. The third represents a combination of storage space for materials and shelter for livestock. These wooden reconstructions with their straw roofs give children a chance to really see and feel what life was like in the Bronze Age in the Alps. Some kids will find this interesting, others may be less intrigued—consult the museum's website to learn more. 🕐 Museo delle Palafitte del Lago di Ledro, Via al Lago 1, Molina di Ledro. Tel: 0464. 508.182, www.palafitteledro.it. Open March—June & September—November, Tuesday—Sunday, 9:00-17:00 (closed on Monday); July—August, daily, 10:00—18:00. Closed off season.

> **Tip:** In July and in August the museum organizes workshops for children and adults. These can be quite entertaining for younger children; call in advance to find out if anything is planned (in English) during your visit.

Our last stop for the day is **Ledro Art Land**. This is one museum where children can run, play, and get a much broader view on what art can be. Twenty contemporary sculptures by local artists using wood, metal and stone await you at points along a gentle trail through the woods. This is a wonderful place to teach children that art isn't just paintings in frames, and to inspire them to craft their own sculptures from sticks, rocks and other things they find in nature. ⊕ Ledro Land Art Open Park (the location is marked on Google Maps), open year-round, free of charge.

If all this fresh air and pristine mountain views leave you hankering for a real picnic, there's one place to go—**Bosc del Meneghi Farm**. Rustic and authentic, the farm is just a couple of minutes from the lake Ledro's shores. Everything here is organic, and you can even say hello to the farm animals. Open April—September, on weekends. It's best to call before coming here, and make a booking. Cell: 389.5150167, www.bosc-del-meneghi.it.

ITINERARY N. 4: A Day at Lake Tenno, the Ancient Village of Canale del Tenno, the Trento Science Museum, and the Caproni Museum of Aviation

On this itinerary, you can relax at a stunning turquoise lake, explore a medieval village that hasn't changed much in the last 500 years, and learn something new at Trento's exciting science museum, aeronautic museum, or both.

> **Tip:** The itinerary can be followed as is, or you could flip it and start at the furthest point, visiting sites so that you see the one closest to your accommodation last. This minimizes the driving time at the end of the day, when everyone is tired, and gives you more flexibility.

Day Trips from Lake Garda

LAKE TENNO

Getting there & parking: Drive north from Riva del Garda along the SS421. Set your GPS to Albergo Stella Alpina, a hotel right on the shores of the lake. There is a small parking lot, and you have to take stairs to reach the lake, so strollers are not an option here.

Lake Tenno didn't exist until the year 1100 when an earthquake rearranged the landscape, so it is fairly new as lakes go. It sits at an elevation of 550 meters with a surface area of two and a half kilometers squared, which features a little island or peninsula (depending on the lake's depth at the time) with a few trees. Its dazzling turquoise water will send you searching for your camera, and in July and August, it's usually warm enough to enjoy a swim or float around on an air mattress like the locals do. Once you've dried off, you can hike from the lake to the lovely medieval hamlet of **Canale del Tenno (Borgo di Canale** on some maps).

CANALE DEL BORGO (BORGO DI CANALE)

Getting there & parking: Take the SS241; Canale is marked on Google Maps. Cars are not allowed in the village, and the lack of parking outside the village is real motivation for the half-hour walk uphill from the lake.

The first record of this ancient village dates back to 1211. The population abandoned it after World War I, but after World War II, families started to trickle back. Today it has only 50 residents, but this absolute jewel punches above its weight and is included in the list of Italy's most beautiful villages. You can visit the tiny local museum, but even just wandering along the cobbled streets will take you back hundreds of years. And if this blast from the past has put you in the mood for more educational fun, head to our next stop, the MUSE science museum in Trento.

TRENTO

Getting there & parking: Head north on the SS421, then take the SS237 and connect to the SS45bis going northeast to Trento. Set your GPS to Parcheggio Aperto (in Via Petrarca) or the Autosilo Buonconsiglio P3, or Parcheggio Fiera (Piazza Fiera 35), all of which are less than five minutes away from Castel Buonconsiglio and Trento's *centro storico*.

Day Trips from Lake Garda

Tourist office: Piazza Dante 24, Trento. Tel: 0461.216000, www.discovertrento.it. Open daily, 9:00-19:00.

Trento is worth seeing, if you have the time. Established at least 2000 years ago, it was a prominent cultural and political force during the Renaissance. As you might guess, it was where the Council of Trent met in the 16th Century, leading the Catholic Church's Counter-Reformation movement (in response to the Protestant Reformation). Trento was part of Austria until 1919, and is now an important city in Italy's economy. The Adige, the second-longest river in Italy, runs through it, adding to its beauty.

In addition to its charm and interesting history, Trento has a number of attractions worth exploring. The Buonconsiglio Castle, the Trento MUSE Science Museum, and the Caproni Aviation Museum are our three favorite things to see here and are the focus of this itinerary. If you just want to recharge and relax, this city's small historical center is bursting with good restaurants and fun shopping options.

Start your visit at Trento's *centro storico*. The **Duomo**, which is dedicated to the city's patron saint—San Vigilio—is well worth a visit. This impressive cathedral was commissioned by Bishop Federico Vanga in Lombard-Romanesque style. 🕒 Cattedrale San Vigilio, Piazza d'Arogno 9. Tel: 0461.231.293. Open daily 6:30—12:00 & 14:20—20:00. Visits are not allowed during mass.

●•••●•••●•••●•••●•••●•••●•••●•••●•••●•••●•••●•••

Mission 1: Two strong animals protect the entryway to the church. Can you find them? What are they?

Mission 2: Inside the Duomo itself, can you find a fresco (wall painting) showing women standing inside a walled city?

●•••●•••●•••●•••●•••●•••●•••●•••●•••●•••●•••●•••

From there, you can continue browsing through the many shops and boutiques of this well-off town until you reach the stern and severe façade of **Castel Buonconsiglio.** The castle served as residence for the bishop-princes who ruled over Trento from the 13th century up to the 18th century. Because it was originally built as a military fortress, the castle looks rather austere, but inside you'll find delicate and ornate artwork and several fascinating rooms to explore, built in many different architectural styles, because the castle was enlarged repeatedly over the centuries. Castel Buonconsiglio has played many roles in its long life including a barracks, a jail, and now an art gallery. Don't miss the Eagle Tower (Torre Aquila) at the southern end of the complex; it features the beautiful and famous *Cycle of the Months*, a series of frescoes that give a detailed view of life in the 15th century. The fresco dedicated to winter was the first one ever to depict a snowball fight! Like many castles, it is surrounded by charming gardens where the kids can run and play. ⊕ Castel Buonconsiglio, Via Bernardo Clesio 5, Trento. Tel: 0461.233.770. www.buonconsiglio.it. Open Tuesday—Sunday, 10:00—18:00 (off season until 17:00); closed Monday.

MUSE SCIENCE MUSEUM (TRENTO)

Getting there & parking: From the main piazza (Piazza Duomo), it's a 15 minute walk to the museum. If arriving by car, set your GPS to Corso del Lavoro e della Scienza. The museum has its own lot.

For science-loving kids, this is a medium-sized but popular stop. Come here to learn about the earth's different climates and ecosystems, and to gain a better understanding of the amazing geology around you in the Lake Garda region. From dinosaur fossils to taxidermied animals to information about environmental sustainability for the future, MUSE offers plenty to engage the imagination. The whole building is designed to illustrate the earth's structure with the upper floors dedicated to mountains and the basement focused on dinosaurs. The most interesting part for most families is the section dedicated to scientific experiments; be sure to stop here, where kids (and adults…) can have some hands-on fun. You can also get an eagle's eye view of the surrounding area from the museum's terrace.

Unlike most other museums, this one has a real heart for younger children. If you have a child five or under who has been bristling while older siblings do things they can't, you can balance things out here. The museum's interactive sensory exhibit is only open to children age five or under. But luckily, they can bring one adult each to immerse themselves in a symphony of light, sound and more. ⊕ MUSE Trento Science Museum, Corso del Lavoro e della Scienza 3, Trento. Tel: 0461.270.311, www.muse.it. Open Tuesday—Sunday, 10:00—18:00 (until 19:00 on weekends); closed Monday.

CAPRONI AVIATION MUSEUM

Getting there & parking: The museum sits right outside Trento, about 10 minutes by car. Set your GPS to Via Lidorno and park at the museum's lot.

For some more modern history, end your day with a visit here to see the models and very cool machines on display. Established in 1927, this is Italy's oldest aviation museum. The collection includes a variety of small aircraft as well as the massive 14,000 kg Transaereo Noviplano with its towering layers of wings and a much more modern Lockheed Starfighter. The museum also features temporary exhibits such as the current one titled Space Girls Space Women highlighting the roles women have played in aviation and space exploration. Guided tours and flight simulation are available on some weekends (call first). ☉ Caproni Aviation Museum, Via Lidorno 3, Trento. Tel: 0461.944.888, www.museocaproni.it. Open Monday—Friday, 10:00—13:00 & 14:00—18:00. Weekends open 10:00—18:00.

All these museums will surely awaken your appetite. Luckily, Trento offers several popular dining options. **Ristorante Pizzeria DOC** in Trento is a beautiful venue, with stonework and a vaulted ceiling. The worst thing we could say is that it is hard to decide what to get with so many delicious pizzas on offer! The risotto, meat pies and pasta are all very good, too. Via Milano 148, Trento. Tel: 0461.262022, www.doctrento.it. Open Monday—Friday, 12:00—14:30 & 18:00—22:00 (the restaurant closes down at 22:00, the pizzeria remains open until 23:45). Weekends, open for dinner only. Closed in August.

Ristorante Rosa D'Oro in Trento offers traditional dishes, classic Italian pasta and pizza and it's also a brewery. This is a solid classic in a good location. Piazza Santa Maria Maggiore, Trento. Tel: 0461.261.792, www.ristoranterosadoro.com. Open daily, 12:00—14:30 & 19:00—23:30.

ITINERARY N. 5: The Nicolis Car Museum, Borghetto sul Mincio, the Sigurta Park, and Cavour Water Park

This itinerary offers great variety: Car fans and history buffs will enjoy visiting the Nicolis transport museum; nature lovers will feel at home at the stunning Sigurta Botanical Garden, and everyone will enjoy a perfect lunch of handmade tortellini at the postcard pretty village of Borghetto sul Mincio.

NICOLIS MUSEUM

Getting there & parking: From Lake Garda take the E70 autostrada (30 minutes). From Verona, take the SS12 (20 minutes). Park at the museum's lot.

Nestled into Villafranca di Verona, a serene town with ancient origins, is a newer museum dedicated to powerful engines. **Nicolis Museum,** which opened in 2000, features a wide range of cars and motorcycles from vintage Alfa Romeos and Ferraris to sleek motorcycles. It even includes bicycles and military aircraft in the mix. If you have a child who loves to take things apart to see how they work, this stop is sure to be a hit. ◎ Museo Nicolis, Viale Postumia, Villafranca di Verona. Freephone: 800.189699, Tel: 045 6303289, www.museonicolis.com. Open Tuesday—Sunday, 10:00—18:00. Closed on Mondays. Children under 5 enter for free, children under 16 pay a reduced fee.

Villafranca also boasts an impressive 12th century **Scaligero Fortress.** And while you can't normally tour the inside, it is well worth having a look at the exterior. It is one of many such fortresses built throughout the area by the Scaligero (Scala) family, one of Verona's ruling dynasties. In the summer months, concerts and shows are held inside.

BORGHETTO SUL MINCIO

Getting there & parking: From Venice, take the A4 and E70 (90 minutes). From Verona, take the SP24 (40 minutes). There's a parking lot at the entrance to the village.

Tourist information office: Piazza Carlo Alberto 32. Tel: 045.795.1880, www.valeggio.com. Open in season.

Our next stop for the day is **Borghetto Sul Mincio**—a tiny village that is big on charm, and has roots that stretch way back to the Longobard era in the 6th century. When the Scaligero family held power, this was an important strategic center, and they built the castle at the mountain top, that looks over the town from its vantage point. Parts of the castle were destroyed by an earthquake in 1117. Today it is in private hands, and it isn't open to visitors.

When the area became part of the Republic of Venice in 1405, the focus shifted to agriculture. The Mincio River and the fertile lands gave rise to farming, and the villagers built mills along the river. Today, some of the mills are still functional. Can anyone in your family spot which ones? As you walk around, don't miss the town's main bridge, the elegant **Ponte Visconteo** (**Visconti Bridge**), which dates back to the 14th Century and hosts one of borghetto's most famous festivals, the *Festa del Nodo dell'Amore* (see Special Events in the Area at the end of this itinerary).

Borghetto sul Mincio can be explored on foot or on a bike; you can rent bicycles at the entrance to the village to pedal along the river. All of that active exploring can make a family hungry. Luckily, Borghetto sul Mincio claims to be the birthplace of tortellini. A local legend tells the story of a soldier and a water nymph who fell in love while the nymph was briefly in human form. She had to return to the water, and before they parted they tied a handkerchief into a knot to symbolize their love. Later, the tortellini was created to replicate that knotted handkerchief in pasta form (the best and tastiest form!). Today the nymph and the soldier are both long gone, but several restaurants serve steaming dishes of this popular dish—see our recommendations at the end of this itinerary.

SIGURTA BOTANICAL PARK

Getting there & parking: From Borghetto sul Mincio, take Via di Circovallazione (one kilometer). From Verona, take the SP24 (40 minutes). From Venice, take the A4 and E70 (90 minutes). Set your GPS to Via Baden Powell, there's a large parking lot there, one block away from the main entrance to the botanical park.

An afternoon stroll through the gorgeous greenery of **Sigurta Botanical Park** is the perfect way to end your day. Once farmland owned by the powerful Gerolamo Nicolo Contarini, these lands were passed from one noble family to another, accumulating more delightful flower beds, lush lawns and herb gardens over the centuries. Stroll slowly or rent a bike to pedal peacefully past little lakes and colorful displays of plants from all over the world. You can even rent a golf cart if you are experiencing tortellini overload or have a tired child who needs a break. If your family is ready for more adventure, try the maze, or if you want to sit back, take the 35-minute train tour. ◴ Parco Sigurta, Via Cavour 1, Valeggio sul Mincio. Tel: 045.637,1033, www.sigurta.it. Family discounts available. Open early March—late October, 9:00—19:00 (March & October until 18:00). Last admission one hour before closing time. Opening times change annually, check the website before coming here.

PARCO ACQUATICO CAVOUR (CAVOUR WATER PARK)

Getting there & parking: From Borghetto sul Mincio or the Sigurta Park, take the SP55 (less than 5 minutes). From Verona, take the SP24 (40 minutes). The Aqua Park has its own lot for guests.

For something more active, and, well, wet, head to Parco Acquatico Cavour. This is a favorite stop for families travelling to this area. If you haven't had you fill at the Gardaland Aquatic Park (see Lake Garda chapter) or Jesolandia (see Day Trips from Venice chapter), or if you actually prefer a smaller, more low-key venue that is more suitable for younger children, this is the spot.

Kids can jump from pool to pool, slide down the many water slides, run in the 'rain forest', climb the slippery 'iceberg', and exhaust themselves while you enjoy a cool drink in the shade. Organized activities such as face painting and pool parties are available daily in high season, usually around 11:00—13:00. (Check the website, as these change constantly.) ◴ Parco Acquatico Cavour, Loc. Ariano, Valeggio Sul Mincio. Tel: 045.795.0904, www.parcoacquaticocavour.it. Open in the summer months only, daily, 09:30—19:00 (last entry at 18:00). Children under 10 years old are eligible for a reduced ticket. Children under 3 enter for free. Discounted afternoon tickets (entry after 14:30) are available (check the website first).

Eating in the Area

BORGO SUL MINCIO AND ITS SURROUNDINGS

There are several good restaurants in this village and the surrounding area (Valeggio Sul Mincio), but prices can be a little high. For some tasty and reasonably priced pizza, try **Bar Ristorante Pizzeria La Goccia.** The ambiance is inviting, and in season you can sit outside, too. Via Magenta 18, Valeggio Sul Mincio, Tel: 0457.950.442, www.ristorantevaleggio.it. Open Friday—Wednesday, 12:00—14:00 & 18:30—23:30. Closed Thursday.

Pastificio Remelli started off as an artisanal pasta shop, but they have recently added a few tables and now they are a restaurant, too, that specializes in chubby tortellini. Book a table in advance; they are always full in season. Via Alessandro Sala 30, Valeggio Sul Mincio. Tel: 045.795.1630, www.pastificioremelli.it. The restaurant is open for lunch Tuesday—Sunday. The pasta shop is open Tuesday—Saturday, 8:30—19:30. Sunday 8:30—15:30, Monday 8:30—13:00.

VILLAFRANCA DI VERONA

Pizzeria La Greca is a pleasant family-run trattoria that sits just around the corner from the Nicolis museum. They offer a selection of meat dishes, salads, and pizza, of course. Viale Postumia, 73, Villafranca di Verona. Tel: 045.630.4499, www.pizzerialagreca.it. Open daily, 12.00—14.30 & 18.30—midnight.

Goosta Piadineria Artigiana is where the locals go for a tasty *panino*. Alternatively, try their *piadina* (flat bread filled with cold cuts, cheese and vegetables). Corso Giuseppe Garibaldi 40, Villafranca di Verona. Tel: 0456.304.950, www.piadineriagoosta.it. Open Monday—Saturday, 12:00—14:30 & 18:30—midnight. Sunday, open for dinner only.

For a homey but well-prepared meal, try **Ristorante Ai Tre Volti.** The kitchen philosophy here is old school, but in a good way—generous and reasonably priced portions, friendly (albeit sometimes slow) service, and delicious classic local dishes such as fried gnocchi, trays of artisanal cold cuts, polenta, and more. Via Messedaglia 215, Villafranca di Verona. Open Tuesday—Sunday, 12:00—22:30. Closed Monday.

Special Events in the Area

The Festa del Nodo d'Amore (the celebration of the love knot) takes place on the third Tuesday in June. The people of Borghetto del Mincio lay large tables along the Visconti bridge and serve delicious tortellini to more than 4,000 hungry visitors. These famous dinners have been going on for more than 20 years, and the tradition has managed to land the village a place in the Guinness Book of Records. To participate, you must buy a ticket in advance for the dinner (around 85 euro per person).

An event that is open for all, on the other hand, is the famous **Sagra dei Tortellini**, which takes place in September. All the restaurants participate, and it's a feast of good food, music, and lively evenings. Find out more at the local tourist office.

On the first weekend of July, visitors will enjoy the **Fiera di Valeggio Sul Mincio,** a three-day event which combines good food, exhibitions, concerts, fireworks, street performers, artisan markets and other cultural initiatives. The program changes yearly, but it's always fun to explore. Find out more about this event and others at the local tourist office.

Antiques and crafts lovers will be glad to know that the village organizes a little **antiques market** on the fourth Sunday of every month, and for foodies, there's usually a small **farmers' market** on Saturday mornings in the main piazza.

The Dolomites

Chapter 6

The Dolomites

Most visitors come to northern Italy to enjoy the marvels of Venice and Lake Garda, and they are right—these are indeed fantastic places to explore. But what many holidaymakers don't realize is that northern Italy offers much more. Just a couple of hours away from the cultivated beauty of Venice and Verona, with their treasure trove of art and history, await the Dolomites, a lesser-known treasure of nature's artwork that is perfect for families. The Dolomites will leave you bewildered by their landscape; half Italian and half Austrian, they offer the best of both worlds, and have even been declared a UNESCO World Heritage Site in 2009.

So why travel to the Dolomites? **Here are our 5 top reasons:**

1. They are stunning, and offer a real contrast to the classic, all-Italian charm of Venice. We wouldn't advise anyone to skip the marvels of *bella Venezia*, naturally, but a couple of days in the Dolomites, surrounded by the incomparable beauty of the mountains, canyons and lakes, will inject your family trip with a well-needed dose of nature and adventure.

2. They are far less crowded. Venice, Verona and Lake Garda can get very busy in the summertime, which detracts from their magic and can overwhelm children. The Dolomites, on the other hand, offer endless trails for kids to explore freely, which means you can really relax and recharge during your vacation.

3. They are cheaper (and at times—significantly cheaper) than Venice and Lake Garda. Hotels and restaurants can be 30% less here. The cable cars and chairlifts are spendy, but you can get family discounts.

The Dolomites

4. This is a family-friendly paradise. Many attractions here are geared specifically towards kids, especially those younger than 14. Children can enjoy a variety of attractions, excellent adventure parks, playgrounds, farm visits, bird shows, rock climbing lessons, petting zoos, horse-drawn carriage rides, alpaca hikes, and more. The **'Special Activities in the Area'** section in this chapter is brimming with options; even if you don't go on a single hike, you can still find a fantastic activity to enjoy outside.

5. The hiking trails in the Dolomites Alps are hard to beat. While many children complain about hiking initially, it's a great family activity and once they get going, they usually embrace the challenge and revel in the sense of adventure. We have listed a number of recommended hikes in this chapter, but we were careful to choose only the easiest ones—trails that give you the most rewarding scenery for the least effort. They are suitable for anyone who is mobile and is relatively fit. Naturally, the local tourist information offices can advise you about more challenging options.

Planning Your Visit to the Dolomites

The Dolomites stretch from the Adige River to the Piave Valley, and extend through the provinces of Belluno, South Tyrol (Alto Adige) and Trentino. In this chapter, we offer 10 detailed, self-led itineraries that focus on the very best that the Dolomites have to offer. As always, these itineraries can be modified, mixed and matched, depending on your family's preferences. Whichever itinerary you choose, knowing what to expect and planning in advance can help you make the most of your time, and avoid the common pitfalls of travel in this area.

First, know that during the summer, some valleys in the Dolomites limit car access to those who are residents or guests at a hotel in the valley. This is done to protect the natural sights from too much traffic. If you've booked your stay in a restricted zone, make sure your hotel provides you with a pass before you travel here. If you are only passing through, you might have to park slightly farther away than you had initially planned, and continue by bus or cable car.

Some visitors are caught off guard by the costs of taking the chair lifts (*seggiovia*) and cableways (*funivia*) that connect various towns with the mountain chalets, hiking trails, adventure parks and ski slopes above them.

You can save significantly if you plan which places you want to see and which lifts you will use in advance. If you are using more than two in the same valley, you can often get a combo-pass for that whole area. You can also find discounted family tickets, and usually a return ticket is better value than two one-way tickets. It also helps to know what the various types of cable cars and lifts are called in Italian: *Funiva* and *cabinovia* both mean cable car. An *ovovia* is a small cable car shaped like an egg. *Seggiovia* means chairlift.

Remember that driving in the Dolomites can be tiring for those unused to mountains, and for children who suffer from motion sickness. The roads are safe and in good condition, but very steep, at times. You can make it easier on yourself by first, making sure you rent a suitable car (powerful but small enough to easily navigate the narrow roads) and second, not overdoing it. Check the Google Earth maps to see what kind of road you will be traveling on, and avoid crossing more than one mountain pass a day (these are known as *pass* or *passo* in Italian). If you don't feel comfortable driving to the most remote nature reserves, stick to the sights and attractions that can be found near the main roads and the autostrada, and require significantly less driving.

Last but not least, remember that for tourists, there are only two seasons in the Dolomites: Summer (late-May—early September), and winter (for skiing). During the rest of the year, several sights, restaurants and attractions close down.

How the Dolomites Came to Be

The Dolomites were created about 280,000,000 years ago, thanks to a combination of three geological phenomena: The transformation of sediments into rock, the rise of a mountain range from the ancient sea, and finally, the remodeling of the rock and glaciers by various agents such as water, mudslides, earthquakes, avalanches and more. The Dolomites have always fascinated scientists, and it was a scientist who named them—French mineralogist Déodat Gratet de Dolomieu was the first to describe and name, in the 18th century, the carbonate rock *Dolomite*, that gives these mountains their pale color.

It may be hard to imagine, but the Dolomites were once a natural habitat for dinosaurs, who roamed this muddy and dangerous terrain during the Triassic period. For experienced hikers, there are some paths that allow you today to follow in the footpaths of the dinosaurs, and see the fossils that indicate their presence, especially around Mount Pelmo. Human presence in the Dolomites goes back to Mesolithic times (some 7,500 years ago), and in recent years, receding glaciers have allowed scientists to learn more about the hunters and gatherers who once lived in caves in these mountains.

Top 10 Family Activities in the Dolomites

1. Take the Sass Pordoi cable car (funivia) to enjoy some of the most spectacular views in northern Italy.

2. Go on a fun horse-drawn carriage ride, or a family hike, in Alpe di Siusi.

3. Experience the Ladin culture and traditional wood carving workshops in Ortisei.

4. Soar through the Alpine forest on a zipline in the mountains.

5. Visit the Marmolada—queen of the Dolomites.

6. Splash around in the beautiful Pellegrino Lake.

7. Discover beautiful waterfalls and mines at the Gilfenklamm canyon.

8. Jump and climb at some of the best adventure parks in Italy.

9. Stroll through the beautiful botanic garden and castle in Merano.

10. Visit the spectacular lakes around Dobbiaco, and stop for a chocolate workshop, too!

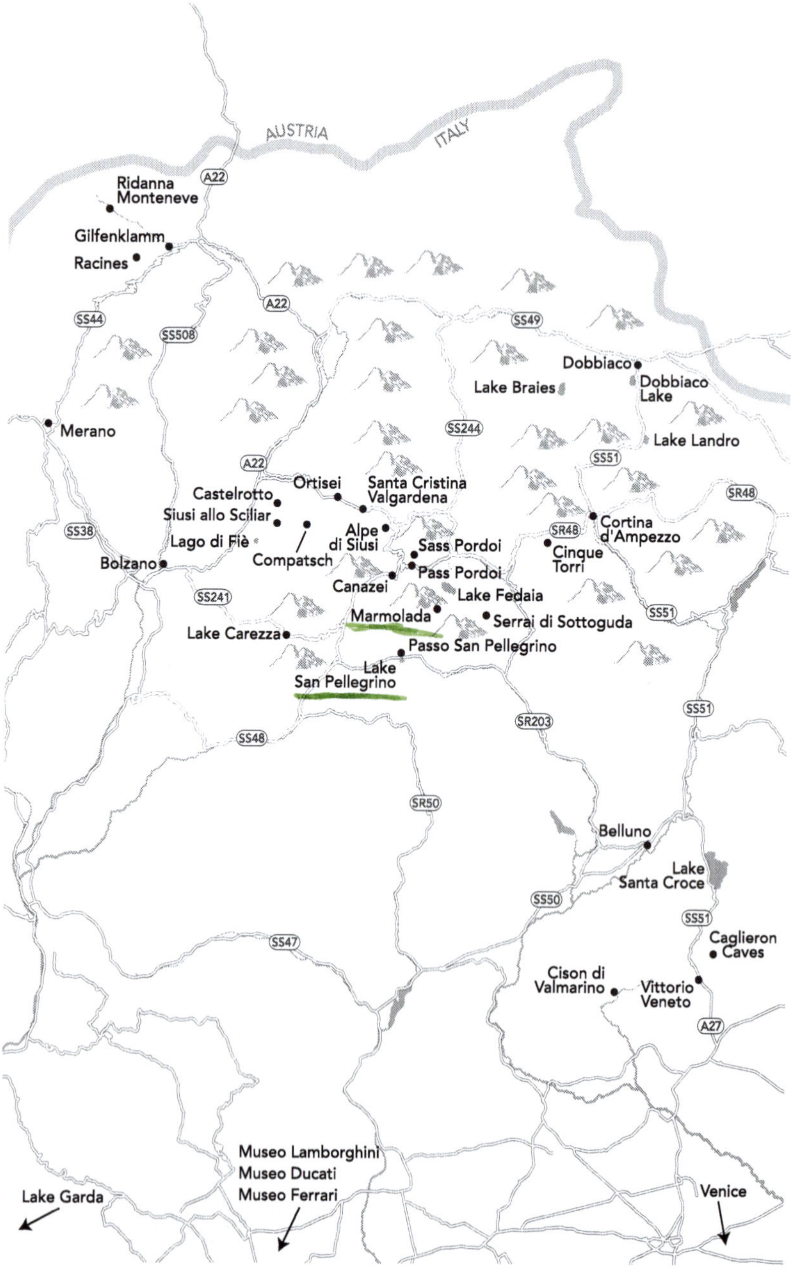
AUSTRIA
ITALY
Ridanna Monteneve
A22
Gilfenklamm
Racines
SS44
SS508
SS49
Dobbiaco
Lake Braies
Dobbiaco Lake
Merano
SS244
Lake Landro
A22
SS51
Ortisei
Santa Cristina Valgardena
Castelrotto
Siusi allo Sciliar
SR48
Cortina d'Ampezzo
SS38
Lago di Fiè
Alpe di Siusi
Compatsch
Sass Pordoi
SR48
Cinque Torri
Bolzano
Pass Pordoi
Canazei
Lake Fedaia
SS241
Marmolada
Serrai di Sottoguda
SS51
Lake Carezza
Passo San Pellegrino
Lake San Pellegrino
SR203
SS51
SS48
SR50
Belluno
Lake Santa Croce
SS50
SS51
Caglieron Caves
SS47
Cison di Valmarino
Vittorio Veneto
A27
Museo Lamborghini
Museo Ducati
Museo Ferrari
Lake Garda
Venice

Day Trips in the Dolomites

Itinerary N. 1: Merano, Trauttmansdorff Castle, and the Merano Alpine Park

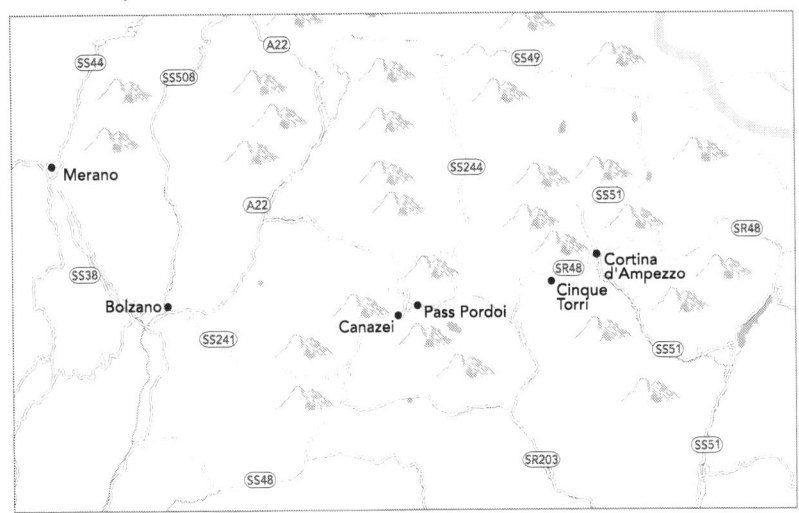

This itinerary begins with a visit to beautiful Merano, which sits only 90 minutes north of Lake Garda. Merano tempts visitors with its charming, colorful architecture, a stunning botanic garden, a castle, hiking trails, and even an adventure park complete with Alpine slides (which are like roller coasters, except the cars run on a track on the mountain, not in the air). And since most of the attractions here are within five minutes of each other, your family will enjoy a lot of very convenient Alpine fun, with very little car time in between.

Getting there & parking: From Verona or Lake Garda, take the A22 autostrada north. Set your GPS to Garage Terme Merano (Piazza Terme, Merano). This large underground lot is just minutes from the town center.

Tourist information office: APT Merano, Corso della Libertà 45, Merano. Tel: 0473.272.000, www.merano-suedtirol.it/it/merano. Open Monday–Friday, 9:00–19:00; Saturday, 9:00–16:00; Sunday closed. Hours may vary off season.

Start your day at Merano's castle. The Empress Elisabeth (Sissi) of Austria-Hungary was a celebrity and trend setter in her day, and she made **Trauttmansdorff Castle** in Merano her winter residence. When you visit

Day Trips in the Dolomites

the castle's famous **botanic gardens,** you will understand why. They include rare and beautiful plants from around the world, and a few animals run freely between the flower beds, so don't be surprised if you encounter a rabbit or a curious peacock! Exotic and tropical creatures including stick insects, giant frogs and hideous spiders live in the glass house terrarium, where they will delight children and make adults quietly uncomfortable. The grounds also feature sensory stations and artist pavilions. The castle dates back to the 13th century, but has been renovated over the years. In the summertime they host a variety of events; check the website before you go to see what is happening. 🕐 Trauttmansdorff Castle and Gardens, Via S. Valentino 51, Merano. Tel: 0473.235730, www.trauttmansdorff.it. Open April 1—October 31, daily, 9:00—19:00 (Fridays in June through August, open until 23:00); November 1—November 15, open daily, 9:00—17:00. Last entry one hour before closing.

Next, it's time for a hike. The **Passeggiata Tappeiner** is the most famous trail in town, and it is suitable for families. This easy, six-kilometer (3.7 miles) route normally takes about two hours, and it is mostly exposed, so water and hats are in order. The itinerary officially starts behind the Duomo, but we recommend that you start near the chair lift station because that avoids the rather steep first section, which can be hard for younger children. You'll enjoy an up-close look at the lush, green Alpine woods and gorgeous views of Merano with its pretty clock tower and red roofs below you. And once you've completed the walk, it will be even easier to indulge yourself with a slice of **Ristorante Unterweger's** famous black forest cake! 🕐 Ristorante Unterweger, Via Gnaid 27, Tirolo (outside Merano, along the Tappeiner trail). Tel: 0473.220.216. Open daily, usually 10:00—18:00.

> **Tip:** The **Gilf Promenade** is an even easier hike in Merano, going from Gilf Canyon at the Passirio River to Castel San Zeno and the Torre delle Polveri tower. This route is very popular with families, too; find out more at the tourist office.

Young children might lack the patience to enjoy a visit to the **Merano Thermal Park,** but parents deserve it and teens will like it, too. They have 13 stylish indoor pools and 12 outdoor pools where you can soak up some relaxation, and there is a wonderful selection of spa treatments available. 🕐 Merano Thermal Spa, Piazza Terme 9, Merano. Tel: 0473.252000, www.termemerano.it. Open daily, 9:00—22:00, the outdoor pools are open from mid-May—mid-September. Spa treatments should be booked in advance.

Merano's historical center is full of interesting shops and restaurants, and there's even a very small **medieval castle** that hides between the boutiques. It is so small that many visitors tend to skip it, but for younger children, the mysterious and dimly lit rooms, filled with antiques, ancient tools and the occasional piece of armor, can be an interesting attraction. ⊙ Castello Principesco di Merano, Via Galileo Galilei 21, Merano. Open Easter—early January, Tuesday—Saturday, 10:30—17:00; Sunday 10:00—13:00; Monday closed. Children under 18 enter for free.

Then, for some child-sized Alpine adventure, take the *funivia* (cable car) up the mountain to **Merano 2000 Park** where the kids can have fun on climbing walls, bouncy castles, trampolines, and, best of all—one of the longest Alpine slides in Europe! The carts (Alpin Bob) on this mountain coaster zoom up to 22 kilometers an hour, which should delight any little thrill seeker. Find out more on their website: www.meran2000.com. This park is also a handy departure point for a hike to the **WaidmannAlm Farm**, which is an easy, stroller-friendly, 45-minute walk away. There your taste buds can feast on meals of local produce on the terrace, while your eyes feast on a perfect, panoramic view. ⊙ Merano 2000 & Alpine Bob Slides, Via Val di Nova 37, Merano. Tel: 0473.234821, www.merano2000.com. Open early May—early November, daily, 10:00—16:30 (until 17:30 in July and August). Family tickets are available, children under 8 don't have to pay to ride the *cabinovia*. Children must be at least 3 years old to ride the Alpine coaster.

Day Trips in the Dolomites

Val di Fassa

The Fassa valley is understandably one of the most popular tourist destinations in the Dolomites, with several exciting *funivias* that lead to jaw-dropping panoramic view points, and intriguing communities of Ladin speakers that still celebrate their ancient traditions. All in all, it's an ideal spot for mountain-loving travelers with children of all ages. Of the many options in this area, we have focused on two popular family attractions: Itinerary N. 2 will take you to Passo San Pellegrino and Pellegrino lake, and itinerary N. 3 will lead you to the town of Canazei, and the impressive Pass Pordoi.

> **Tip:** You will need to take a chairlift or cable car to reach most of the fun here. If you plan or riding two or more cable cars, it's might be worthwhile to get a Val di Fassa combo card. Ask about family discounts, too: www.fassa.com/it/PanoramaPass.

Itinerary N. 2: Passo San Pellegrino, Rifugio Fuciade, Lake Pellegrino & Moena

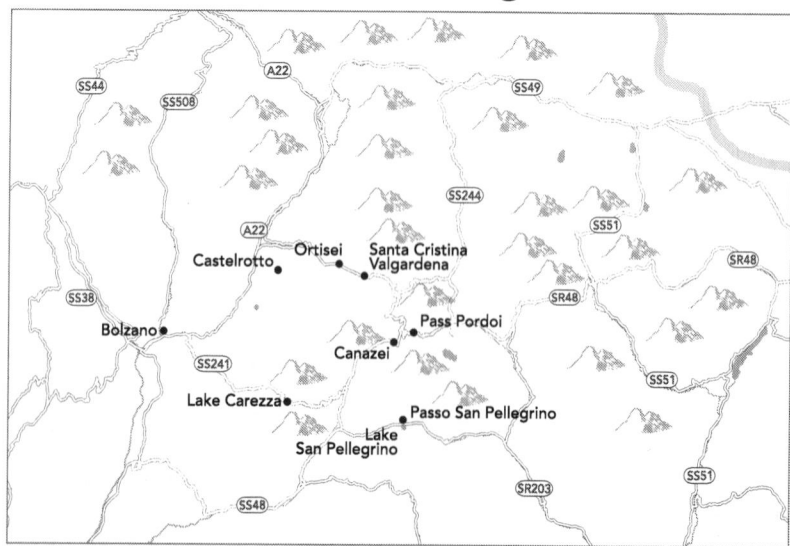

Getting there & parking: Set your GPS to Passo Pellegrino, which sits on the SS346 road, next to Hotel Arnika and Hotel Cristallo (both are marked on Google Maps). Select the road that passes through Moena, and not the SP81 that goes through Passo Rolle (it's a more difficult drive).

Tourist information office: Moena Tourist Office (APT Moena), Piaz de Navalge 4, Moena. Tel: 0462.609.770, infomoena@fassa.com. Open April–December, Monday—Saturday, 8:30—12:30 & 14:30—18:30; Sunday closed.

This half-day itinerary begins with a fun 90-minute hike to a chalet called **Rifugio Fuciade** (*rifugio* means mountain hut in Italian) along an easy, family-friendly path. Start at the **Parcheggio Passo San Pellegrino** parking lot, which is as far as you can go in summer because of traffic restrictions. Follow the trail to the small mountain hotel called **Rifugio Albergo Miralago** (Loc. Lago delle Pozze , Passo San Pellegrino Soraga, Tel: 0462.573.791, www. albergomiralago.com) which overlooks a little lake (Lago delle Pozze). This is where the real hike begins, as the road winds up the hill through a forest of pine trees. After about 20 minutes the views open up, and large alpine meadows dotted with wildflowers stretch in every direction. The kids have space to run around freely, roll in the grass and have a blast. Continue and follow the main path to **Rifugio Fuciade—La Baita,** and avoid the other paths branching off it, which aren't as accessible or suitable for families. The rifugio itself is a magical little place, run by husband and wife team Sergio and Emanuela. It is a cozy spot for a hearty, homey meal, and we especially love their creamy polenta with locally made sausages. In the summer, hiking is the only option to reach this baita; in the winter, they offer horse-drawn carriage rides through the snow covered forest, too! ⊙ Rifugio Fuciade, Localita' Fuciada, Passo San Pellegrino, Soraga. Tel: 0462.574.281, www.fuciade.it. Open daily in high season, though hours of operation tend to vary, call first.

Now, with your stomachs full, you are ready to hike back down to the starting point and proceed to the second part of the itinerary. **Lago (lake) di San Pellegrino,** is located just a few minutes from the parking lot and it is clean enough for you to jump in, and splash around. ⊙ Lago San Pellegrino, GPS coordinates: 46.376539, 11.784780.

Once you've dried off, you can go and explore **Moena**. Scenic wooden houses decorated with colorful flowers at every balcony are this lovely town's calling card. Moena means 'fertile land' in Ladino, and this verdant spot is lush enough to justify its name. You could end your day here, with a dinner at a good restaurant, though families with toddlers might want to make one more stop, at Fiabilandia, a popular playground in town that is suitable for younger children. ⊙ Fiabilandia, Strada de Massort, Moena. Cell: 338.223.7153. Open daily in high season, opening hours vary, call first.

264
Day Trips in the Dolomites

Itinerary N. 3: Lake Carezza, Canazei, and the Panoramic Pass Pordoi

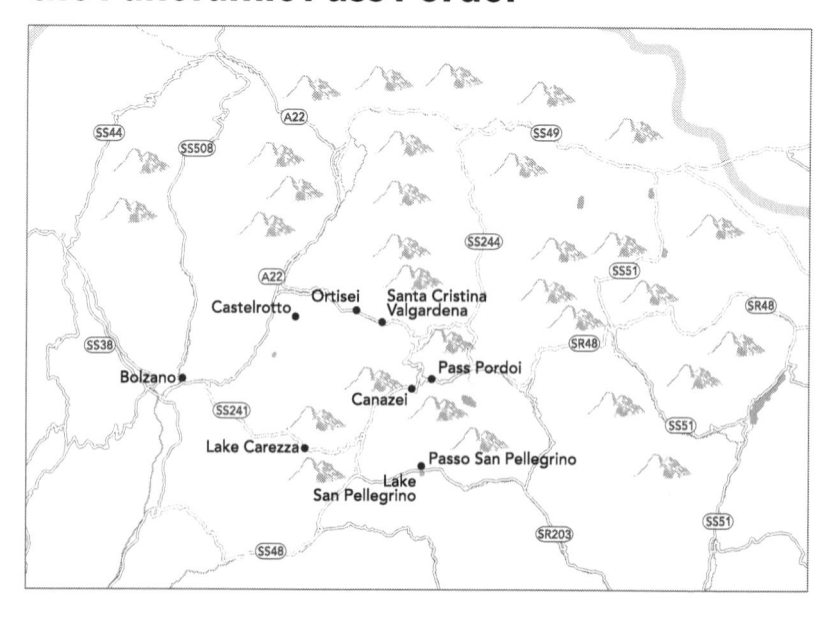

Day Trips in the Dolomites

If you only have half a day in Val di Fassa, the one thing you absolutely should not miss is a trip up the popular Pordoi funivia. While it is the second most famous cable car in the Dolomites (after the Marmolada), it is our first pick because the spectacular summit offers moon-like views: vast, stark and incredibly beautiful. If you are coming from Lake Garda or Bolzano, you can easily combine this funivia ride with a visit to Lake Carezza, followed by a drive through Pass Pordoi (the mountain pass connecting the towns of Canazei and Arabba), and a visit to Canazei itself.

Lake Carezza

Getting there & parking: The lake is just 35 minutes east of Bolzano. Take the SS241 and set your GPS to the large parking lot called Parcheggio Lago Carezza (marked on Google Maps, might appear as Karerseestraße on other maps). There is an underground tunnel that safely connects the parking lot with the lake itself.

Lake Carezza is one of the first lakes you will come upon when entering the Dolomites, which means that even if you don't have the time or energy to venture deep into the mountains, you will still be able to enjoy the beautiful views here. In the Ladin culture, lake Carezza is known as **Lec de Ergobando,** the rainbow lake, because of its spectacular colors. According to a local legend, once upon a time this lake was crystal clear, and in the middle of it lived a beautiful nymph. A sorcerer fell in love with her, and built a rainbow bridge to reach her, disguising himself as a salesman so she would not know his true identity and run away. But the nymph exposed his tricks and escaped, and the sorcerer, devastated, shattered the rainbow bridge into a million pieces that fell into the lake, giving it its colors. Note that this lake isn't suitable for swimming, and you can't sit directly on its shores, you can only walk along the trail that surrounds it, to admire its beauty.

> **Tip:** Instead of hiking, how about flying? The Catinaccio Zipline in Vigo di Fassa is located halfway between Lake Carezza and Canazei, and will enable you to do just that! See our full description at the end of this itinerary, under 'Special Activities in the Area'

Canazei

Getting there & parking: from Lake Carezza, continue on the SS241 (90 minutes). Set your GPS to Via Roma 30, Canazei, and park in that area. Via

Roma is just one minute from Canazei's main piazza (Piazza Marconi).

Tourist information office: Piazza Marconi 5, Tel: 0462.609.600. Open daily, 8:30—12:30 & 15:00—19:00. Canazei has one of the largest tourist offices in the valley; stop by to pick up a map and to learn about any guided tours and events planned during your stay.

Perched at 1,464 meters above sea level on the northern edge of Val di Fassa, Canazei is the highest village in the valley. This quaint town is part of Ladinia, the area where the geographic isolation provided by the mountains allowed the ancient language of Ladin to survive despite encroachment by Italian and German. The language is still spoken by some, and the colorful Ladin traditions and celebrations live on (see 'Special Events in the Area' at the end of this chapter). Known as Cianacéi in Ladin, Canazei offers views of the peaks of Marmolada (see Itinerary **N. 6** in this chapter), Sassolungo and the Sella group, several artisanal food shops to tempt hungry foodies, riverside parks and play areas (you can rent a bike and go for a ride), hotels and restaurants.

Pass Pordoi & Pordoi Funivia

Getting there & parking: From Canazei, drive along the SS48 (also known as the *Strada delle Dolomiti*) to reach the Pordoi Mountain Pass and the Pordoi Funivia. You'll find the funivia right alongside the SS48 road, in front of the Hotel Col di Lana (25 minutes from Canazei, it's also marked on Google Maps and Waze). There's a large parking lot for visitors.

The dramatic views that you'll see on the drive from Canazei will put you in the right mood to soar up to 2,950 meters above sea level and visit the Pordoi panoramic point. The four-minute ride up the funivia can be unnerving, but it is also truly spectacular. The observation deck feels like the absolute top of the world—we can't think of a better place to order a hot chocolate and enjoy the view. If you are feeling adventurous, you can also venture off for a little hike through the surreal landscape, and we'd recommend keeping it simple with children: Take the shortest path from the *funivia* station to **Rifugio Forcella Pordoi,** about 20 minutes away. The other trails are longer and involve serious hiking; this is the only family-friendly option here. In any case, call the Rifugio Forcella owners first, to check that the path leading there is open and clear (Cell: 368.355.7505) and be sure you don't miss the last *funivia* back down! ⊘ Funivia Pass Pordoi—Pass Pordoi Panoramic Cable Car, on the SS48. www.canazei.org. Open late-May—Mid October (precise opening times vary yearly), 9:00—17:00 (last admission at 16:00). Children pay a reduced fee.

Why the Dolomites Are Red at Dawn and Dusk

The Dolomites are known as the 'pale mountains', but they aren't pale first thing in the morning or at sunset—they are gloriously red. Scientists call this phenomenon *Enrosadira*, and explain that it happens due to an optical illusion when the light is reflected at certain angles off ice particles and various sediments on the rock. But the ancient Ladin inhabitants of the Dolomites had a different explanation in mind. According to them, it was the doing of Laurin, the king of dwarfs! Laurin was a well-known mythological creature in these valleys, and his beautiful rose garden was his pride and joy. When he lost a terrible battle with the Gothic King Theodoric the Great, he couldn't bear the idea of his enemy enjoying his roses. Laurin quickly put a spell on the garden, so that no one could see its beauty by day or by night. But the king of dwarfs was no lawyer, and there's a loophole in the spell—dawn and dusk. During those times, between day and night, the stunning red of his roses shines on.

Val Gardena

An hour northeast of Bolzano is the Val Gardena, family fun central. As one of five regions in the Dolomites with a majority of Ladin-speaking inhabitants, locals take great pride in their heritage, and traditional wood carving and craft shops can be found on every corner of the three main towns in the valley—Ortisei, Selva Val Gardena, and Santa Cristina.

Tourists, especially families, are warmly welcomed here. Kids receive discounts in hotels, dozens of activities are geared for families, and bikes and strollers can be borrowed for free (or a minor fee) from many local sports shops. The well-equipped tourist offices in Ortisei, Santa Cristina and Selva Val Gardena can provide you with more details about the various trails and services available in this area.

268
Day Trips in the Dolomites

There are many ways to explore this valley, but we will focus on our two favorite options: A visit to picturesque Ortisei and a hike to the peak of the Seceda mountain (see itinerary N. 4) is excellent for tweens and teenagers; and a tour of Santa Cristina and the Monte Pana Activity Park (see itinerary N. 5) is perfect for toddlers and younger children.

Itinerary N. 4: Ortisei and Seceda Summit

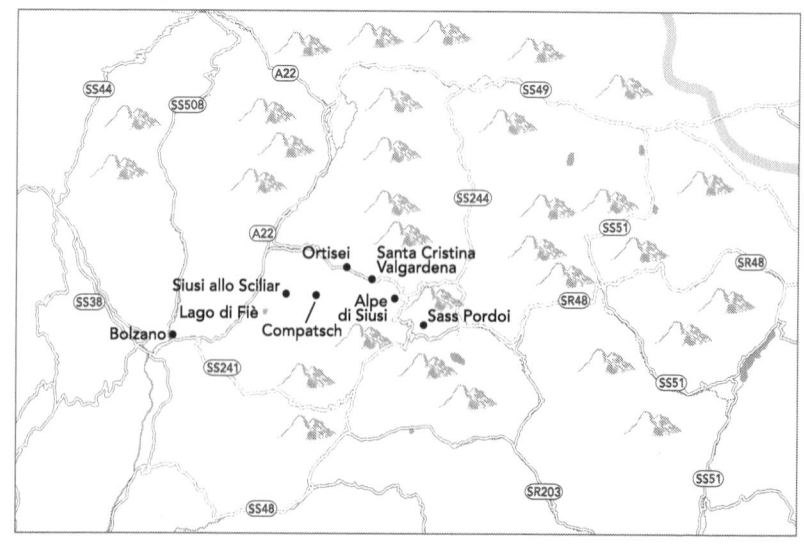

Ortisei

Getting there & parking: From Bolzano, take the SS12 and then the SS242. From Canazei, take the SS242 and cross the Gardena Pass (this is one of the most beautiful roads in the Dolomites, but it's also a serious one hour drive between the mountains). You can leave your car at the large lot by the Seceda Funivia (Via Val d'Anna 2, Ortisei; five minutes by foot or by escalator from the *centro storico*). Another popular lot can be found by the entrance to the Ovovia Alpe di Siusi, on Via Setil 9.

Tourist information office: APT Ortisei, Strada Rezia 1, Ortisei (near the church). Tel: 0471.777.600. Open daily, 9:00—12:00 & 14:00—18:00 (on Sunday the office may open later in the afternoon).

Begin your day in the town of **Ortisei,** which in the Ladin language is known as Urtijei—the place of nettles. Famous for its intricate, traditional wood carving, here you can stroll through a pedestrian shopping area admiring the local crafts and cheerful, brightly colored architecture. Maybe you'll find the perfect, exquisitely detailed wooden souvenir, or maybe you'll just have a nice coffee and a piece of apple strudel (a local specialty) and enjoy the fresh mountain air. Ortisei is picturesque in the summer, but it is absolutely delightful in the winter.

> **Tip:** Even without getting on a single funivia, kids still have plenty of places to jump and run in Ortisei. There's a small play area for toddlers and preschoolers at the **Parco Pubblico Spielplatz,** and for older children, the popular **Col de Flam Adventure Park** near the Seceda lift station is a hit. 🕐 Col de Flam adventure park, Str. Val d'Anna 10, Ortisei. Tel: 333.880.6080, www.coldeflam.it. Open June 15—September 15, daily, 10:00—19:00 (last admission at 18:00).

Once you've taken in the charms of Ortisei, it's time to head to the mountains. Many visitors don't realize this, but there are actually three different cable cars that depart from Ortisei, taking people up three different mountains: the **Resciesa Funicular** (www.resciesa.com), the **Alpe di Siusi Ovovia** (www.alpedisiusi-seiseralm.com) and, finally, our recommendation, the **Seceda Funivia.** The Seceda funivia is easily accessible, and the cable car will take you up to the stunning Seceda summit, where the mountain is topped with sheer slabs of earth that almost look like frozen waves. From here you can embark on a hike or even enjoy a sky-high playground. This funivia is a two-part journey: First you take the ovovia up to the Furnes summit, and then you take the seggiovia (chair lift) all the way up to the Seceda summit. Signage tells you about the most prominent peaks surrounding you, including the Brenta Group, the Adamello and Ortles Groups, and the Otzal and Stubai mountains all the way to Großglockner. 🕒 Seceda Funivia, Via Val D'anna 2, Ortisei. Tel: 0471.796.531, www.seceda.it. Open June—mid-October, daily, 8:30—17:30.

Once you've reached the peak, more magnificent views await you: Hiking trail no. 5 is a short and popular choice for many, and leads from the Seceda seggiovia station to the Curona Hut Seceda, a delightful chalet at 2,175 meters elevation with a café. An even easier option would be to hike to the playground at Cuca Baita, just minutes away, which also has a nice little restaurant.

To return, you can go the way you came, or you can choose a more challenging path and follow the trail leading to Rifugio Fermeda (www.fermeda.com). The trails passes through lovely alpine meadows, a botanic garden and a small lake, until you reach the Cabinovia Col Raiser funivia (www.colraiser.it) and take it down the mountain. You'll then have to take a bus back to Ortisei.

> **Tip:** If you plan on doing any of the hikes, buy a detailed map showing all the trails and lifts at the tourist office. Make sure you have the proper gear, too, and that you stick to trails that are suitable for the fitness level of everyone in your group. Remember, the altitude can affect you so don't assume a distance you find easy at sea level is going to be as easy for you here.

Itinerary N. 5: Santa Cristina and the Panaraida Park

Getting there & parking: From Ortisei, continue along the SS242 (20 minutes). From Bolzano, take the SS12 and then the SS242. There's a large parking lot next to the Santa Cristina Ski school and Hotel Cristallo, at the angle of SS242 and Via Dursan.

Tourist information office: Strada Chemun 9, Santa Cristina. Open Monday—Saturday, 8:30—12:00 & 15:00-18:30; Sunday 8:30—12:00. Tel: 0471.777800 / 0471.790137. The office can also advise you on the weekly tours and family activities organized in high season in town.

If your children are too young to enjoy the other hikes in this chapter, this itinerary is just the right size for them. Visiting Santa Cristina and the Panaraida (Monte Pana) park is a perfect morning or afternoon activity for the younger alpine adventurers. Quiet and quaint in the summertime, Santa Cristina becomes a tourist magnet in the winter, when it hosts the famous Saslong ski run and the Super-G and Downhill men's races in the FIS Ski World Cup. For shoppers, Santa Cristina boasts many Ladin wood carving shops with beautiful items. Even the simple, pale buildings with wooden trim radiate tranquility, and you can prolong your stay by enjoying a peaceful stroll on the Val Gardena Promenade, which was formerly a rail line.

Day Trips in the Dolomites

The PanaRaida Adventure Trail (park) is one of the few adventure parks in the Dolomites geared specifically towards toddlers and younger children. It starts right off the Seggiovia Monte Pana and goes in a loop through the meadows where you encounter 10 adventure stations along the way. The children can soar on a giant forest swing and zoom from tree to tree in a wooden cable car. The water play section is sure to delight with its miniature mill, and there's a picnic area, an intriguing labyrinth, and tree houses. In short—little ones have hours of hands-on fun here! Naturally, this half-day of attractions can easily be combined with the Ortisei itinerary. 🕐 Monte Pana Chair lift, Via Pana, San Cristina. Open mid-June through mid-September, daily, 8:30-16:30. Find out more here: www.valgardena.it/en/families/playgrounds/panaraida.

Day Trips in the Dolomites

Itinerary N. 6: The Marmolada, Lake Fedaia, and the Serrai Canyon

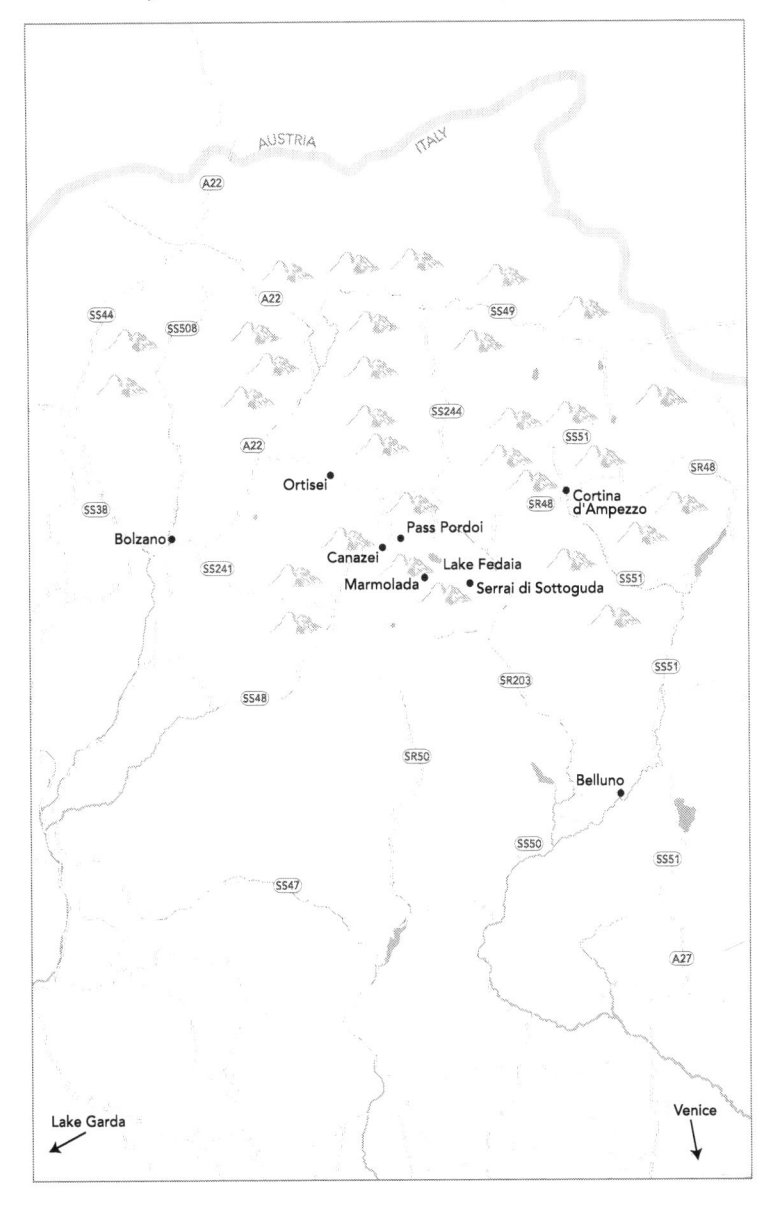

The Marmolada is the most famous peak in the Dolomites, a majestic sight surrounded by suitably beautiful treasures, including little waterfalls, an impressive canyon and a crystal blue lake. The suggestions in this itinerary don't require much walking, which means they are suitable for young children, too, though there are several more challenging hikes here for older and more adventurous teenagers.

Serrai di Sottoguda Canyon

Getting there & parking: From Canazei, take the SP641 heading east to the town of Rocca Pietore and the entrance to the Serrai Canyon (35 minutes). Park at the entrance to the reserve.

Start your day at the **Serrai Canyon,** where you can easily scale your visit to your family's interest and ability by either walking up or taking the little tourist train that runs from the town of Sottoguda (in the summer). Carved by receding glaciers and the Pettorina Torrent, the Serrai is, in places, a narrow gorge between dramatic, sheer cliffs. The long and narrow Franzei waterfall adds to the almost surreal sense of how small we are compared to the enormity of this landscape. Serrai Canyon also boasts some man-made features such as the Sant'Antonio church, and a statute of the Madonna dei Serrai in a natural grotto—a beautiful collaboration between man and nature.

The Marmolada

Getting there & parking: From Canazei or from Serrai di Sottoguda, take the SP641. There's a parking lot by the funivia station (marked on Google Maps).

Next, it's time for an audience with the queen of the Dolomites—the Marmolada. The highest point in the Dolomites, the Marmolada can even be spotted from Venice on a clear day. But seeing it up close is, naturally, a very different experience. The north side is fairly flat, while the south side has a long ridge of sheer cliffs. This was the border between Italy and Austria-Hungary until after WWI, and as such it was the front during the war. Soldiers hid here—Italians tucked into the craggy south side and Austro-Hungarians concealed in tunnels they dug into the north side. As the glacier on the north side retreats, it occasionally reveals evidence of the men who fought on these freezing ridges, and sacrificed so much.

You'll take two cable cars to reach the very top of Marmolada (they are included on one ticket), and will eventually reach Punta Roca, the highest point of the mountain, at a staggering 3,265 meters high. Believe it or not, you'll find a restaurant there if you want a bite to eat in front of some of the most awe-inspiring views in Europe. 🕒 Funivia Marmolada, Loc. Malga Ciapèla 48, Rocca Pietore. Tel: 0437.522984, www.funiviemarmolada.com. Open July—September, 9:00—16:00. In the winter it is open for skiing (call first). Bring a sweater or fleece; it can get very chilly at the summit.

Lake Fedaia

Getting there & parking: From the Marmolada, drive down the same road to the lake (marked on Google Maps).

End your itinerary with a visit to Lake Fedaia. This artificial, crystal blue lake sits just minutes from the Marmolada (by car) and is the result of the dam that was built here. If this dam seems rather familiar, you are not wrong—it appeared in the film *The Italian Job*. That isn't the lake's only brush with fame—in the 1950, an exclusive physics lab operated here, where a number of Nobel Prize winners worked and conducted their secretive research.

Day Trips in the Dolomites

Itinerary N. 7: Dobbiaco, Lake Braies and the Tre Cime di Lavaredo Nature Reserve

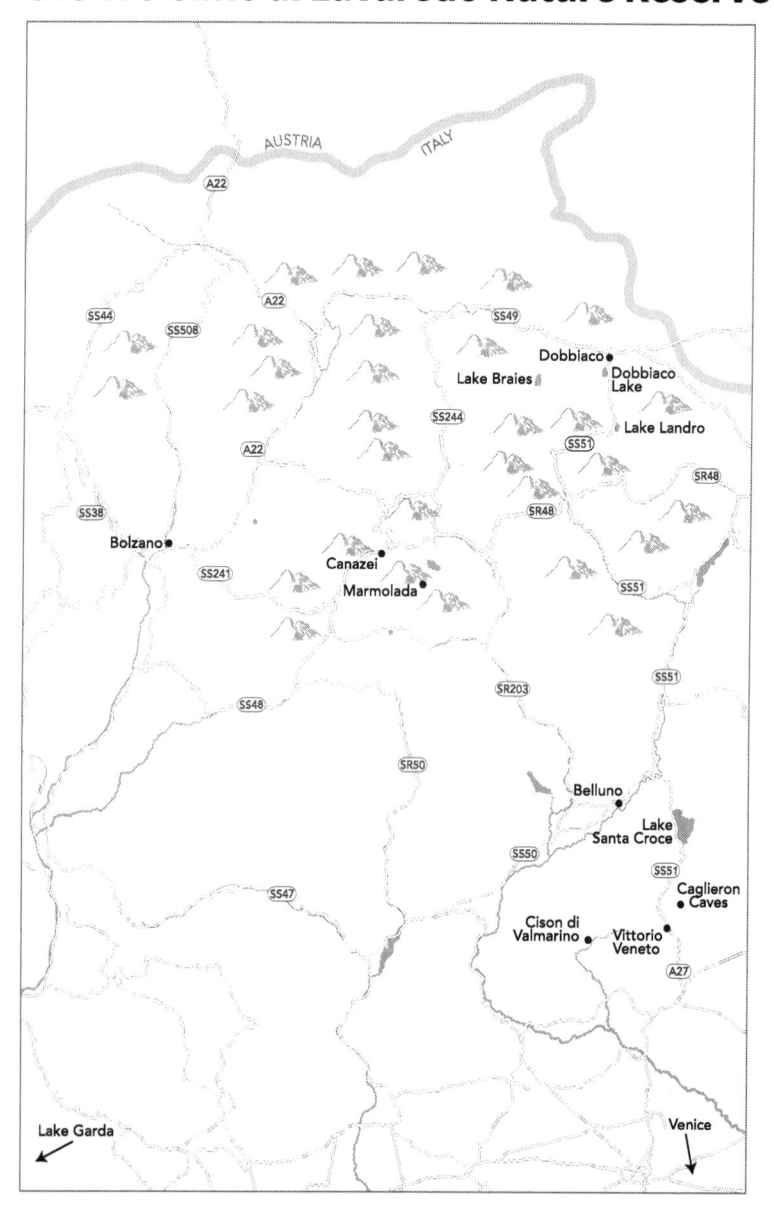

Day Trips in the Dolomites

This fun, flexible itinerary is one of our favorites because it combines sumptuous alpine scenery, the tranquility of Dobbiaco and three beautiful lakes in the countryside. You can modify the itinerary to suit your personal tastes, but however you arrange it, you can look forward to a day of family fun and unforgettable views. If you are coming from Venice, consider breaking the long drive to Dobbiaco by making a pit stop at Lake Santa Croce and the Caglieron caves, which are en route and are described in detail in the 'Day Trips from Venice' chapter.

Dobbiaco, Lake Dobbiaco, and the Tre Cime Reserve

Getting there & parking: From Venice, take the A27 autostrada up north in the direction of Brunick (2.5 hours).

Tourist information office: Associazione Turistica Dobbiaco, Via Dolomiti 3, Dobbiaco. Tel: 0474.972.132, www.tre-cime.info/it/dobbiaco. Open: Monday—Friday, 9:00—12:30 & 15:00—18:00 (July—August open non-stop until 19:00). Saturday, 9:00—12:00. In July and August open on Sunday, too.

Start your Alpine day in Dobbiaco, which sits just 15 minutes from the Austrian border. This picturesque town was composer Gustav Mahler's favorite retreat, and he would come to his little cabin here to draw inspiration from the abundant natural beauty and serenity. The town celebrates its Mahler connection with a classical music festival every summer.

You can see, hear and even taste the Austrian influence in every corner of Dobbiaco. The locals speak German, and the restaurants serve almost only Austrian specialties. Dobbiaco is very easy to navigate and has many bike rental shops and wide bike paths that lead to various attractions in the countryside. The town's center features mostly restaurants and is only partially interesting; it can be skipped in favor of other family-friendly attractions, such as Dobbiaco's **Wild Animal Park,** where you can visit lynxes, raccoons, goats, pigs and deer that are tame enough to feed and even pet. 🕐 Dobbiaco Animal Park (Parco Zoologico in Italian, Gustav Mahler Stube in German), Carbonin Vecchia 3, Dobbiaco. Tel: 0474.972.347, www.gustavmahlerstube.com. Open daily in the summer, 9:00—18:00. Off-season closed on Thursday. Children under 13 pay a reduced entry fee.

Then, if your children are wild about chocolate (and who isn't?) you can drive over the border to the town of Heinfels, Austria to the **Loacker**

Day Trips in the Dolomites

Chocolate Factory (15 minutes from Dobbiaco, by car). The smell of chocolate alone will get everyone excited, but an even better way to enjoy this attraction would be to join their pastry workshop. This should be booked in advance, and details are on their website: www.loacker.com. 🕐 Loacker, Panzendorf 196, Heinfels Tirolo, Austria. Tel: 00-43-48426060. Open daily, 9:00—17:00 (until 18:30 in high season).

For the best and most child-friendly lunch in town, drive back to Dobbiaco and head to **Reierhof**, a restaurant and farm with a playground and petting zoo that kids will love. 🕐 Reierhof, Via Pater Haspinger 12, S. Maddalena Val Casies. Cell: 3489529370 www.reierhof.com. Open mid-May—late-September for lunch only, closed Tuesday.

> **Tip:** If you are packing a picnic to enjoy at one of the nearby lakes, you can pick up some delicious cheese and yogurt at **Latteria Tre Cime – Mondolatte,** Via Pusteria 3, Dobbiaco. Open daily, mid-July—mid-September, 8:00—19:00 (10:00—18:00 on Sunday).

Once you've seen all that Dobbiaco has to offer, either drive along the SS51 or bike to the **lakes**. The nearest one is **Lake Landro** (only five minutes away), and while it is quite small, it's also very accessible, and a perfect spot for a picnic with some serious views. The next lake along the road is Lake Dobbiaco, but before you reach it, make sure you make a stop en route, to enjoy the stunning view of the mountain peaks at **Punto Panoramico Tre Cime.** Set your GPS to Cafe-Ristorante-Hotel Tre Cime, Via Landro 6, and walk 100 meters to the wood-clad panoramic deck to marvel at the beauty before you. It's quite rare to find a panoramic viewpoint right off the road that doesn't require any special climbing or driving or cable cars!

Lake Dobbiaco, also known by its German name Toblach See, is about seven kilometers further down the SS51 road from Punto Panoramico Tre Cime. This is one of our favorite undiscovered spots in the area. While not as famous as Lake Braies (which we describe below), it really is the perfect spot for families. As accessible as it is gorgeous, the stunning turquoise water is framed by the grey mountains and green grass. Follow the stroller-friendly walking trails along the lake shores to discover ducks, picnic areas and paddle boats to rent.

Lake Braies

Getting there & parking: from Dobbiaco, take the SS49 (20 minutes); the lake is marked on Google Maps. There are three (rather pricey) parking lots for visitors; the earlier you come, the better your chances of finding a spot in the parking lot N. 1, which is right by the lake. Otherwise, you'll have to park farther away in one of the other two lots, and walk.

Lake Braies is one of the most popular attractions in the Dolomites. Dramatic cliffs and pine-covered slopes swoop down to the crystalline waters of this exquisite mountain lake, but so do crowds of people, which can detract from the sense of magic and serene natural beauty at times. Many of the lakes in the Dolomites have hotels on their shores, but Lake Braies's **Hotel Pragser Wildsee** has a history worth knowing. At the end of WWII, the Nazis brought a group of high-profile prisoners from Dachau and other concentration camps to one of the last points the SS still controlled—South Tyrol. Amid confusion about where to hold them and panic at the looming arrival of the Allies, 139 prisoners from 17 countries were liberated. Among them were family members of Claus von Stauffenberg and Carl Friedrich Goerdeler (two of the men behind the famous failed attempt to assassinate Hitler on July 20, 1944); Léon Blum (the former French prime-minister) and the Lutheran priest Martin Niemöller (famous for his anti-war poem: "First they came for the Socialists, and I did not speak out because I was not a Socialist .... Then they came for me and there was no one left to speak for me."). Once they were liberated from the claws of the SS, the prisoners were welcomed to the Hotel Pragser Wildsee as their first step on the road to freedom and recovery.

The hiking trails around the lake are well sign posted from the entrance road, but first you'll have to take your eyes off the stunning Croda del Becco mountain rising to 2,810 meters to dominate the skyline. The western shore is good for young children, and it is stroller-friendly. The eastern shore is harder to navigate and rather steep, so we'd advise against trying with a stroller.

Itinerary N. 8: The Gilfenklamm Gorge, Racines, and the Ridanna Monteneve Mines

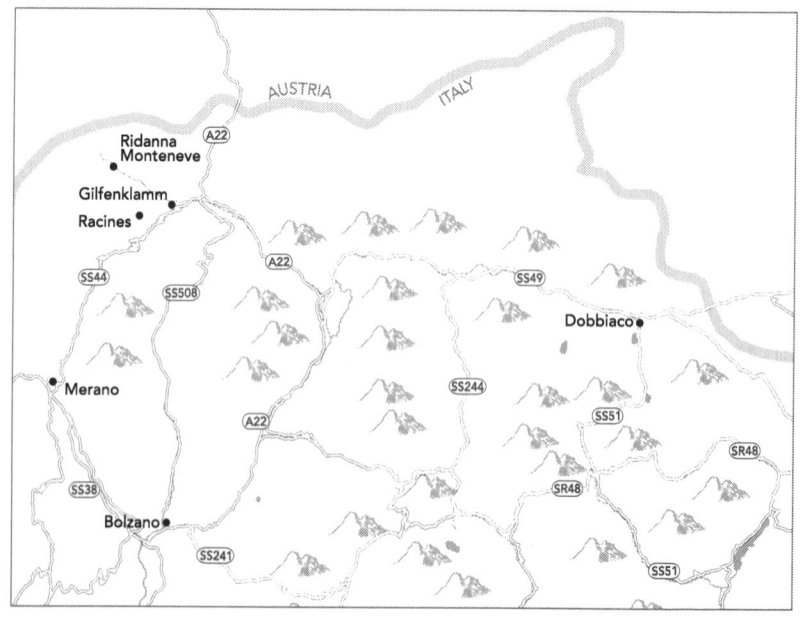

Day Trips in the Dolomites

This action-packed, fun-filled day explores a different side of the Dolomites. Instead of heading up to one the summits to marvel at panoramic views, you'll splash around in Gilfenklamm Gorge and then go below the earth's surface at the World of Mines of Ridanna Monteneve. Between those two points, there's a hike and a visit to an alpine playground. You can make this a two-day excursion from Lake Garda by adding half a day at a nearby lake (Dobbiaco, for example, is only 90 minutes away), and some time relaxing in one of the quaint little mountain villages.

Stanghe Waterfalls at Gilfenklamm Gorge

Getting there & parking: From Lake Garda, take the A22/E35 up north to Vipiteno (2.5 hours). The entry to the stanghe waterfalls is near the Racines sports' center, and the Jaufensteg Albergo (hotel). There's ample parking there.

Gilfenklamm Gorge is extremely popular in high season, so we strongly recommend arriving early (by 11:30 it is usually crowded). Once you behold this living work of nature's art, you'll understand why. The river slices through the gorge, with rocks of various colors rising from the water and lush plants sprouting wherever they can. The exciting trail here includes a series of metal and wooden bridges, and in spots it takes you under low cliffs where you will feel like real explorers when you duck to fit through. It leads you to the Stanghe waterfall, and once you have had your fill of admiring the sparkling water plunging down, you can hike back the way you came. You'll follow the same trail, but with one difference: you are going to be all wet! Most children love this, especially on hot days, but it is good to be prepared and have dry clothes to change into. ◎ Gilfenklamm, Stanghe di Racines, Racines. Tel: 0472.760.608, www.sterzing-ratschings.it.

Day Trips in the Dolomites

Adventure Time!

Just five kilometers from the gorge, at the town of Racines, you will find **Parco Mondo Avventura Montagna,** an alpine playground with slides, ponds, monkey bars and more. You'll encounter some farm animals wandering around, and there's a small adventure park nearby that younger children will like. To reach it, set your GPS to the Cabinovia Racines-Giovo parking lot, take the cable car up the mountain, and follow the easy, one-kilometer trail to the park itself. Open mid-June—late September, daily, 8:30—17:00. In case of bad weather, call before coming here to make sure they are open. Tel: 0472.659.153, www.ratschings-jaufen.it. For older kids, the **Skytrek Adventure Park** in Vipiteno is a much better option. They have adventurous climbing routes, obstacle courses, and more. The park is very close to the Gilfenklamm Gorge, and is open April—September, Wednesday—Sunday, 10:00—18:00; July—August, open daily. May close down in case of bad weather, even in season (call first). Nordpark Sterzing—Parco Nord Vipiteno, cell: 345.865.2530, www.skytrek.it.

Ridanna Monteneve Mines

Getting there & parking: From Gilfenklamm, take Via Stanghe towards the town of Racines (20 minutes). The mines are right outside Racines, and are marked on Google Maps. There's parking at the entrance.

Once the kids have dried off, it's time to head to the mines and see what's below the surface of the Dolomites. At the **World of Mines Ridanna Monteneve** you'll don a helmet and head down dark (stroller-accessible, for the most part) paths. You have a choice of tours that last between half a day and 90 minutes; the 'compact tour' is two hours long, includes plenty of hands on activities for kids, and will be perfect for most families. You'll learn how the technology of mining evolved through the ages, and a bit about minerals, too. The tours are child-friendly, so they will have fun and won't object to the sneaky science lesson. The mines are chilly, bring a fleece and scarf to bundle up. Not all tours are available in English—call before your visit to make sure. ◴ Miniera Ridanna Monteneve, Localita' Masseria 48, Racines. Tel: 0472.656.364, www.bergbaumuseum.it. Open late March—early November. Guided tours available Tuesday—Sunday, 9:30, 11:15, 13:30 and 15:15. In August the mines are open on Monday, too. Booking in advance is recommended: ridanna.monteneve@museominiere.it.

If somehow you still have any energy left, the small but beautiful **Wolfsthurn Castle** is just 10 minutes from the mines and is the perfect place to end your day. To reach it, continue along Strada Kalchern; the castle is marked on Google Maps, too. Known as the 365 window palace, this Baroque mansion houses today a hunting museum, filled with taxidermied animals (which might interest some children, but upset others). The castle's richly decorated rooms provide visitors with a peek into the lives of the noble families who once lived here, and there's also a beautiful garden, complete with walking trails that are fun to explore. In season, the staff organize artistic workshops for children—call first to find out if anything is available in English, too. ◴ Wolfsthurn Castle–South Tyrolean Museum of Hunting and Fishing, Kirchdorf 25, Ratschings/Mareit. Tel: 0472.758.121, www.wolfsthurn.it. Open April—mid-November, Tuesday—Saturday, 10:00-17:00; Sundays and Holidays, 13:00—17:00. Closed Monday.

Itinerary N. 9: Alpe di Siusi, Bullaccia Summit and a Horse Carriage Ride

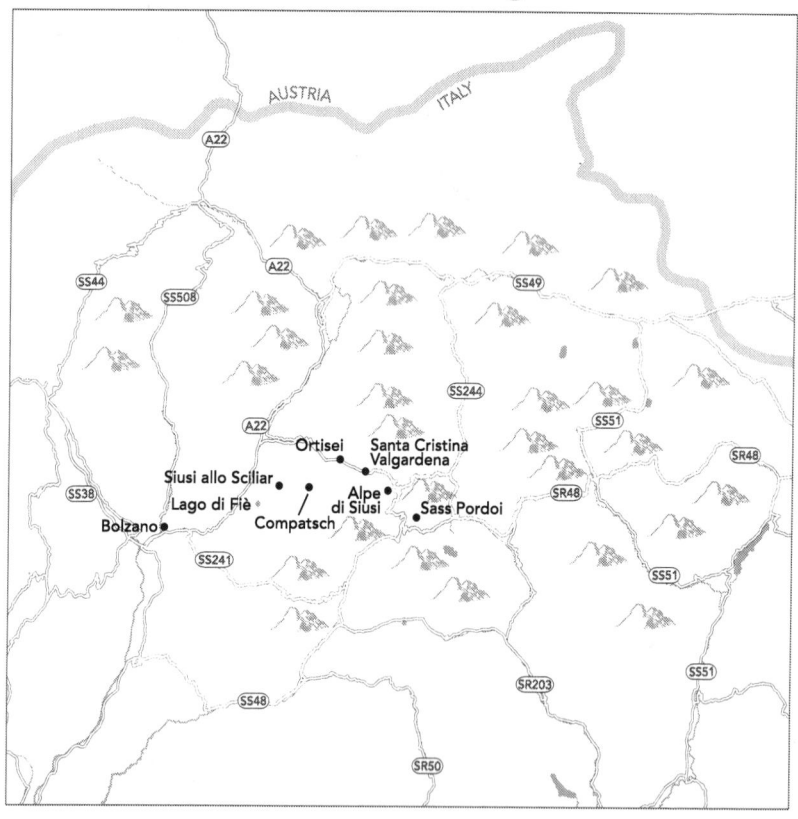

Getting there & parking: Take the A22 autostrada, exit at Bolzano Nord and proceed to one of the towns within the Alpe di Siusi plateau (Castelrotto, Fiè Allo Sciliar, or Siusi). It's worth noting that you can also access the Alpe di Siusi from the other side of the plateau, by taking the ovovia from Ortisei. In the summertime, road restrictions apply, and between 9 a.m. and 5 p.m. you won't be able to go any further than the town of San Valentino (unless you have a special pass). To avoid finding yourself blocked halfway, drive to the town of Siusi, park your car in the large lot, and take the Cabinovia up to the Alpe di Siusi plateau. Alternatively, you can also drive to Castelrotto, park there, tour the town, and then take the bus to the Siusi cabinovia.

Day Trips in the Dolomites

The Alpe di Siusi is a stunning area, and the largest high-altitude alpine meadow in Europe. Green meadows roll down the slopes looking like the setting of a fairy tale, and in winter when it snows, the same slopes are filled with skiers. The many hiking trails in this popular family destination include some easy, kid-friendly routes, and you can enjoy a day of exploring the spectacular scenery from the vantage point of a cable car. The Cabinovia Alpe di Siusi will take you from the town of Siusi up to **Localita' Compatsch**. We recommend buying in advance the full ticket, which includes the funivia to Compatsch and the subsequent seggiovia from Compatsch up to the Bullacia (Puflatsch, in German) summit. ◐ Cabinovia Alpe di Siusi, Via Sciliar 39, Siusi. Tel: 0471.704.270, www.seiser-alm.it.

> **Tip:** Compatsch is the starting point for many hikes as well as fun horse-drawn carriage rides across the meadows! Find out more about the various trails at the Compatsch Tourist Office (near the cabinovia, open in season only, Località Compatsch 50, Tel: 0471.727.904). You can also consult the 'Special Activities' section at the end of this chapter.

As soon as you descend from the chairlift, you will see the views and the path that leads to Puflatsch Restaurant (Ristorante Bullaccia, in Italian). This is an excellent place to stop for lunch, with gorgeous views and delicious food. ◐ Puflatschhütte (Bullaccia), Alpe di Siusi. Tel: 333.9047182 / 0471.727.839, www.puflatsch.eu/en.

Once you've eaten, it's time for a hike. The Compatsch trail is one of the nicest and most popular options, and it is suitable for families. Start there, and then take Trail No. 30 for a 90-minute walk to the town of Saltria. From Saltria you can walk back down, or take the bus back to where you left your car.

> **Tip:** Whichever hike you choose, we recommend you first stop by the tourist office to pick up an updated map of the trails, make sure that all trails are open and clear, and verify the bus schedule.

Day Trips in the Dolomites

The Marinzen Hike

An alternative to the popular Alpe di Siusi trails would be to drive to the beautiful village of Castelrotto, and take the Marinzen seggiovia (chair lift) to the Marinzen mountain. From there you can either hike to Puflatsch-Bullaccia, or stay in the area and walk just 15-20 minutes to the delightful Schafstallhütte Baita (mountain hut) which features a restaurant, a petting zoo, a large playground, and even a fish pond for fishing (the necessary equipment can be rented at Marinzenhütte). Find out more at the Castelrotto Tourist Office: Piazza Kraus 1, Castelrotto. Tel: 0471.706333. Open Monday—Saturday, 9:00-12:00 & 14:00—18:00. Sunday closed.

End your day in this area with a drive to **Lake Fié,** a reminder that small is beautiful. This lake is located in the **Parco Naturale Sciliar-Catinaccio** (nature reserve), so you'll have to leave your car in the lot and hike in. Feel free to jump into Lake Fié for a swim; it is one of the cleanest lakes in the Dolomites. This is the perfect spot to relax, lounge on a deck in the sun, or rent a little boat and paddle away. Drink in the gorgeous mountain views, and if you are hungry, you can hike to **Malga Tuff Alm**, a particularly nice mountain chalet that sits just a short distance from the lake and has a petting zoo and playground as well as a restaurant (www.tuffalm.it). To reach it, follow trail number 1b (check your map before departing), which starts behind hotel Waldsee (www.hotel-waldsee.com). As you walk up, you'll pass another small lake (for fishing) and several wooden sculptures of animals. ◷ Malga Tuff Alm, Fie' allo Sciliar. Tel: 0471.726090, www.tuffalm.it. Open Easter—September, Wednesday—Thursday for dinner only; Friday—Sunday, 11:00—23:00.

Day Trips in the Dolomites

Itinerary N. 10: Cortina d'Ampezzo and the 5 Torri Historic Open Air Museum

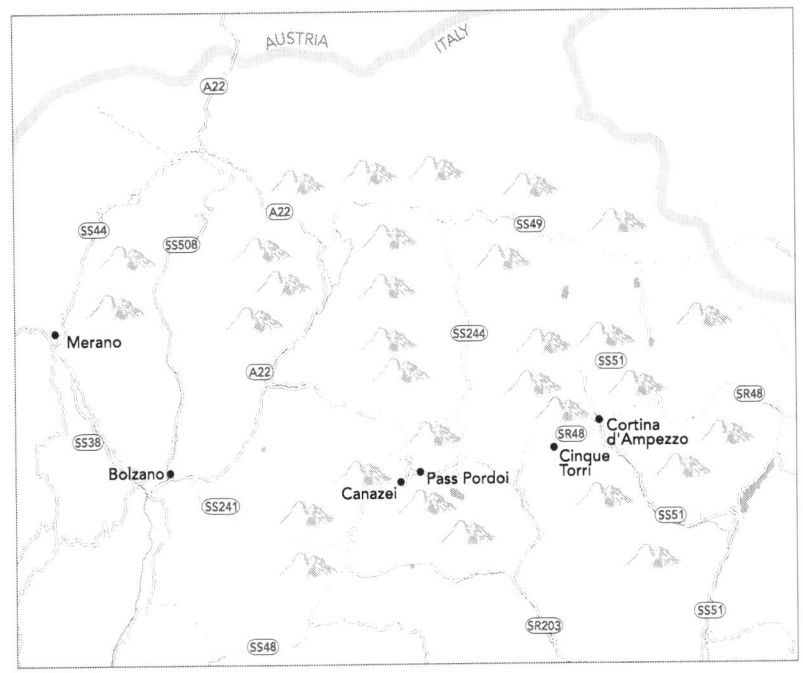

This half day trip offers some truly dramatic views, and goes well with the Lake Santa Croce itinerary (see the 'Day Trips from Venice' chapter), the Dobbiaco itinerary, or the Marmolada itinerary because of its geographic proximity. You can use these itineraries to create a circular two-day Dolomite adventure that starts and ends either in Venice or in Bolzano.

Cortina d'Ampezzo

Getting there & parking: From Venice, take the A27 autostrada, then the SS51. There is a large parking lot by the Cortina d'Ampezzo bus terminal, at Via Guglielmo Marconi 25.

Start your morning in Cortina d'Ampezzo, the Aspen of Italy, which sits two and a half hours north of Venice. The drive here is not very interesting, initially, until you pass the town of Pieve di Cadore, where the landscape suddenly changes dramatically. In the winter, Cortina d'Ampezzo is a hot ski destination with expensive hotels and chic designer boutiques that cater to well-heeled tourists from across Europe. The town was immortalized in a number of films (The Pink Panther, in 1963, and the James Bond film *For Your Eyes Only*, in 1981), and before that, the 1956 Winter Olympics were held here. In the summer, Cortina is much calmer, and is a good starting point for excursions though there isn't much to see or do in the town itself. Unless you have teens who love to shop, and a budget to indulge them, a short visit and a *gelato* break here will suffice, in favor of more interesting attractions nearby.

Once you leave Cortina, take the SR48 toward Passo Falzeron (Falzeron mountain pass). This is a beautiful drive, and we recommend stopping at either **Disco Bar Belvedere** or **La Locanda Del Cantoniere Di Bellodis Ivanoor** on the way for coffee and some apple strudel in front of the stunning view. Then, continue on the SR48 until you see the sign for **Funivia 5 Torri,** which is your next stop. 🕐 Disco Bar Belvedere, Località Pocol, 38, Cortina d'Ampezzo. Cell: 333.279.3363, www.belvederecortina.com. Open daily in July—August, 10:00—20:00; open in the weekends only for the rest of the season. 🕐 La Locanda Del Cantoniere Di Bellodis Ivano Localita' Vervei 1, Cortina d'Ampezzo, Strada statale 48 delle Dolomiti. Tel. 043.686.6275, www.locandadelcantoniere.it. Open June—September, 12:00—15:00 & 19:30—21:00. May close on Tuesdays.

Cinque Torri (5 Torri) Park & Open Air Museum

Getting there & parking: From Cortina, continue for 16 km (35 minutes) on the SR48 until you see the sign for Funivia 5 Torri (marked on Google Maps as Cinque Torri). There's ample parking at the entrance.

With so many chairlifts and itineraries in the Dolomites, the Funivia 5 Torri has somehow remained under the radar. But it's a secret we are happy to share with our readers, because the views here are just astounding. Dramatic formations jut upward from the peaks, with paths running between the cliffs allowing you a very close up look at the strange beauty of the sheer, naked rock. Below you is classic alpine scenery, with rolling verdant meadows that offer glorious skiing in winter.

This area is popular not only with hikers, but with history lovers, too. This was an important battlefield in World War One, and the entire area before your eyes is now an open-air museum, dedicated to the thousands of soldiers who hid and fought here. In fact, the reason you can easily

Day Trips in the Dolomites

walk along the paths on this difficult terrain is because the Italian troops stationed here a century ago built them to move supplies. Watch the ground as you walk; if you are lucky, you might spot bits of barbed wire, shrapnel from explosives, and other war debris.

It pays to read a bit about WWI before you arrive because there is not much signage or explanation here. This was the front-line between Italy and Austria-Hungary, and troops from both sides burrowed into the mountainside and the ice and fought furiously. It is almost inconceivable that such beauty was the backdrop for so much violence and misery. The Austro-Hungarians wanted to push past the Italians and sweep down the Alps to seize Venice and encircle the Italian army. But the Italians managed to hold firm and stop them in what some describe as the most treacherous conditions of WWI. But it was not a quick matter of one decisive battle. Italians were stationed here for two years, battling both the opposing army and nature itself in what became known as the White War. In these stunning alpine peaks, 18,000 lives were lost—more to avalanches, the 'white death', than to warfare. ◉ Funivia 5 Torri—Museo Lagazuoi, Passo Falzarego (17 km from Cortina d'Ampezzo). Tel: 0436. 867301, www.lagazuoi5torri.dolomiti.org. Open May—October, 9:00—16:40. To reach the summit you'll need to take the cable car, then the chairlift. Children under 15 pay a reduced fee.

> **Tip:** For lunch, the baita right by the chair lift (Rifugio Scoiattoli www.rifugioscoiattoli.it) is one of the most popular choices. The food is very good, much of it is locally sourced, and the ambiance is lively and friendly.

KIDS' CORNER

More About... The Animals of the Dolomites!

Pssst, you! Yes, you! Do you love nature and animals? If so, the Dolomites are for you. Put on your walking shoes, and take out your spy binoculars—it's time to go on an adventure and discover which animals hide in these mountains.

When you think of mountain animals, you might think of wild goats, and you'd be right. Chamois are a small goat-antelope, native to the Alps. They are brown in spring and summer, then turn grey in the winter to blend in with the snow and camouflage themselves from predators. If you see one, watch quietly and you might see a dozen more—they live in herds. Mouflon are a type of wild sheep that can be found between the soaring ridges of the Dolomites. They have distinctive curled horns (watch out!), and are more vocal that most forest animals. In fact, they were politely asked not to audition for the next season of The Dolomites' Got Talent... Other animals here include the lynx and brown bear, which are closely monitored by the park zoologists and environmental scientists, to protect them. When you walk along the meadows in the high altitudes be extra quiet, as sometimes large groups of chatty marmots hide behind them! Even if you can't spot any of these animals during your hikes, don't be disappointed—you

KIDS' CORNER

can still find proof of their presence. Just look carefully at the ground, and you will see the tracks in the mud left by paws and hooves. Can you guess which tracks belong to which animals?

Naturally, there are many birds in the Dolomites, too. Listen for woodpeckers in the forests, as well as Rock ptarmigans, and the largest grouse in the forest, the capercaillie. Listen carefully, you might hear the female's cackling call between the trees! Check YouTube for the sound before you leave on your trip, and try to identify it during your hike. These dark birds have distinctive red patches around their eyes and the males like to spread their tail feathers like peacocks to impress and attract the females. Golden eagles, Eurasian eagle owls, and different types of owls live here too. At night, these nocturnal birds of prey sweep the forests and catch little rodents for a tasty dinner.

Are you Ready for a challenge? Take our super Dolomites Quiz!

Question one: What is "Enrosadira"?

    a. A witch who lives in the Dolomite forests and eats pickled squirrels.
    b. A large mythical bird.
    c. A natural phenomenon, also known as "Alpenglow", which describes the changing colors of the Dolomites throughout the day, from pink to orange to pale grey to bright red.

Question two: Which of the following animals can be found in the Dolomites?

    a. Brown bears.
    b. Grizzly bears.
    c. Polar bears.
    d. Winnie the Pooh bears.

Question three: What was the name of the scientist who gave the Dolomites their name?

    a. Doldol Dolimitisky Mc.Dolomiten (AKA – the Dol man).
    b. Dèodat de Dolomieu.
    c. Mr. Potato Breath.

Question four: How old are the Dolomites?

    a. One million years.
    b. four hours.
    c. 280 million years.

Eating in the Dolomites

Many tourists are surprised when they discover the cuisine of the Dolomites is often not Italian, but Austrian-German. This region became a part of Italy only in 1919, and is still heavily influenced by its neighbors: You'll see German place names, experience some Ladin and German culture and traditions, and taste heavier dishes with roots in Austria. Because most children prefer pizza and pasta over the traditional German cuisine, we've focused our recommendations specifically on Italian style restaurants, to please all. In addition to the restaurants recommended here, know that all the baita (mountain chalets) listed in the itineraries are also restaurants, and they tend to have the best traditional food (booking a table in advance is always recommended).

MERANO

Restaurant Pizzeria Mosl cooks up huge pizzas that will delight kids and adults. It's very popular, so advance booking is recommended. The restaurant is located right outside Merano, at Via Priami 1, Loc. Obermais, Merano. Tel: 0473.210780. Open Thursday—Tuesday, 10:30—14:30 & 17:00—22:45 (the restaurant closes at 20:45, the pizzeria at 22:45). Wednesday closed.

Kirchsteiger is one of our favorites in Merano's historic center. Enjoy a range of dishes including their popular pizza in a comfy, warm, family-friendly atmosphere. Via Dante Alighieri 22, Merano. Tel: 0473.230365. Open in season, Friday—Tuesday, 12:00—14:00 & 18:00—21:30; Thursday closed.

ORTISEI

Cafe' Pasticceria Demetz is a solid, convenient option for families with a selection of sandwiches, cakes, and hot beverages. Via Rezia 44, Ortisei. Tel: 0471.796157, www.cafedemetz.com. Winter: from 07:45—20:30; Summer, 07:45—19:30. July & August until 23:00.

Ristorante Pizzeria Erica offers the usual selection of kid-friendly pizza and pasta in a relaxed environment. It's a nice find in an area with so many high-end restaurants. Via Purger 5, Ortisei, Tel: 0471.796348. Open year round, Thursday—Tuesday, 12:00—14:30 & 18:00—23:30. Wednesday closed.

CANAZEI

Ristorante La Stua dei Ladins offers tasty pizza, pasta and antipasti platters with local cold cuts and cheese and a side order of rustic charm. The food is good, and it is worth going just to see the incredible woodwork, especially the wooden ceiling. Streda de Pareda 33, Canazei. Tel: 0462 600316. Open Wednesday—Monday, 20:00—23:30; Tuesday closed. In high season (mid-July—mid-September) open daily.

Ristorante Mini is not technically in Canazei but in nearby Campitello di Fassa. This tiny gem is worth the drive for the tasty food and charming atmosphere. Strada de Morandin 27, Campitello di Fassa. Tel: 0462.750168, www.minirestaurant.it. Open Tuesday—Sunday for dinner, 18:00—21:00. Monday closed. Opening hours may vary, call first and book a table, as they are always full.

DOBBIACO

Restaurant Winkelkeller is a popular choice for a typical Tyrolese meal. They are full every night of the week, so book in advance to enjoy their polenta, sausages and potato dumplings. Graf-Kuenigl-Strasse 8, Dobbiaco, Tel: 0474.972022, www.winkelkeller.it. Open Thursday—Tuesday, 12:00—14:00 & 17:30—21:00; Wednesday closed.

Ristorante Lago di Landro, right on Landro Lake and five kilometers outside of Dobbiaco, offers simple, tasty and reasonably priced food in a lovely setting. Via Landro 8, Dobbiaco. Tel: 0474.972399. Open year round 08:00—21:00 (off season until 18:00).

GILFENKLAMM & VIPITENO

Knappenstube is right near the mines, in the town of Racines, and features hearty, traditional yet sophisticated Tyrolese fare in a relaxed environment. Masseria 48, Racines. Tel: 0472.656471, www.knappenstube.com. Open Tuesday—Sunday, 11:30—14:00 & 18:30-20:30. Closed Monday.

Pizzeria Seidner is a family-friendly choice with tasty pizza. Vicolo Ralser 1, Vipiteno. Tel: 0472.765437. Open Monday—Saturday, 11:00—14:00 & 17:00—22:30. Sunday closed. Opening hours may vary in the winter.

Sleeping in the Dolomites

> **Tip:** The Dolomites offer over 1,500 B&B, hotels, and self-catering accommodations. However, these are not your only options. For families, an even better choice is often a farm stay. Many of the farms in the Dolomites are also B&Bs where your children can meet the animals, learn how food is harvested and even see how cheese is made. Find out more here: www.redrooster.it.

VAL GARDENA

Hotel Posta in Santa Cristina is an eco-friendly, family-friendly option with reasonable rates. They offer a children's activity area with crafts and cookery, a climbing wall, organized hikes and a spa. Via Dursan 32, Santa Cristina Valgardena. www.familyhotelposta.com.

Hotel Biancaneve in Selva di Val Gardena has a stunning location. In addition to the gorgeous setting, you'll find a variety of children's activities including swimming and skiing (in the winter) as well as babysitting services. They raise the bar for child-friendliness by providing swim diapers, baby carriers and strollers. Str. Cir 36, Selva di Val Gardena. www.biancaneve.it.

Residence Cesa Callegari offers self-catering apartments with fully equipped kitchens in Selva di Val Gardena. It's just a 10-minute walk to the Funivia and ski lift and two kilometers to the Piz Sella cable car, and you'll find a playground and barbecue facilities on site. There's shared laundry facilities and free Wi-Fi. Callegari Cesa village, two kilometers away, has shops and restaurants. Via Plan 52, Selva di Val Gardena. www.callegari.it.

ALPE DI SIUSI & CASTELROTTO

Hof Zerund in Castelrotto lets families experience everyday life on an alpine farm on a small, comfortable scale. They have four apartments, the largest of which accommodates up to six people, in a gorgeous, traditional setting with fantastic views. The children can meet ponies, cows, bunnies and goats and enjoy the farm's playground all while learning about traditional and modern farming. Paniderstrasse 43, Kastelruth (Castelrotto). www.hofzerund.com.

Bad Ratzes sits at 1,200 meters (3,937 feet) just three kilometers away from **Seis / Siusi,** on 22 hectares of grounds. It's an ideal Dolomites hideaway with all the essential scenery: a lush meadow, a crystal-clear stream and an ancient pine forest complete with views of Mount Sciliar. You can gaze at the stars by a roaring bonfire, take archery lessons and learn how to build from nature. Address: Via Ratzes 29, Siusi. www.badratzes.it.

RACINES

Alphotel Tyrol is a four-star option located in the most northern part of the Dolomites, near the Gilfenklamm Gorge and the Austrian border. They offer a spa overlooking the lake and some fantastic children's activities. Enjoy the petting zoo, adventure playground and go-kart track for starters. Racines di Dentro 5, Racines. www.alphotel-tyrol.com.

MERANO

Taser offers both hotel and chalet accommodation at their beautiful, secluded 1,450-meter-high location. You reach Taser by cable car, and you'll find a little petting zoo, a Tyrolese restaurant, a playground and a host of activities. This eco-friendly option is focused on families and healthy living. Schennaberg 25, Scena (Merano). www.familienalm.com.

Special Events in the Dolomites

Dolomiti Balloon Festival: Every January, **Dobbiaco** (see Itinerary 7) hosts a fantastic hot air balloon festival with daytime and night displays of dazzling, colorful and whimsical balloons. www.balloonfestival.it.

Cavalcata Oswaldo von Wolkenstein: This is a massive competitive equestrian event with challenges unlike standard horse competitions. Held in and around Siusi (see Itinerary 9) every June, teams of riders compete at jousting, racing and feats of agility. But this isn't just for the horsey set; this is one of the largest festivals in the region with food, music and period costumes. Find out more here: www.ovwritt.com.

Night Concerts at Castel Proesels: Every summer concerts, movies, art exhibitions and other events are organized in the stunning Castel Proesels, 16 kilometers outside of Bolzano. www.schloss-proesels.it.

Segra di Urtigei: Ortisei (see Itinerary 4) celebrates its most famous village festival in early July. Men and women in distinctive traditional costumes dance and play music and fill the streets. There are concerts, too. Contact the tourist office for details regarding the precise yearly program.

Val Gardena Folklore Festival: On the first Sunday of August, the valley celebrates its heritage with traditional costumes, music, food stands and more.

Concerts: Many open-air concerts are held throughout the Dolomites in the summer, and the local tourism office is the best place to find out what is happening.

Special Activities in the Dolomites

ZIPLINE

Catinaccio Rosengarten Fly Line in the Val di Fassa (see itinerary 3) is a unique way to see the Dolomites. Instead of hiking, you can fly! This is a combination of a seggiovia and a zipline that lets you soar for a kilometer through the forest for an amazing view of Pordoi, Sella and Larsech mountains. Take the **Catinaccio Funivia cable car** up the mountain, and the zipline starts near the station at an altitude of 1,805 meters. Anyone who weighs between 20 kg and 120 kg can get on the fly line. It's near the restaurant and chalet called **Baita Checco e il Negritella,** which is a nice spot for lunch. While your teenagers are zooming through the forest, the younger members of the family can enjoy a high-altitude **playground** called **Kinder Park Ciampedie,** which is located right next to the zipline. Catinaccio Impianti Funivia, Strada de Col de Mè 10, Vigo di Fassa. Tel: 0462.763242, www.catinacciodolomiti.it. Open mid-June to mid-September, June 11—September 19, daily, 9.00—12.30 & 14.00—17.30. (August until 18:00). Combined tickets for the Seggiovia (chair lift) and the fly line are available. Children under 14 pay a reduced fee. **Kinder park,** Scuola di Sci Vigo di Fassa Piazza J.B.Massar 1. Tel: 0462.763.125, www.scuolascivigo.com/kinderpark. Open in high season daily, 9:30—17:30.

RAFTING AND CANYONING

If your teenagers need to let off some steam doing something seriously crazy, fun, and wild, then rafting along the rivers of the Dolomites may just be the solution. **Multisport Extreme Waves** offers rafting and hydrospeed excursions, canyoning, tarzaning, mountain biking, an adventure park and climbing trails. There's also a play area with bouncy castles and a soccer field for toddlers. They are located near the **Adamello Nature Reserve,** one hour south of Bolzano, and 30 minutes from Lake Esmeralda. Tel: 0463.970808, www.extremewaves.it

Acqua Terra is another option for fun and wet rafting tours for the whole family, as well as other adrenaline-pumping activities such as canyoning down the waterfalls and organized hikes. They operate in two locations: **Val Venosta** and **Val Passiria.** Tel: 0473.720.042, Cell: 336.611.336, www.acquaterra.it

Day Trips in the Dolomites

HELICOPTER RIDES

Want a bird's eye view of the Dolomites? You could treat yourself to an exciting helicopter tour. **Airway Helicopters** charge 99 euro for a 15-minute flight or 199 euro for a more comprehensive 30-minute tour. Other activities such as joining the helicopter team for a day or parachuting are also available. Flights leave from **Merano** (see Itinerary 1). www.airway.it

ADVENTURE PARKS

> **Tip:** Most adventure parks in the Dolomites are open from mid-May–mid-September, but some only operate July through September. Hours of operation tend to vary, check the park's website. Additionally, some parks close in inclement weather even in the middle of the high season, so always call in advance before driving there.

The **Dolomiti Action** adventure park (near **Canazei** and Vigo di Fassa, see Itinerary 3) offers a range of adventure trails from easy children's routes to challenging adult courses. Try your hand at ziplining, climbing nets and other thrills as you navigate the alpine forest. Cell: 328.865.1993, www.dolomitiaction.com. Open daily in high season.

Day Trips in the Dolomites

Adventure Dolomiti in Molina di Fiemme offers just as much fun with adventure courses for young children at least 80 cm in height, as well as laser tag, rafting and more. The park is located one hour south of Bolzano, near the Cavalese Waterfall Nature Reserve. Their website is only in Italian, but you can telephone to speak to them directly. (English-speaking representatives are usually available.) Cell: 329.2743.226 / 327.319.5985, www.adventuredolomiti.it.

Sores Park is 45 minutes north of **Trento** with nine different adventure courses where kids and teenagers can climb, jump along rope bridges, develop their skills and abilities and build confidence while having a blast. Ask about discounted family tickets. To find the park, set your GPS / google maps to Hotel Rifugio Sores and from there follow the signs. Tel: 0463.463500, Cell: 329.692.7869 / 327.135.1386. www.sorespark.it. Open July—mid September, daily.

Villnoess Dolomites High Ropes features nine different adventure courses for different levels of ability, with suspension bridges, balance beams, cable pulleys and more. The park is located near **Ortisei** and Alpe di Siusi (see Itinerary 9), at the foot of the Geisler Mountains. They even have a barbecue area, in case all that adventure makes you hungry! Tel: 0472.840.602, www.hochseilgarten-villnoess.it. Open mid-June—mid-September, daily, 09:00-18:00.

Xsund is an adventure park in Terlano, near **Bolzano**. Their range of offerings includes adventure courses, boating, and an archery course (though many children might find it upsetting; the targets are detailed models of animals including deer, bears and boars). Tel: 0471.257.944, www.xsund.it. The park is open from mid-March to mid-November.

Otzi Rope Park is also near **Bolzano**, and features a giant swing, rope ladders and a range of adventure courses. Even toddlers can go on some things here. Open July—August, 9:30—16:30. www.hochseilgarten.bz.

Cortina Adrenalin Center is a good option for families with both younger and older kids visiting the **Cortina d'Ampezzo** area (see Itinerary 10). They have a cool playground with a mini-adventure course for kids who don't meet the 120-cm height requirement, and 14 courses ranging from easy to exhilarating. You can also book canyoning activities in advance through the center. www.adrenalincenter.it. Open late-June—mid-September, daily. GPS coordinates: N 46.54467; E12.12876.

HORSEBACK & CARRIAGE RIDES

> **Tip:** when contacting any horse farm in the Dolomites, always ask whether the activity you are interested in is suitable for tourists who don't speak German (or Italian), too. Also, try to provide the owners with precise information about the participants to avoid disappointment, including the age of the children, their level of riding experience, and any restrictions, concerns or health issues that you may have.

Fattoria Cavalcailvento does horseback excursions, pony rides for the little ones, carriage rides, and other fun activities in Cavedine (15 minutes from **Trento**). Advance booking required. www.cavalcailvento.it.

Farm Gstatschhof is a farm stay in **Castelrotto—Alpe di Siusi** that also offers fun horseback lessons and excursions in the valley. www.gstatschhof.com.

Seiser Alm Carriage Rides lets you choose a route for a relaxing, fairy-tale carriage ride based on what you want to see in the Alpe di Siusi area and what you want to pay. www.seiseralm.it/en/summer-dolomites/other-activities/horse-carriage.html.

Maneggio Reitstall offers riding lessons, horse and pony excursions and a playground in picturesque **Santa Cristina,** in the heart of the Gardena valley. www.maneggio-montepana.com.

Pozzamanigoni is a hotel, restaurant and equestrian center in **Selva Val Gardena.** In addition to the usual lessons and excursions, they also have an indoor riding arena, which is used by professional riders from the area. www.pozzamanigoni.it.

Maneggio Ortisei even lets you bring your own horse for trekking and lessons, but don't worry if you left your pony at home. You can also use one of theirs. www.maneggio-ortisei.it.

Sunny Ranch in Cavereno in the eastern Dolomites near **Cles** offers pony rides, horse treks and wagon rides. Call in advance to book a spot. www.sunnyranch.it.

Agritur Bontempelli is a popular farm with horse and pony rides, as well as other activities in a particularly beautiful setting, deep in the eastern Dolomites and the **Adamello nature reserve.** Their activities are especially suitable for toddlers and younger children. www.maneggio.net.

Sulfner Farm is a well-known horse farm located 20 minutes west of Merano (see Itinerary 1), and is particularly suitable for experienced riders. But even complete newbies who have never been near a horse before can have a good time by joining one of their carriage tours along stunning trails. www.hotel-sulfner.com.

HIKE WITH ALPACAS AND LLAMAS

Kaserhof Farm outside of **Bolzano** is a delightful ranch where people, alpacas, horses, ducks and cats all live together in harmony. In addition to guided tours of the farm that little ones will love, on Wednesdays and Fridays you can go trekking with their cheeky alpacas and llamas! It's a fun and novel way to explore that will impress the kids. (The animals lead the way, you don't ride them.) Booking in advance is necessary. www.kaserhof.it.

GUIDED HIKES & KID-WORKSHOPS

Val Gardena Tours: there are several guided tours and activities for families organized throughout the summer in Val Gardena (Gardena Valley). You can consult the full program and book a spot in advance here: www.valgardena.it and here: www.valgardena-active.com (most activities are for kids 6-12 years old).

ROCK CLIMBING

Mauro Bernardi is an experienced rock climber and Val Gardena native who offers guided rock climbing tours. Try your hand (and foot…) at an up-close encounter with the pale mountains. www.val-gardena.com/maurobernardi.

MOUNTAIN BIKING

MBT Bike School & Rental gives bike-loving youngsters a great way to explore on two wheels for a high-energy outing. www.mtbschool.it.

SWIMMING

Maradolomit Pool is an alternative to swimming in the lakes in Val Gardena. They have indoor and outdoor pools as well as a sauna. www.mardolomit.com.

VISIT A BIRD CENTER WITH A SHOW

The Gufyland Bird Center near **Merano** rehabilitates injured birds to release them back to the wild and also puts on unique shows with birds of prey twice daily. Seeing these majestic raptors and owls swooping around up close inspires a new level of appreciation for wild things. Via del Castello 25, Tirolo (may appear on some maps in German only: Gufyland, Schlossweg 25, Dorf Tirol). Tel: 0473.221.500, www.gufyland.com. Open early April—early November, 10:30—17:00. Shows take place at 11:15 and 15:15, but it's always best to call ahead to make sure these hours haven't changed. Children under 13 pay a reduced entry fee.

BECOME A FARMER FOR A DAY

Fattoria Didattica Il Leprotto Bisestile is a stunning little farm located 20 minutes south of **Trento** near Lake Caldonazzo. This is the sort of place young children will love—with turtles, chickens, donkeys and rabbits, it's a cheerful spot. Book one of their organized activities and stay for a light picnic of organic products produced on the farm. Their jam is delicious! www.illeprottobisestile.com.

Fattoria Didattica En Galavra, just half an hour east of **Trento**, offers discounts through the tourism card association. Children can get hands-on farm experience feeding sheep, collecting eggs and visiting the goats. While the website is in Italian, you can phone the owners, who speak English, to book. www.fattoriadidatticaengalavra.com.

Agriturismo Solasna gives children a chance to meet some farm animals, make and sample cheese, and create crafts. There's also a restaurant. They are in **San Giacomo di Caldes,** near Cles and the Adamello nature reserve. www.agritursolasna.it.

MINI-GOLF

Fantolin Golf in the beautiful village of Moena (near Canazei, Val di Fassa, see Itinerary 3) features a cute, 18-hole mini-golf course, a go kart track and a playground. www.fassa.com/IT/FantolinGolf.

TOP OF THE TOP

Chapter 7

Top of the Top

- ☼ Visit the stunning, gold-covered Basilica di San Marco (see Venice Chapter).

- ☼ Enjoy a wild day of fun at the popular Gardaland Amusement park.

- ☼ Take the Funivia up to Sass Pordoi, for incredible views of the Dolomites (see Dolomites Chapter)

- ☼ Learn how to become a real Venetian gondolier with a gondola rowing lesson (see Venice Chapter).

- ☼ Create your own Venetian Mask (see Venice Chapter)

- ☼ Enjoy a hands-on tour of the Leonardo da Vinci Museums (see Venice Chapter)

- ☼ Splash around at the waterpark in Jesolo (see Day Trips from Venice Chapter)

- ☼ Visit Juliet's house and pretend to be Romeo or Juliet (see Verona chapter)

- ☼ Climb to the top of the Campanile (Bell Tower) in Piazza San Marco to enjoy the incredible view (see Venice Chapter).

- ☼ Tour the ancient Roman Arena (see Verona Chapter)

- ☼ Enjoy the spectacular view of Verona from Castel San Pietro (see Verona Chapter)

- ☼ Splash around and tour the activities at Canevaworld (see Lake Garda Chapter)

- Visit the beautiful and poetic town of Sirmione (see Lake Garda Chapter).
- Jump and climb at one of the many adventure parks around Lake Garda (see Lake Garda Chapter)
- Go on a fun horse-drawn carriage ride, or a family hike, in Alpe di Siusi (see Dolomites Chapter)
- Visit the Marmolada—queen of the Dolomites (see Dolomites Chapter)
- Discover beautiful waterfalls and mines at the Gilfenklamm Canyon (see Dolomites Chapter)
- Take the cable car from Malcesine up to the top of Monte Baldo (see Lake Garda Chapter)
- Have an adrenalin-filled adventure at some of the best adventure parks in Italy (see Dolomites Chapter).
- Visit the Exciting Ferrari, Lamborghini and Ducati Museums (see Day Trips from Venice Chapter)

Top Five Places to Splash Around on a Hot Summer Day

- The beach at Lake Garda (see Lake Garda Chapter)
- Jesolo Aquapark (see Day Trips from Venice Chapter)
- Canevaworld Water Park (see Lake Garda Chapter)
- Lake Tenno (see Dolomites Chapter)
- Lake Molveno (see Day Trips from Lake Garda Chapter)

Top Five Places to Enjoy Stunning Panoramic View

- The Campanile (Bell Tower) on Piazza San Marco (see Venice Chapter)
- The Marmolada (see Dolomites Chapter)
- Sass Pordoi (see Dolomites Chapter)
- Terrazza Panoramica dei Brividi (see Lake Garda Chapter)
- Castel San Pietro (see Verona Chapter)

Top Five Cultural Attractions to Enjoy

- Peggy Guggenheim Collection (see Venice Chapter)
- Palazzo Ducale-the Doge's Palace (see Venice Chapter)
- Basilica I Frari (see Venice Chapter)
- Verona's historical center (see Verona Chapter)
- Basilica San Marco (see Venice Chapter)

Top Attractions for Kids who Love Nature, Animals, and Science

- The Natural History Museum in Venice (see Venice Chapter)
- The MUSE Science museum in Trento (see Dolomites Chapter)
- The Ridanna Mines (see Dolomites Chapter)
- The Two Leonardo da Vinci Museums in Venice (see Venice Chapter)
- The Family hikes in the Dolomites (see Dolomites Chapter)
- The Varone Waterfalls (see Lake Garda Chapter)

INDEX

5 (Cinque) Torri Open Air Museum...288
Accademia Gallery Venice...97
Acqua Terra Tours...298
Adventure Dolomiti...300
Agritur Bontempelli...302
Agriturismo La Filanda...222
Agriturismo Solasna...304
Agriturismo Spigollo...186
Airway Helicopter Tours...299
Ai Tre Archi...138
Albatross Mobile Homes...223
Al Gatto Nero...139
Al Giardinetto...138
Alpaca Ranch Garda...231
Alpe di Siusi...284
Alphotel Tyrol...296
Al Vecchio Fontec...217
Ambassador Suite Hotel...224
Ambiente Acqua Diving...233
Antico Doge Hotel...141
Aqualandia Water Park...160
Arche Scaligere...178
Arsenale...114
A Tribute to Music Hotel...141
B&B Villa Beatrice...185
Baia delle Sirene Beach...207
Bardolino...205
Bar la Toletta...136
Bar Lido di Assenza...207
Barlot Ranch...231
Basilica dei Frari...91
Basilica della Salute...100
Basilica di San Marco...104
Bastione...209
Biennale Venezia...143
Bistrot de Venise...139
Black Death (plague)...131
Boat Rentals Lake Garda...200, 227
Borghetto Sul Mincio...247
Bosc del Meneghi Farm...242
Boscopark Adventure Park...1855
Bridge of Sighs...111
Bullaccia...284
Burano...119
Busatte Adventure Park...230
Ca d'Oro...88
Cafe' Pasticceria Demetz...293
Caglieron Caves...150
Campanile (Venice Bell Tower)...106
Camping Bella Italia...222
Camping Village San Francesco...223
Canale del Tenno (Borgo)...243
Canazei...265
Canevaworld...200
Canoa Kayak Club...228
Canyon Adventure...234
Caproni Museum of Aviation…246
Ca Macana Masks...146
Ca Rezzonico…95
Carta Alta Masks...147
Castel Beseno...238
Castel Brando...151
Castel Buonconsiglio...244
Castello Principesco di Merano...261
Castelrotto...286
Castel San Pietro Panoramic Terrace...180
Castelvecchio Fortress and Museum...169
Catinaccio Rosengarten Fly Line...297
Cavour Water Park...229
Chorus Association Ticket...75
Cicheti...136
Circolo Nautico Brenzone...232
Cison di Valmarino...153
Col de Flam Adventure Park...269
Combination Tickets Venice...75
Compatsch...285
Conca Beach...232
Correr Museum...112
Cortina d'Ampezzo...287
Crazy Wheels Quad Tours...231
Cremeria Bulian...199
Cremeria di Lazise...205
Disco Bar Belvedere...288
Dobbiaco...277
Dobbiaco Animal Park...277
Dolomiti Action Adventure Park...299
Ducati Museum…157

Index

Elena Rosso Beads...147
Events in Lake Garda...225
Extreme Waves Rafting...298
Fallani Venezia...147
Family-Friendly Beaches in Garda...215
Fantolin Mini-Golf...304
Farini...134
Farm Gstatschhof...301
Fattoria Cavalcailvento...301
Fattoria Didattica En Galavra...304
Fattoria Didattica Il Leprotto Bisestile...304
Ferrari Museum...155
Festa della Sensa...142
Festa del Redentore...142
Fiabilandia...263
Fly 2 Fun Pragliding...232
Fontego delle Dolcezze...140
Foresta del Cansiglio...152
Forest Park Adventure Park...237
Gardaland...200
Garda Outdoor...234
Garda Surf & Sail...232
Garda Touring Association...233
Gardens in Verona...184
Gardone Riviera...212
Gelateria Blu Garda...214
Gelateria Scaligeri...199
Giardini della Biennale & Sant'Elena...82
Giardini Pubblici Venice...82
Giardino Heller (Heller Botanic Garden)...213
Gilf Canyon Trail...260
Gilfenklamm Gorge...281
Go Kart Jesolo...162
Gondola Rowing Lesson...146
Goosta Piadineria Artigiana...250
Grotte di Catullo...199
Gufyland Bird Center...303
Hard Rock Café...134
Hilton Skyroof Bar...81
Hotel Accademia...185
Hotel Baitone...222
Hotel Biancaneve...295
Hotel Bolivar...165
Hotel Campagnola...224
Hotel La Gioiosa...224

Hotel Posta...295
Hotel Pragser Wildsee...279
Hotel Ristorante Alpino...219
Hotel Tivoli...141
Hotel Violin d'Oro...141
Human Chess in Marostica...144
I Frari Basilica...91
Il Giardino dei Sapori...218
Il Girasole...218
Il Vittoriale...213
Jesolo...159
Jesolo Military Museum...162
Jesolo Palace...165
Jesolo Supermarkets...164
Jesolo's Best Beaches for Families...163
Jewish Ghetto Venice...117
Jonathan Aviation Collection...147
Juliet's house...173
Jungle Adventure Park...186
Kaserhof Farm...302
Kirchsteiger...293
La Bottiglia...137
La Giostra della Rocca...144
Laguna Escursioni Venice...146
Lake Braies...279
Lake Carezza...265
Lake Dobbiaco...277
Lake Fedaia...275
Lake Fié...286
Lake Garda Water Ski Center...232
Lake Landro...277
Lake Ledro...239
Lake Molveno...236
Lake Pellegrino...263
Lake Santa Croce...152
Lake Tenno...243
La Maison della Crepe...140
La Marachella Pizzeria...164
Lamborghini Museum and Factory...156
La Mela Verde...140
Latteria Tre Cime...278
Lazise Play Village...205
La Zucca Vegetarian Restaurant...49
Leonardo da Vinci Museum Campo San Rocco...92
Leonardo da Vinci Museum Campo San

Index

Barnaba...96
Le Vie Degli Asini...240
Libreria Acqua Alta...80
Lido...118
Limone Sul Garda...211
Loacker Chocolate Factory...277
Locanda Del Cantoniere...288
Locanda La Corte...141
Loggia del Consiglio...177
Malcesine...208
Malga Tovre Farm...237
Malibu Beach Camping Village...165
Maneggio Ortisei...302
Maneggio Reitstall...302
Maradolomit Pool...303
Marciana Library...112
Marco Polo...125
Marega Mask Shop...94
Marinzen Hike...286
Marmolada...274
Mauro Bernardi Rock Climbing...303
MBT Bike School...303
Merano...259
Merano 2000 & Alpine Bob Slides...260
Mezzolago Beach...240
Mmove Hikes...233
Moena...263
Molina di Ledro Beach...240
Molveno Cable Car...236
Monte Baldo Funivia (Cable Car)...209
Mountime Rock Climbing...233
Murano...120
Museo delle Palafitte (Pile Dwelling Museum)...241
Museo Storico Navale (Venice Naval Museum)...115
MUSE Science Museum Trento...245
Museum Tours for Families Venice...78
Natural History Museum Venice...86
New Jesolandia Luna Park...162
Nicolis Car Museum...247
Nico's Café...137
Ninfee Park...229
Noale Renaissance Festival...145
Oasi del Panino...163
Old Wild West...134
Ortisei...269

Osteria del Maso...237
Osteria Macafame...184
Otzi Rope Park...300
Padiglione delle Navi (Venice Ship Museum)...115
Palafitte Lounge Bar...205
Palazzo dei Capitani...208
Palazzo Ducale (Doge's Palace Venice)...108
Palio dei 10 Comuni...144
Palio della Marciliana...145
PanaRaida...271
Parco Avventura Polsa...230
Parco delle Cascate di Molina (Molina Waterfall Park)...206
Parco Grotta Cascata Varone (Varone Waterfall)...210
Parco Natura Viva Safari...204
Parco Savorgnan Venice...82
Parma a Tavola...183
Passo Falzeron...288
Passo San Pellegrino...262
Pass Pordoi...266
Pastificio Remelli...250
Peggy Guggenheim Collection...99
Piazza Bra...170
Piazza delle Erbe...175
Piazza San Marco...103
Pizzeria Capri...164
Pizzeria La Goccia...250
Pizzeria La Greca...250
Pizzeria Leon d'Oro...220
Pizzeria LungoLago64...219
Pizzeria Seidner...294
Pordoi Funivia...266
Pozzamanigoni...302
Punta San Vigilio...207
Pur Beach...240
Regatta Storica...143
Reierhof...278
Relax Restaurant...219
Reptiland...210
Resciesa Funicular...269
Residence Cesa Callegari...295
Residence Hotel Palazzo Della Scala...224
Residence Nuove Terme...223
Restaurant Pizzeria Mosl...293

Index

Restaurant Winkelkeller...294
Rialto Bridge...89
Ridanna Monteneve Mines...282
Rifugio Forcella Pordoi...266
Rifugio Fuciade...263
Rifugio La Montanara Cafe'...237
Rifugio Scoiattoli...289
Rimbalzello Adventure Park...230
Riovalli Parco Acquatico...229
Ristorante Ai Tre Volti...250
Ristorante Al Gondoliere...219
Ristorante Alvise...135
Ristorante del Brenta...237
Ristorante Emiliano's...217
Ristorante Lago di Landro...294
Ristorante La Stua dei Ladins...294
Ristorante La Vecia Mescola...183
Ristorante Mini...294
Ristorante Paradiso Perduto...219
Ristorante Pizzeria Erica...293
Ristorante Pizzeria Nastro Azzurro...184
Ristorante Riviera...139
Riva degli Schiavoni...113
Riva del Garda...209
Roman Theater...180
RossoPomodoro...135
Row Venice Gondola...146
Sailing Dulac-Pier Windsurf...232
Salò...214
San Giorgio Island...114
Santa Cristina Valgardena...271
Santa Maria dei Miracoli Church....80
San Trovaso Squero (Gondola Garage Venice)...97
Sant'Anastasia Church...179
San Zeno Church...182
Sapori in Cantina...218
Scala Contarini del Bovolo...90
Scaliger Castle Malcesine...208
Scaliger Castle Sirmione...198
Scuola Grande di San Rocco...93
Sea Life Jesolo...161
Seceda Summit...268
Serrai di Sottoguda Canyon...274

Sigurta Park...247
Sirmione...198
Skytrek Adventure...282
Sores Park...300
Stanghe Waterfalls...281
Sulfner Farm...302
Sunny Ranch...302
Surf Segnana...232
Suso Gelateria...139
Tappeiner Trail...260
Taser...296
Taverna Scalinetto...135
Tenuta La Borghetta...223
Terrazza del Brivido (Panoramic Terrace)...211
Torbole Beach...232
Torcello...121
Torre dei Lamberti...176
Torri del Benaco...207
Trattoria Clementina...218
Trattoria San Trovaso...136
Trauttmansdorff Castle and Botanic Park...259
Treccani Ristorante Pizzeria...219
Tre Cime Reserve...277
Trento...243
Tropicana...161
Val di Fassa...262
Val Gardena Tours...303
Venezia Unica Card...75
Venice Carnival...141
Venice Clock Tower...105
Venice Kayak...146
Venice on Board Rowing Lesson...146
Verona Arena...170
Verona Duomo...181
Via Mazzini...173
Villaggio Turistico Lugana Marina...224
Villnoess Dolomites High Ropes...300
Vogalonga...143
Voices from the Middle Ages Cittadella...145
White Gelateria...139
Wolfsthurn Castle...283
Xsund Adventure Park...300

Photo Credits

Introduction: By Olena Z/Shutterstock; By Gabriele Maltinti/Shutterstock.com; By Roman Babakin/Shutterstock.com; By bymandesigns/Shutterstock.com. Chapter 1: By Samot/Shutterstock.com; By Mariia Golovianko/Shutterstock.com; By Jolanta Wojcicka/Shutterstock.com; By Nataliya Hora/Shutterstock.com; By HildaWeges Photography/Shutterstock.com; By Mariia Golovianko/Shutterstock.com; By Anna Levan/Shutterstock.com; By Jeramey Lende/Shutterstock.com; By Alessandro Cristiano/Shutterstock.com; By Catarina Belova/Shutterstock.com; By Everett Historical/Shutterstock.com; By Alex Donnelly/Shutterstock.com; By faber1893/Shutterstock.com; By Irina Papoyan/Shutterstock.com; By sbellott/Shutterstock.com; By Evgeniya Moroz/Shutterstock.com; By PlusONE/Shutterstock.com; By Federico Rostagno/Shutterstock.com; By Evgord/Shutterstock.com; By Paolo Gallo/Shutterstock.com; By mountainpix/Shutterstock.com; By Dubova/Shutterstock.com; By Sailorr/Shutterstock.com; By gueriero93/Shutterstock.com; By Everett Historical/Shutterstock.com; By Kostyantyn Ivanyshen/Shutterstock.com; By Csaba Peterdi/Shutterstock.com; freepik.com; By MoreVector/Shutterstock.com; By Boris-B/Shutterstock.com; By arturasker/Shutterstock.com; By Oh lun la/Shutterstock.com; By Samot/Shutterstock.com. Chapter 2: By StevanZZ/Shutterstock.com; Ariela Bankier; Photo courtesy of the Ferrari museum all rights reserved; By Elizaveta Galitckaia/Shutterstock.com. Chapter 3: By Yasonya/Shutterstock.com; ChiccoDodiFC/Shutterstock.com; By Manuel Hurtado/Shutterstock.com; By cge2010/Shutterstock.com; By Olena Z/Shutterstock.com; By Walencienne/Shutterstock.com. Chapter 4: By Vladimir Berny/Shutterstock.com; By xbrchx/Shutterstock.com; By slavapolo/Shutterstock.com; By pointbreak/Shutterstock.com; By Arsenie Krasnevsky/Shutterstock.com; By Rostislav Glinsky/Shutterstock.com; By l-ing/Shutterstock.com; By VaLiza/shutterstock.com; By Sunychka Sol/Shutterstock.com; By xbrchx/Shutterstock.com; By gorillaimages/Shutterstock.com; By Simon Dannhauer/Shutterstock.com; By Danny Iacob/Shutterstock.com; freepik.om; By Oksana Yurlova/Shutterstock.com; By FamVeld/Shutterstock.com; By Anna Om/Shutterstock.com. Chapter 5: By Luca Lorenzelli/Shutterstock.com; By Michele Righetti/Shutterstock.com; By Bildgigant/Shutterstock.com; By saad315/Shutterstock.com; By GoneWithTheWind/Shutterstock.com. Chpater 6: Ariela Bankier; By Philip Bird LRPS CPAGB/Shutterstock.com; By Pawel Kazmierczak/Shutterstock.com; By Brocreative/Shutterstock.com; By Mikadun/Shutterstock.com; By Gaspar Janos/Shutterstock.com; By Tomsickova Tatyana/Shutterstock.com; By Stefan1085/Shutterstock.com; By Tanya May/Shutterstock.com; By Fesus Robert/Shutterstock.com; By DiegoMariottini/Shutterstock.com; By underworld/Shutterstock.com; By Mostovyi Sergii Igorevich/Shutterstock.com; freepik.com; By Ammit Jack/Shutterstock.com; By Olesia Bilkei/Shutterstock.com; By SUSAN LEGGETT/Shutterstock.com. Chapter 7: moosa art/Shutterstock.

Printed in Great Britain
by Amazon